Praise for

LIVE YOUR OPUS

"If you're a high achiever who hustled your way to success but lost yourself along the way, this book delivers. Janine Mathó offers a grounded, practical path to align your ambition with what matters most to you."

MEL ROBBINS, *New York Times* bestselling author of *The Let Them Theory* and host of *The Mel Robbins Podcast*

"*Live Your Opus* is a wake-up call for high achievers who are ready to stop running on empty and start living on purpose. If you've been chasing success, always wondering when 'enough' would finally hit—this is your essential guide."

DORIE CLARK, executive education faculty at Columbia Business School and *Wall Street Journal* bestselling author of *The Long Game*

"So many of us reach a moment, quiet and often hidden, when success begins to feel strangely hollow and the life we've worked so hard to build no longer fits. In *Live Your Opus*, Janine Mathó meets that moment with uncommon grace. This is not a book of easy answers, but a brave and generous companion for the inner work of returning to oneself. With clarity and care, Mathó helps us remember something essential, something we may have known once but lost track of along the way: that vitality, meaning, and contribution are not separate paths, but one path walked in alignment with the truth of who we are."

STEPHEN COPE, author of *The Great Work of Your Life*

"Janine holds what most coaches can't—your ambition, your doubt, your vision—and helps you turn it all into clarity and power. I watched her carry this work from the shadows into the world. In *Live Your Opus*, she offers that same rare gift to every ambitious person: a path back to self-trust, energy, and a kind of success that doesn't cost you what matters most. More than just wisdom, Janine offers high achievers the clarity they spend years chasing, delivered with heart, strength, and truth."

NIMROD MASHIAH, Olympic athlete, three-time world medalist, and elite performance strategist

"In a world wired for fear and addicted to certainty, *Live Your Opus* is a powerful invitation to reclaim mastery over your own mind and design a life led by purpose. Janine doesn't just ask us to dream—she shows us how to disarm the survival-driven wiring that keeps us small so that we can live our dreams. This book is a must-read for anyone who wants to live their highest potential and shape a future where dreams aren't just personal aspirations—they're the responsibility we carry to model what's possible for the next generation."

LINA ASHAR, founder and CEO, Dreamtime Learning

"A playbook for presence and purpose, Mathó lifts the veil on burnout, energy, and what really matters. *Live Your Opus* is a toolbox to help anyone wanting to live their best life."

PROFESSOR KERENSA JENNINGS, Fellow of the Royal Society for Arts, Manufactures and Commerce (FRSA)

"The use of musical metaphors such as composition and opus is a brilliant and original way to draw the reader into what becomes a true odyssey of self-discovery and creation. Part One offers a thoughtful approach to the vital act of taking charge of our minds, our choices, and the small details of our daily lives. Part Two provides a masterful blend of practical exercises, provocative insights, and moving stories of real people who have transformed their lives. It inspires the reader to begin their own journey, one small, mindful step at a time. This is the kind of book that, if it were required reading in every high school around the world, would change how we define success and how we live in pursuit of it."

CLAIRE HARBOUR, trusted advisor to C-suite leaders and founders, author, and disruptor

LIVE YOUR OPUS

RECLAIM YOUR ENERGY, REDEFINE SUCCESS, AND CREATE A LIFE THAT TRULY MATTERS

JANINE MATHÓ

amplify
an imprint of Amplify Publishing Group

amplify
an imprint of Amplify Publishing Group

www.amplifypublishinggroup.com

Live Your Opus: Reclaim Your Energy, Redefine Success, and Create a Life That Truly Matters

For more information, please contact:
Amplify Publishing, an imprint of Amplify Publishing Group
620 Herndon Parkway, Suite 220
Herndon, VA 20170
info@amplifypublishing.com

Library of Congress Control Number: 2025912145

CPSIA Code: PRV0925A

ISBN-13: 979-8-89138-577-1

Printed in United States

For Richard, thank you for encouraging me to explore all that's within, to leave what no longer fit, and to grow into what could be—together.

CONTENTS

Introduction

YOU ARE YOUR GREATEST WORK

On January 6, 2020, when I was forty-eight years old, I found myself flat out in bed unable to eat, sleep, or function. Somehow, even though it seemed like I was at the height of my career and had worked hard to achieve everything I thought I wanted, my life had fallen apart. For the first time, I felt like a failure. I didn't even know who I was anymore, and neither did anyone else.

Just six weeks earlier, I had been living my dream: I'd moved to England in 2018. I was a Cuban American in London holding not one, but two, international roles within an FTSE 100 company. I had a great network of friends and enough income to see my husband and three children regularly despite us living an ocean apart.

Work was demanding, but not difficult. I was a highly respected—and rewarded—high performer; like many people in such roles, stress came with the job. I traveled extensively in my role, which I enjoyed as it gave me the opportunity to see the world. I was thinner than I'd been in years, which I thought was a good thing at the time, and my calendar was full of opportunities I'd worked hard to earn. I had great colleagues and was happy to be working for a purpose-driven company that supported my career growth.

My husband was, and still is, the love of my life. We juggled caring for our nearly grown children and our international lifestyle. We had two homes to keep, a dog and a cat to care for, meals to prepare, and family and community gatherings to organize and host.

Reflecting back, it was an extraordinary, yet, somewhat hectic, life. One that my eighteen-year-old self, left to fend for herself after my parents' divorce, would have envied. I loved my life; it was a true adventure—and a privilege. I was genuinely happy and deeply grateful for the opportunities around me.

But there was another side to it all, a side that I barely acknowledged, a side that is still very hard for me to be honest with myself about. Despite the many upsides, I spent the bulk of my time working upward of eighty hours a week for months at a time. My sleep had been terrible for longer than I could remember. I was tired to my core, and because I suffered from fibromyalgia, I was chronically achy. Although I looked well enough, I did wonder if this was what forty-eight was supposed to feel like.

Constantly on the go, I was emotionally drained from dealing with a difficult boss and ongoing restructuring. I was building teams up and taking them down on top of juggling two jobs, international moves, and my family. My life took two iPhones to manage, an assistant, cleaners, and a lot of helpful friends, airline miles, and (if I'm honest) money. I hoped the pace would slow down eventually; it never did.

Somehow, my life was both remarkable and exhausting. Do you know what I mean? It was a good life, and, because it was the only one I knew, I probably would have continued that way for a long time.

But what happened next changed my life forever.

THE CRASH

My mother was killed in a car accident in Florida in November of 2019, and that was the beginning of the end.

The grief was overwhelming and unfamiliar. I was under pressure to return to work quickly, so I was back in the office a week after planning and attending the funeral, burying myself in projects and deadlines to keep the pain at bay. But inside, I was fraying at the seams, more than even I realized.

I'd powered through crises before—poverty in my early career, family emergencies, big moves, even a divorce. I thought I could handle it all. Only this time, I couldn't.

When my mother died, the cracks in my life became fractures. Burnout symptoms bled into bereavement, which quickly unearthed unresolved childhood trauma. Six weeks later, just after love-filled family Christmas and New Year's celebrations in London, my body and mind reached their limit. My doctor ruled me "unfit to work," a status unique to the UK, and put me on medical leave. For the first time ever, I was forced to stop.

A CHANCE TO CHANGE

During those first weeks on leave, I was too depleted to do much of anything. Resting felt foreign, like a betrayal of everything I'd been taught about success. I tried to resist it, but, as my body began to heal, I started to see just how far I had pushed myself—and how much I had lost along the way. I focused on getting better because I wanted to feel like myself again, so I could get back to "normal" as soon as possible. I had a life to live, after all.

Those first eight weeks were the worst. If you've ever been in this place before, you'll understand that while my corporate life had drained my physical, emotional, and spiritual energy, going on leave topped it off by stripping me of everything I thought defined me.

Without a title and an organization to affiliate with, I was antsy and unmoored. I didn't know what to do with myself or my time. I was a stranger to myself. Without my job to fill up my days, I was confronted with many questions I'd long avoided: Who am I outside of my title, paycheck, and responsibilities? What does success mean to me? What kind of life and career do I truly want to build? And the most challenging question: How did I end up here? The answers didn't come easily, or, in some cases, at all.

It took time for me to settle down enough to accept the help I needed, but it turned out that acceptance was the first step. Once I gave in and accepted the break as the gift it was, I began to recover.

While a Morning Pages practice (a form of journaling) helped me reflect, therapy helped me work through long-buried childhood trauma and the unresolved grief I had over losing my mother. Mindfulness practices (which I found annoying at first), movement, and time in nature gave me tools to reconnect with my body and quiet my overactive mind.

Despite the progress, I still struggled with questions of identity and worth. I didn't understand how I was supposed to pick up the pieces of my life and go back to work without falling back into the same patterns; I wasn't even sure what those patterns were yet.

At the suggestion of a friend, I sought out a coach. I was skeptical at first. I didn't need motivation; I needed to make sense of the wreckage. But I also knew I couldn't do it alone.

In our first session, he asked me a question that stopped me in my tracks: "What if your value isn't defined by what you achieve? What if it's defined by who you are?"

At first, I didn't know how to answer. I wasn't even sure I understood the question; it seemed radical. I had spent my entire life believing that success and worth were earned through effort, achievement, and external validation. In fact, external markers like degrees, title, pay, purchasing power, and what other people thought of me were important; they let me know that I had succeeded. Didn't they? So, if I wasn't succeeding by those terms, what did I have left?

Still, his question piqued my curiosity. Don't get the wrong idea; I didn't have a grand revelation. There was no huge breakthrough moment. But I did begin to wonder: What if he was right? What if I've been measuring myself with the wrong yardstick?

And, in that moment, my mind cracked open just a little bit, wide enough to let in a flicker of possibility. Maybe, just maybe, there was another way to live. One where I wasn't constantly running on empty. Where I wasn't rushing around frantically, striving to keep pace with myself. Where I was smiling at the end of each day instead of collapsing. Maybe success isn't always about doing more. And maybe I could define success by who I am, the life I choose to live, and the impact I create in the world, rather than by what I achieved.

The problem was, I still wasn't sure who I was. But I was committed to doing whatever work I needed to do to find out. As I recovered, I took comfort in creating structure and small rituals—writing in the mornings, sitting quietly for five minutes even when it made me anxious, walking without a destination, spending time with my dog in the park and on hikes, playing with ingredients in the kitchen, and connecting with close friends who helped revitalize me.

Gradually, I began to feel more like myself, not the version of me that had been performing or producing, but the one underneath all that. I still had no grand plan, no clear next step. But I did have a new intention: To create a life that felt at least as good on the inside as it looked on the outside.

I now realize that was the moment I stepped onto the path I now call healthy high achievement. I still wasn't sure how I was going to live this kind of life. But I'd finally stopped running and started listening. I was ready to go after what I wanted and live in alignment with who I was.

What I discovered wasn't a softer life. It was a *stronger* one—more honest, more intentional, and, yes, more ambitious, but in an entirely different way. A way rooted in vitality, clarity, and meaning. It was a way of living and working that I never knew existed.

WHAT I LEARNED

While I was going through this experience, there was one thing I was clear about: I never wanted to go through burnout again. And the feeling ran deeper than that: I never wanted *anyone* to go through what I had been through. My coaching session had unlocked a deep curiosity in me. I was determined to understand how and why I had ended up in this place and what I could do to prevent it in the future for myself and others.

I had a lot of questions: How could I build a full and ambitious life and career while staying healthy and true to who I am? How do I uncover what is most meaningful to me and make that the central force in my life? What is success, really? How might I stay steady when life is always changing? I wondered how others dealt with setbacks, reinvention, career pivots, identity crises, and other massive moments of change that life throws at us.

Although I had only previously experienced success without well-being and balance, I was hopeful about this new idea that I could define success by who I am. I intended to figure out for myself how to build a healthy, meaningful, and sustainable life and career without giving up my ambitions.

Armed with that hope, I took my twenty-five years of expertise in learning, leadership, and the future of work and filled in any gaps by talking with professionals, experts, and devouring books on transitions, neuroscience, positive psychology, creativity, well-being, and longevity, to name a few.

I pored over the data from every future-of-work report and every study on employee engagement or the state of the workplace that I could find. I went deep into spiritual traditions and ancient wisdom, and I studied mindfulness, meditation, Ayurveda, yoga, energy, and Buddhist and Vedic principles. I read autobiographies and texts from all of these fields.

And I interviewed people of all ages, including high-achieving entrepreneurs, business leaders, and academics, about their personal and professional journeys and reinventions. I ultimately interviewed hundreds of people, and I continue to do so today.

I quickly learned that I wasn't alone in this quest. The questions that haunted me about success, identity, purpose, meaning, and sustainability are universal. They have been going on for as long as humans have been sharing stories. People around the world have experienced these moments in different forms and found them as jarring and humbling as I did. Since the pandemic, as people increasingly ask themselves these questions, their perspective has shifted from what they do for a living to how they want to live.

The second thing I learned is that I wasn't the only person experiencing this kind of crisis. The first book I read on the topic was *Thrive*, by Arianna Huffington; I also took her LinkedIn Learning course. I was shocked to learn that someone I admired, a woman I considered powerful, smart, and beautiful, had also gone through a form of burnout. Her openness in sharing her story as a force for good made me feel kinder and more accepting of my own situation, and it further fueled my curiosity.

Today, more people than not are experiencing burnout, depletion across their physical, emotional, mental, and spiritual energy, and a disconnection from themselves, their purpose, and each other. So many of us are searching for more—more meaning, impact, love, joy, connection, time, money, health, and a way to sustain our energy and success. The reasons range from poor experiences in life or at work to the bewildering state of our world.

Gallup's 2024 research on "The Great Detachment" and Voluntās' "Global Meaningfulness Index 2024" reveal a deepening crisis: People are staying in jobs that drain them, while meaning feels increasingly elusive, even in the wealthiest, happiest nations.[1] Forty-five percent of leaders report feeling overwhelmed most of the time, and seven out of ten people at any time are experiencing symptoms of burnout and chronic stress. Women of all ages and Gen Z are suffering disproportionately.

These trends reflect a collective depletion of energy, morale, and connection, what I call an "emotional recession." An emotional recession, like an economic one, signals a widespread and unsustainable depletion, not of money, but of energy, morale, and human connection. It's not just burnout; it's a collective sense of detachment and exhaustion from ourselves, one another, our world, and the work we do.

Imagine trying to power a city with a depleted grid. That's what our workplaces are like in this emotional recession. The energy that fuels innovation, collaboration, and growth is running dangerously low, with burnout, disconnection, mental health struggles, and the search for meaning acting as rolling blackouts across industries.

This malaise has grown beyond the workplace. Disconnection from meaningful work is one of the greatest disconnections of our time because it leads to further loneliness, depression, and mental health challenges. It is impacting our individual lives, our families, our children, and our communities.[2]

The way that most of us have been and are still being taught to achieve isn't fit for the pace and character of today's world; the old playbook of productivity at all costs no longer works. As leaders and individuals, we must evolve and learn how to foster meaning, connection, and sustainable practices that align our work with life's deeper purpose—and that requires new paradigms.

Through all of this, I was beginning to see a pattern even as I recovered: This wasn't just about me. It was about all of us.

THE NEED FOR A NEW MODEL OF SUCCESS

The old model of success is broken, not just for me, but for so many of us. We've followed all the rules, hit the milestones, climbed the ladders, only to arrive and find ourselves exhausted, empty, overwhelmed, or unsure of what everything was for.

Through my experience, research, and hundreds of conversations, I started to see something more clearly than ever before: We're not the ones failing. The system we've been told to succeed within is failing us. We keep chasing success the way we were taught, in a system we inherited, but something inside us knows: It's no longer working, not in this new world we live in.

This realization isn't just conceptual; it's deeply personal. Because what's at stake isn't just your performance or productivity; it's your life. What's at stake is your energy—your capacity to show up with vitality, clarity, presence, and meaning. If you lose that, everything else begins to fray. It's time not only to redefine success, but to reclaim your life from the inside out.

And so, I began to ask a different set of questions. I wanted to move beyond what needed to change out there and into what needed to shift within us.

What emerged were not conclusions, but truths about healthy, meaningful lives that I have come to live by, and they sit at the heart of this book.

- **You are the sole composer of your life.** Forget what they taught you when you were in grade school, or, if you're like me, what you told your children while they were in grade school: Success doesn't require external validation. True fulfilment comes from living in alignment with your values and who you are. There is no right way. Be creative, make joy, chase dreams, stand in awe, and then let go and enjoy the ride.

- **You are your greatest work—own it.** To know who you are, you must invest in knowing yourself and own your story, all of it. Every win, every loss, every blemish. The things that happen to you in your life are not good or bad or otherwise; you shouldn't inflate or ignore them. Your experiences are fuel for your journey. Hiding from them, like I had done too many times in my journey, only disconnects you from yourself and your path.

- **Success is best when ambition and well-being coexist.** Contrary to what most of us have been taught, ambition and well-being are not opposites. The most successful, high-achieving people prioritize their self-care, energy, and well-being above all else. If you doubt me, look first at Olympic-level athletes. They understand that rest and well-being aren't rewards for their effort; they are integral parts of it. Getting these to coexist requires intention, commitment, present focus, and the long view. It can mean raising the bar and letting go of old patterns to master yourself in new ways and across every dimension: physical, emotional, mental, and spiritual. Trust me, the journey is worth it.

- **The only constant is change.** This sounds obvious given everything happening in our world, but life is always changing. This attachment and need most of us have for continuity is human, but it's unattainable. We have all learned this lesson at least once with the pandemic, yet, still default to the false idea that there are actually constants in our lives, when the only constant is change. Instead of resisting change, you can develop the tools to stay steady and to grow and thrive through it.

These realizations showed me that there is a better way to live. That it is possible to build and sustain a different kind of success where I don't trade my well-being or lose myself in pursuit of my ambitions.

WHAT CAME NEXT

What I learned sent me off on a journey that would do more than change my life; it eventually became the foundation of what I now call the Opus Way, a practical, powerful method to reclaim your energy, define success on your terms, and create a life that truly matters. And it has already changed the lives of many people.

As I learned about well-being and success, I experimented on myself. Over time, and with a lot of dead ends, I developed a framework for living that energized me in a whole new way.

Soon, friends—and strangers—noticed the change in me. They would stop me at the grocery store or on walks to tell me how vibrant, even glowing, I looked. Although these kinds of interactions felt strange, they were the nudges I needed to keep going, to follow my heart's direction and find a way to live an ambitious life that was also healthy, meaningful, and sustainable, all without sacrificing my energy, well-being, or any of my ambition.

In time, friends began asking for advice, and I started to share my methods with them. In my mind, I was beginning to live my Opus. But I didn't share those words with anyone yet; they sounded too lofty. My Opus? That's an inflated way to talk about life, isn't it? "Who do you think you are?" I could hear my parents' voices ask of me. But, as friends were inspired and experienced transformations of their own, they referred others to me. It was then that I had an epiphany: Maybe this way of living and working could help others.

In 2024, I created a program, called Project Opus, to support entrepreneurially minded women in creating and living their Opus. I brought together everything I had learned at the time and shared it with them. Within just ten weeks, they also enjoyed great personal and professional transformations—seeds that are still growing today. Since then, people have continued coming to me to learn more about my approach. It has now grown into this book and more.

Over the past five years, I've learned that you can achieve a more ambitious, meaningful life and career than you ever dreamed of and feel great while doing so, but only if you're willing to take a long look in the mirror and reclaim yourself, envision success on your terms, and stay committed to seeing that vision through.

If someone had said that to me back then, I'm sure I wouldn't have believed them. I know if I hadn't hit rock bottom, I would have continued forward in that same frantic, busy, and scattered way of being, perhaps until I retired. Instead, I now live a life that inspires me every day, one that I had always dreamed of but hadn't had the wherewithal to create. An energetic and inspiring life where I'm also calm, focused, joyful, ambitious, and measured. Today, I am living my Opus.

The best thing about this way of living is that you don't need to wait until you hit rock bottom. It's available to anyone, including—and especially—you.

You have already picked up this book, which is here to guide you on a journey to build a life you fully love, a life that is ambitious, meaningful, healthy, and uniquely yours.

WHERE THE WORK—AND THE MAGIC—BEGINS

This book will help you build something that many of us quietly crave: a life that feels as good, or hopefully even better, on the inside as it looks on the outside. One where your well-being rises to meet your ambition, and where you can grow, contribute, and lead as you build enduring success—without burning out or losing yourself in the process. A life powered by energy, not just time or effort, and designed to last.

The Opus Way is a proven method, yes, but more than that, it's a mindset. A way of aligning who you are with how you live so that your achievements reflect your essence, not just your effort. It gives you the tools to navigate a world that moves fast and demands much even as you stay grounded in your own vitality, clarity, and truth.

WHY "OPUS"?

In music and in other artistic pursuits, an *opus* is a significant body of work. It marks a piece that matters. I chose that word because the people I admire most aren't just chasing goals; they're creating lives that matter. They live with intention, lead from the heart, and build with depth. That's what you're here to do, too.

To help you do that, I built this book around the three integrated components of the Opus Way:

- **The Opus Change Continuum.** A framework to help you understand how you respond to change emotionally and energetically, so you can meet yourself with clarity and compassion.

- **The Opus 8 Energy System.** Eight core energy principles, organized into three dynamic tiers—Stability, Alignment, and

Endurance—that help you replenish, direct, and sustain your physical, emotional, mental, and spiritual energy for a life of deep meaning and momentum.

- **The Live Your Opus transformation process.** A four-stage journey—Connect, Dream, Compose, and Embark—that activates the Opus 8 energy principles and helps you bring your Opus to life with clarity, intention, and momentum.

Together these elements form a complete system, supporting you in owning your energy, navigating transition and growth, and sustaining what matters most.

And just so you know, you're not doing this alone. You'll find tools, guided practices, and messages from me at LiveYourOpus.com. This is your journey, and you get to move through it in the way that feels right to you. If you want an even more personalized experience, the *Live Your Opus Workbook* is also shared there to help you go deeper and stay consistent.

I have organized this book such that you can start to grow right from the beginning, in part one, "Your Opus Begins Here." Before you can move forward with clarity, you need to understand how change really works, why some shifts feel exhilarating, and others feel impossible. In part one, you'll discover the different elements of the Opus Way and learn how to use them to build steadiness and shape a version of success that actually feels good. And you'll have tools—like the Opus 8 Compass—to help you tune in, choose what you need most, and move forward with intention, no matter where you are. By the end of part one, you'll know how to reclaim your energy, and have a new way of seeing yourself and your path forward.

In part two, "Transform Your Life in Twelve Weeks," you'll step into the transformation process. This is where the real work begins, but, don't worry, it's well-paced. Here, you'll continue to reconnect with your energy and use it to refine your vision for your life and take meaningful action, grounded in practices that sustain you. By the end of these twelve weeks, you'll be living your Opus, not just imagining it.

The work that you do in this book will go beyond changing your life for a season. Here, you'll create something that lasts. In part three, "Take the Journey of a Lifetime," you'll learn how to sustain your Opus over time: how to stay aligned as your energy, values, and vision evolve. Because real growth isn't a finish line; it's a way of being.

NO MATTER WHERE YOU ARE

One of the most common questions I'm asked is, "Does the Opus Way work at my stage of life?" My answer is always yes. Because your Opus is just not about *where* you are; it's about *who you are becoming.*

Each stage of life brings its own challenges, its own shifts in identity and purpose. We like to believe that if we work hard, make good choices, and find the right people or path, life will eventually settle into place. But life rarely works that way. It is not static. It does not follow a straight line. It shifts. It evolves. And so do we.

What I call "Raise the Bar" moments, those nudges that ask you to reimagine who you are and what's next, can show up at any time. Whether you're launching your career, navigating midlife, caregiving, leading at the highest levels, or standing at the edge of a new chapter, these moments whisper (or shout): *This version of life no longer fits. It's time to grow again.*

These are the moments that call us to advance, not retreat. But instead of expanding by raising the bar, most of us shrink our dreams to fit our current reality. We tell ourselves that we should be grateful, even if we feel unfulfilled. We cling to old identities because we fear starting over. And we struggle, not because we're incapable, but because we've never been taught how to navigate these transitions.

Sometimes, everything on the outside looks fine, but deep down, you know something's shifting. Maybe you land a job that you worked so hard to get, only to realize the values around you don't align with your own. Or maybe you've built your career, only to wake up one day and realize you don't know who you are outside of work.

Maybe you've climbed the ladder, and the view isn't what you had hoped. Or you're stepping into something new, but instead of feeling ready, you feel uncertain, exposed.

And what about the end of your professional journey? The truth is, for many, retirement in today's world brings just as many questions as it answers: Now what?

These moments of apprehension aren't stop signs. They are invitations to expand, refine, and realign. They are invitations to raise the bar on what you're willing to create, experience, and become.

These moments can show up at any time, in every season of life. And, although they may look different, depending on your life stage, the inner questions they stir are strikingly similar. Most of us try to navigate these moments alone, drifting, doubting, second-guessing ourselves while waiting for clarity. But it doesn't have to be that way.

No matter what stage you're in, the Opus Way can help you recognize when you've outgrown an identity so that you can reconnect with your energy and values, navigate change with clarity, and craft a version of success that feels true to you; it's a framework that meets you wherever you are and evolves with you as you grow.

Find comfort in knowing that regardless of where you are right now, whether you're just beginning or standing at the edge of something new, there is always a way forward. Not by waiting or forcing, but by listening and choosing. By stepping into what comes next with intention and trusting in your own unfolding. Every chapter of your Opus is still being written. And the pen will always be in your hands.

And the beautiful part? You don't have to know exactly where you're going—only that you're ready to begin.

So, even if you're reading this book alone on your sofa, in your bed, or between train stops, you're not alone. I'm here with you. And thousands of others are walking this path too. And if you want company, I'd love to welcome you at LiveYourOpus.com.

HOW THIS BOOK WILL CHANGE YOUR LIFE

Before you begin, a gentle warning: Doing this work will change your life—for good. Although you can use this book in many ways, living your Opus is ultimately about learning to work *with* your energy, not against it. It's a practice of aligning your life with what truly matters to you so you can live, love, lead, and grow with integrity, joy, and endurance.

You'll connect with your innermost desires and begin to act on them. Along the way, you'll release other people's expectations and face your deepest fears, not to be fearless, but to harness those emotions as fuel. You'll learn how to generate your own joy, create an impact on the world that's meaningful to you and those you serve, tend to your corner of purpose, and let go of the noise that doesn't serve you.

This work will stretch you. It may be uncomfortable and, at times, even scary. But when you begin to take full responsibility for your choices, your energy, your attention, you'll start to see someone different in the mirror. Not just someone who looks different, but someone who feels different—stronger in body, steadier in heart, clearer in mind, and more connected to your spirit. That's what happens when all four energy domains begin to align.

When you first feel that glimmer of new energy, you'll willingly continue to endure the greatest discomfort of your life and career: facing yourself today to become the person you want to become, living the life that you want to live. And it will be exhilarating!

As you grow, commit, construct, and communicate your life to others in a way that honors your true self, life will begin to respond in kind. Doors will open that you didn't expect to open. People in your life will behave differently. And new people, aligned with your way of being, will appear. You become magnetic because you're living in coherence with who you are.

This is a life without the Sunday scaries or hiding from Monday mornings. A life where you wake up grounded, energized, and grateful, regardless of what the world is serving up. It's a life built on presence rather than performance. One filled with moments of clarity, resonance and, yes, many joyful pinch-me experiences.

This is a life with a mission, driven by questions that matter. A life where meaning is not an afterthought, but a compass. One where your intellect, your body, your heart, and your spirit all get a seat at the table.

When you begin to Live Your Opus, you will be utterly amazed each day with yourself, your life, and your career; it's something that not even dreams can prepare you to feel, an intense feeling of joy and calm that continues to surge. It is not a perfect life; there's no such thing. But it is the closest to perfect that I've found, because it is true.

Your life isn't just about what you achieve; it's about who you are and who you are becoming. Since you're the world's leading expert on yourself, you already have everything you need to get started. So, let's go.

Part One

YOUR OPUS BEGINS HERE

You've taken the first step. You made it here, which means something inside you is stirring. It might be a nudge, a longing, or a full-on shout that it's time for a change. You don't need to have the whole picture or know what you want today or in five or ten years. Right now, you just need a thread to follow and a willingness to see where it leads.

This part of the book is where you start to feel your feet on the ground. It's the lay of the land. The rhythms. The tools. The essentials. The ones that help you move through your life with more clarity, more purpose, and a whole lot more vitality.

We'll cover what the Opus Way is, how it works, and the many ways you can use it. On this journey, you will remember who you are and learn how to build a life that actually fits.

Before you move forward, pause for a moment. Plant your feet. Take a breath. And remember that you're not here by accident.

Chapter One

THE OPUS WAY: A Path to Healthy, Meaningful, Sustainable Success

Before anything new can begin, inside or out, you need three things: a sense of where you are, a memory of what matters, and the courage to choose a way forward.

That's what the Opus Way is: a practical, powerful method to reclaim your energy, reimagine success on your terms, and build a life that truly matters. A life rooted in your values. Aligned with your energy. Built with intention and shaped by action. Healthy enough to sustain and honest enough to grow with you over time.

And let me say this early: The Opus Way doesn't just encompass your work life *or* your personal life. You don't live in compartments. You are one person, in one body, mind, heart, and spirit, and you live one life. That insight, which Danish philosopher Morten Albæk wrote about so powerfully in *One Life*, is a foundation of this work.

If your success costs you your well-being, it isn't really success. If your work thrives, but your relationships or health are crumbling, that's not alignment. And if your personal growth doesn't show up in how you lead, contribute, or build, then it's just a nice idea, not a lived experience.

The Opus Way brings your life into coherence. It helps you build something that *works as a whole.*

Let me walk you through the three interconnected parts that make it work:

- **The Opus Change Continuum** helps you locate yourself emotionally and energetically. It allows you to understand your true starting point at any given moment so you can respond with self-awareness and compassion.

- **The Opus 8 Energy System** is a life-aligned framework of eight core principles that help you generate, renew, and direct your energy across four essential domains: physical, emotional, mental, and spiritual. Grouped into three dynamic tiers—Stability, Alignment, and Endurance—the Opus 8 meets your evolving needs, giving you the strength, clarity, and focus to define success on your terms and build a life that truly matters. Together with the Change Continuum and the Four-Stage Transformation process, the Opus 8 helps you not only generate energy, but use it wisely, so your growth isn't just ambitious, but aligned and enduring.

- **The four stages of the Live Your Opus transformation process**—Connect, Dream, Compose, and Embark—give you a clear, grounded pathway to activate those energy principles and move forward with intention. It's the structure that turns your insights into action and your vision into reality, helping you create change that sticks. It prepares you for the transition that you'll make as you begin to Live Your Opus. This is the journey we'll walk together over the next twelve weeks (and return to whenever you need it).

These elements don't stand alone; they work together as a complete, integrated system. Each piece meets you where you are and helps you move forward with clarity, care, and momentum. This is not theoretical or surface-level self-help; it's a practical, field-tested approach rooted in deep research and real-life experiences.

I designed the Opus Way over years of interdisciplinary study and shaped it in the real world with hundreds of clients, deep research across fields, and the lived experiences of those navigating profound personal and professional change. Their insights helped to shape this framework into something practical, flexible, and deeply human.

The Opus Way rests on a wide foundation, drawing together disciplines that are rarely taught side-by-side, yet are deeply related in real life. The Opus Change Continuum reflects insights from research on emotional responses to change and transition. The Opus 8 Energy System builds on what we know helps people stay grounded, focused, resilient, and live longer, healthier lives. The four-stage Live Your Opus transformation process mirrors natural cycles of change found in human development, behavioral psychology, and even the creative process, each of which follows a rhythm of reflection, visioning, planning, and action.

This work is not abstract. It's real. It's flexible. And it's meant to serve you in this season—and every season after.

As you begin today, you don't need to be ready or certain. But you do need to be open, curious, and willing to take the next step.

Now, before we go further, let me ask you something simple but important: *Why are you here*? Not here on earth (though that is a big question). I mean, why did you pick up this book today? What were you feeling when you opened to this page? What were you hoping to find?

Maybe something in your life is not working.

Maybe something's been whispering to you.

Maybe you're tired of pretending that what you've built so far is enough.

Or maybe you're just trying to stay upright in the middle of a transition you didn't choose.

Whatever you're facing, you don't have to know the full answer to this big question just yet. But take a moment to pause and feel into it. What do you want to get from this journey? What do you *need* from it?

Write it down. Whisper it to yourself. Say it in the shower tomorrow morning. That intention will help you find your footing in the pages ahead.

STARTING WHEREVER YOU ARE

Change isn't always a grand, cinematic moment. Sometimes it looks like staring at your calendar and realizing you don't want to do any of it. Sometimes it's the quiet ache that says, *this isn't it.* And sometimes, change comes barging in—unexpected, unwanted, and messy.

It's okay if you're feeling uncertain right now. Or tired. Or excited. Or quietly hopeful. Or a strange mix of all four. However you're feeling, the important thing is to be honest with yourself about where you are right now.

This is where we begin: Not by fixing. Not by leaping ahead. But by noticing. Naming. And meeting ourselves, kindly, right here, wherever we are.

When we talk about change, we're often talking about transition, the space between the life you had or are living and the one you want to build. And if that space feels messy? That's because it *is.*

Years ago, I came across the work of transition expert William Bridges. He described transitions as having three stages: an ending, a neutral (or middle) zone, and a new beginning. Each transition requires us to let go of the old while navigating the uncertainty of what's next.[3] That framework changed the way I understood my own life. Especially during my burnout recovery, when everything in me wanted to get "back to normal" as quickly as possible.

I now appreciate that healing, growing, and beginning again—they're not tidy. Transitions take time. They ask you to let go before you know what's next. And they rarely come with perfect clarity.

You see, transitions are different than change. In the words of William Bridges, " … change is situational. Transition, on the other hand, is psychological … Without a transition, a change is just rearrangement of furniture. Unless transition happens, the change won't work, because it doesn't take."[4]

Transitions don't just happen to us; they happen *within* us. You're not just adjusting your schedule or your job or your goals. You're adjusting who you are or who you thought you were supposed to be. That kind of shift can feel shaky at best, like losing your way before a new path appears.

Learning this helped me breathe. It reminded me that I wasn't broken. I was simply between stories. I didn't need to be fixed or have all the answers. It was okay that I felt uncomfortable and that I sometimes wanted to resist it all. And it was okay for me to take time to mourn the way things had been.

So, where are you in this moment? Are you standing at an ending, letting go of something that no longer fits? Are you in the messy middle, uncertain, searching, not quite there yet? Or are you standing on the edge of something new, ready, even if slightly afraid?

Don't rush to decide. We're about to explore the Opus Change Continuum, a simple tool that can help you locate yourself emotionally and energetically, with honesty.

The Opus Change Continuum will help you name where you are right now, not where you were six months ago, not where you wish to be in six months from now, but where you are in this very moment. It's a way to bring clarity, compassion, and traction to whatever place you're in.

Are you hesitating? Navigating? Building something steady? Exploring possibilities? Or ready to spark something bold?

There's an archetype for each of those modes, and you'll likely recognize yourself in more than one. That's okay. You're allowed to be complicated. What matters is noticing how you're responding to the season you're in so you can support yourself accordingly.

Before we dive into the Continuum, take a breath. Literally, just one deep, steadying inhale. And ask yourself:

- What is the change I'm sitting inside of right now?

- What am I holding that's heavy, or tender, or waiting to be said?
- What kind of support would actually feel good right now?

There's no gold star for speed here. There is only honesty. And that honesty? That's your compass. Wherever you are, it's your starting point, and you're allowed to begin from right there.

Let me say this a little louder for the people in the back: You are allowed to begin from right here. Because that's where you are. And I'll be with you every step of the way.

THE OPUS CHANGE CONTINUUM

One of the biggest myths about change is that it's linear, as if we wake up one morning, have a breakthrough, make a plan, and never look back. That's not how it works. Real change is messy. It loops and stutters. Some days you're full of fire. Other days, it takes all you've got to just not shut down.

That's why I created the Opus Change Continuum: to help you name where you are, so you can meet yourself with more clarity and compassion. Think of it as a snapshot of how you're relating to change right now, in this moment.

There are five archetypes on the Continuum:

- **Hesitators pause.** They need time, safety, and clarity. They're not lazy or resistant; they're discerning. Their wisdom is in waiting until something feels true. But sometimes, that waiting turns into staying stuck.

- **Navigators love a plan.** They're thoughtful, prepared, and strategic. They can map out a path forward with precision. But when life doesn't go according to the map? That's when it gets hard. Flexibility is the growth edge here.

- **Builders move slowly, steadily.** They focus on what's solid, what works. Their strength is in creating something stable. But sometimes, they forget to leap when opportunities strike, preferring to stay in their comfort zone.

- **Explorers are curious and open.** They're the idea people, the ones who follow the spark, try things, and experiment. Their challenge is focus. With so many doors to open, it's easy to forget which one actually leads home.

- **Catalysts are on fire.** They're vision-driven and action-oriented. They start movements, shift systems, and light the way. But, sometimes, they burn too hot. They move fast and forget to rest, until something forces them to stop.

No archetype is better than the others. They each represent valid ways of being. You might see yourself in more than one. You might resonate with one archetype at work and one at home. You might move through several in a single week. The Continuum isn't static; it's a mirror to help you understand your own pace, tendencies, and needs.

Figure One. The Five Archetypes of the Opus Change Continuum

Let me give you an example from my own life. I was a lifelong Catalyst. But, when I first stepped away from my work after burning out, I was a Hesitator even though I didn't want to admit it. I kept saying I just needed a break, and then I'd go back to "normal." The truth was that my definition of normal was unsustainable. I didn't know what would come next. I just knew I couldn't keep going the way I had been.

Slowly, with help, I moved toward the Builder archetype. I began setting up rhythms that felt nourishing as I tested new ways of working and found my footing again. I then became an Explorer, imagining new directions and asking bigger questions. Eventually, my Catalyst-self returned. But this time, wiser. Calmer. Rooted.

That's the power of seeing yourself clearly. Not to judge, but to understand. To support yourself—not force yourself. Before we move on, I invite you to do a quick self-check:

- Which archetype feels most like you today?
- Is that how you usually respond to change, or is something different happening now?
- What kind of support, rhythm, or permission do you need at this point?

You'll find more depth about each archetype in Tools to Live Your Opus, so, for now, choose the one that resonates the most with how you feel today.

And remember, you don't have to be anywhere other than where you are.

THE OPUS 8 ENERGY SYSTEM

Once you know where you are on the Opus Change Continuum, the next question becomes: How do I support myself from here? That's where the Opus 8 comes in. The Opus 8 Energy System is a life-aligned framework of eight principles that help you generate, renew, and direct your energy to what matters most to you.

Grouped into three dynamic tiers—Stability, Alignment, and Endurance—these principles help you to reclaim your energy and channel it into meaningful, aligned action so that your growth and success are sustainable over time.

The Opus 8 is rooted in high-performance research which confirms that your ability to lead, create, connect, and thrive depends not just on your time or talent, but on your energetic capacity across four essential domains.

Physical energy is your foundation, fueling your stamina, supporting recovery, and allowing you to meet the demands of daily life with strength and resilience.

Emotional energy shapes your internal world, influencing how you relate to yourself and others, how you respond to stress, and how you access joy, empathy, and motivation.

Mental energy is your focus, directing your attention, supporting clear decision-making, and helping you bring consistency and intention to your thoughts and actions.

Your spiritual energy is your deeper "why" and connects you to your values, sense of meaning, and something greater than yourself. It's the energy of purpose, alignment, and inspiration.[5]

The Opus 8 builds on this foundation and expands the lens. Once you cultivate your physical, emotional, mental, and spiritual energy, the Opus 8 helps you to determine where you'll direct that energy, and to what end.

The eight principles of the Opus 8 will help you do more than nurture or replenish your energy; they will help you channel that energy in a way that's healthy and meaningful over the long run. As Figure Two shows, I've organized them into three tiers: Stability, Alignment, and Endurance, each one builds on the other and, together, they form an integrated system.

Figure Two. The Opus 8 Energy System

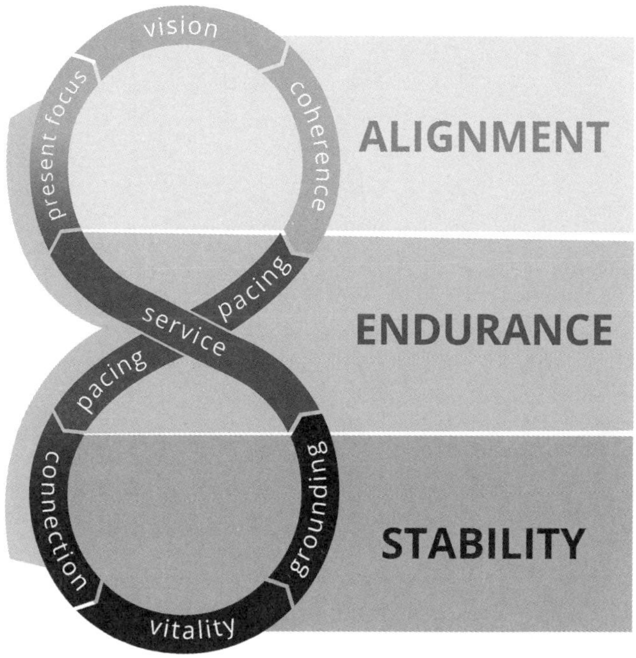

You activate the Opus 8 principles in your life through practices, habits, rhythms, and tools. You won't use all eight principles equally at every moment. Depending on your archetype, or even just the day you're having, certain principles will matter more than others. Whatever you're moving through, the Opus 8 Energy System can meet you there. Let's begin to explore each of the tiers and principles now.

Stability Principles

These are your roots. Beyond helping you survive a hard season, Stability principles allow you to become someone who thrives, period.

Figure Three. Stability Practices

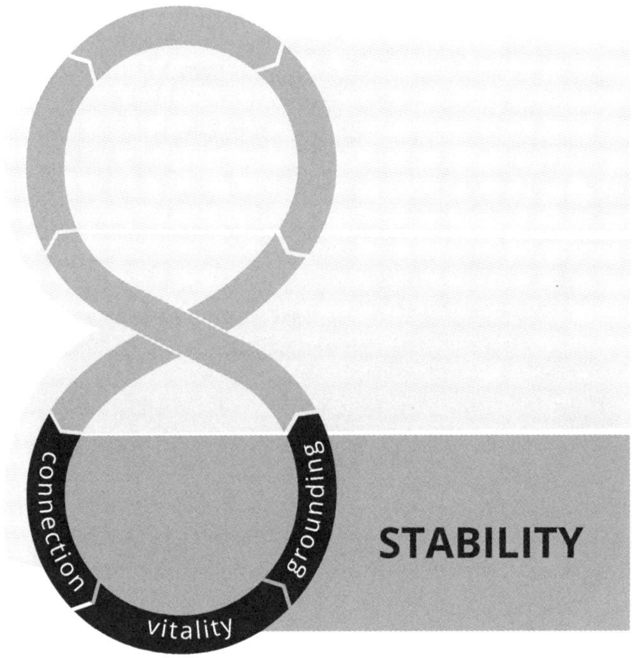

- **Vitality is your energetic foundation.** It underpins your physical stamina, emotional regulation, and overall resilience. When your body is rested, nourished, and moving, and when your basic physiological needs are met, your capacity to recover, relate, and respond expands.

- **Connection is your emotional anchor.** It reflects the quality of your relationship with yourself and others. The act of connecting restores your emotional energy by tethering you to empathy, trust, and care, reminding you that you don't have to carry everything alone.

- **Grounding is your return to center.** It's the capacity to regulate your nervous system and stay present in the face of uncertainty. Grounding practices like breathwork, meditation, walking, or journaling help restore spiritual steadiness and make room for clarity.

When I hit burnout, I didn't need a strategy or plan like I thought I did; I needed the kind of energy generated by Vitality, Connection, and Grounding. I was depleted, but I thought I could fix my life from the neck up. Healing only started, though, when I restored my energy by focusing on sleep, nutrition, quiet, friendship, and slow mornings—when I took my energy seriously and began to cultivate and replenish it with care. It was then that I remembered what it meant to feel like a human again.

That's what these principles do. They help you remember your humanness.

Alignment Principles

When practiced, Alignment principles help you filter out noise and direct your energy toward what actually matters. When your energy is well-aligned, it flows more freely and is more easily replenished.

Figure Four. Alignment Principles

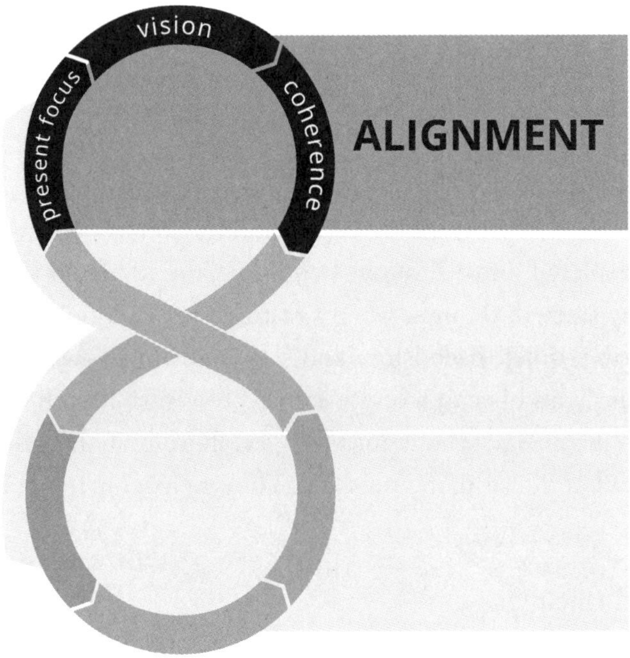

- **Vision is your North Star.** It doesn't need to be perfect. But you do need to know what you're moving toward. A meaningful future vision draws on your spiritual energy and, when well-held, helps replenish it by offering direction, purpose, and hope.

- **Coherence means that your values, goals, and daily actions are in alignment.** Without it, life often feels disjointed or unnecessarily draining. Coherence supports your emotional and mental energy, ensuring they're used in ways that reflect what matters most to you and, in doing so, strengthens them.

- **Present Focus is the art of staying here, in this moment, this breath, this step.** It helps you calm reactivity and choose clearly, even amid chaos. Practicing Present Focus stabilizes and strengthens your emotional and mental energy by bringing you back to what's essential now.

Together, these principles sharpen your mental and spiritual energy. They help ensure your actions are not only productive, but purposeful and life-giving.

When I work with people who feel scattered or stuck in "doing" mode—overworking, overcommitting, overplanning—it's almost always these Alignment principles that need attention.

You may have big dreams. But if your calendar and habits don't reflect them, you'll keep feeling off. These principles help bring your inner life and outer life into harmony.

Endurance Principles

I learned the hard way that progress is a marathon, not a sprint. Progress isn't just about starting strong—it's about continuing, with care, over time. Endurance principles help you sustain energy across all four essential domains (physical, emotional, mental, and spiritual) so that growth becomes energizing, not exhausting. These are the practices that allow your success to last and your impact to deepen without losing yourself along the way.

Figure Five. Endurance Principles

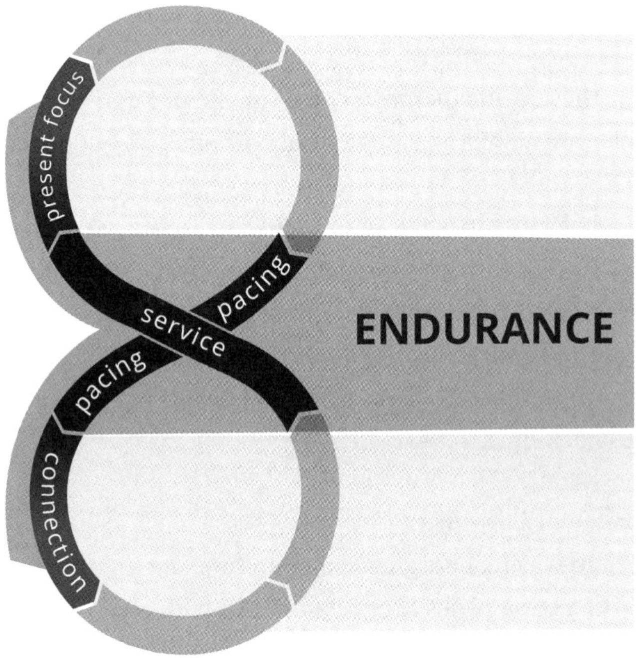

- **Service means contributing to something larger than yourself.** It infuses your life and work with purpose and reconnects you to your why. Service activates your spiritual and emotional energy by offering a sense of connection, compassion, and meaning.

- **Pacing is a rhythm—an intentional dance between effort and recovery.** It protects your energy, especially physical and mental, and prevents burnout. Pacing practices help you to sustain your momentum without requiring constant intensity. It's how to keep going without losing yourself.

There are two other Endurance principles; they draw from the Stability and Alignment principles, but take on renewed meaning here. The definitions below have been tilted toward how they help you sustain yourself and your work.

- **Connection** means nurturing the relationships (with yourself and others) that help you endure and thrive over time.

- **Present Focus** practices allow you to stay rooted in what's real now, helping you make the most of your time, energy, and relationships in a sustainable way.

When I meet high achievers who say, "I can't slow down," or "I don't have time to stop," I often ask: "What are you afraid will happen if you do?" The answers are always telling. The fear is usually not about slowing down. More often, we're afraid of losing what we've linked our worth to. Pacing unhooks that. It lets you stay in the game without losing your soul. Endurance isn't just about lasting—it's about continuing to grow in a way that nourishes who you are and what matters most.

WHERE YOU ARE NOW AND WHAT YOU NEED

Now, I know that's a lot to take in. You don't need to memorize or master all of this right now. Just remember: the Opus 8 aren't traits to possess—they're practices to live. Each one helps you generate, direct, and renew energy across your physical, emotional, mental, and spiritual dimensions. And each one becomes real only when you embody them through your habits, decisions, and daily rhythms.

You don't need to work with all the energy principles at once. Instead, start where you are. If you're depleted, begin with Stability to restore your foundation. Once you're steady, Alignment helps clarify your direction and focus your energy where it matters most. From there, the Endurance tier supports your long-term momentum so growth feels energizing, not exhausting.

So, take a breath and ask yourself:

- What do I need most right now?
- Which archetype resonates most with where I am today? Which energy principle feels like an invitation?
- What's the one thing I could begin practicing today, however simple or imperfect, to support myself?

You can use the table below to guide you, matching the archetype that resonates now with the Opus 8 tier and practices that can support you. At the end of this book, in Tools to Live Your Opus, you can further explore the Opus 8 (Tool 2) and use the Opus 8 Compass (Tool 3) to gain a deeper snapshot of where your energy might be leaking and where it is abundant.

These are your tools now. Return to them whenever you need; they are here to meet you wherever you are. In the pages ahead, we'll bring these practices to life through action, intention, and rhythm, so that your Opus becomes not just something you dream, but something you embody.

Table One. Supporting Your Energy, Wherever You Are

ARCHETYPE	PRIMARY CHARACTERISTICS	SUPPORTIVE OPUS 8 ENERGY TIERS	ACTIONS TO TAKE
HESITATOR	Feeling stuck, uncertain, afraid to take action	Stability	Lean into Grounding and Connection: Build steady routines to reconnect with yourself and get grounded. Restore physical, emotional, and spiritual energy by seeking support from others, establishing rhythm, and practicing mindfulness.

ARCHETYPE	PRIMARY CHARACTERISTICS	SUPPORTIVE OPUS 8 ENERGY TIERS	ACTIONS TO TAKE
NAVIGATOR	Over-reliance on structure, struggles with being flexible when things don't go to plan	Alignment and Endurance	Lean into Present Focus practices to help adjust your vision with clarity, even when plans change. Use Pacing practices to protect your emotional and mental energy and prevent burnout.
BUILDER	Slow but steady progress, may play it safe or resist bold action	Alignment, Stability, and Endurance	Lean into Vision and Coherence: Align your actions with your values and purpose; stretch and take small risks by experimenting. Service and Connection renew emotional and spiritual energy, anchoring your growth in what matters most.
EXPLORER	Visionary, easily distracted, struggles with follow-through	Alignment and Endurance	Lean into Vision, Pacing, and Present Focus: Focus your mental energy and reduce emotional overstimulation using clear structures and boundaries. Evaluate new opportunities through those lenses before saying yes.
CATALYST	Changemaker, moves fast but risks burnout	Endurance, Stability, and Alignment	Lean into Connection, Present Focus, Pacing, and Service: Prioritize rest and recovery, and create systems that support sustainable progress. Anchor your work in deeper meaning to restore spiritual energy and stay aligned with your purpose.

THE FOUR-STAGE PROCESS: ATTAINING HEALTHY, MEANINGFUL, SUSTAINABLE SUCCESS

You now have a sense of where you are—your current relationship with change—and you've been introduced to the eight energy principles that form the foundation of the Opus 8 Energy System. These principles are not just ideas to understand, but energies to cultivate. But insight alone isn't enough. Transformation doesn't live in our thoughts; it lives in our bodies, our behaviors, and our choices. It unfolds over time, through rhythm, reflection, and action.

That's why the Live Your Opus journey is designed as a four-stage process: Connect, Dream, Compose, and Embark. More than just steps, they're stages of becoming. Each one builds on the last. Each one invites you to explore and implement a particular kind of energy, attention, and growth. Each one supports you in aligning your outer life with your inner truth.

Together, these stages form a repeatable framework for transformation; one that you can return each time life asks you to evolve, begin again, or deepen your sense of purpose. Whether you are navigating a career shift, rethinking or redesigning your life, or simply reconnecting with who you are, the four-stage process will meet you where you are and guide you to where you're ready to grow.

Part two of this book walks you through these stages over twelve weeks. And, if you're ready to go even deeper, the *Live Your Opus Workbook* offers additional tools and space to support your ongoing transformation.

Connect

Who are you, really, and what do you need to do to come home to yourself? Before you leap forward, you have to come home.

Connect is the foundation. It's the part of the journey where you get honest about what's working, what isn't, and what you've maybe been avoiding. You build a deeper relationship with yourself. You reconnect with what matters. And you start tending to your energy, your truth, and your voice. If you've been operating in survival mode, or just running too fast or on autopilot, this stage is where you start to wake back up.

A Catalyst might need this stage to slow down and reconnect with meaning. A Hesitator may find the courage to listen in for the first time in a long while. Either way, in the Connect stage you set your compass. Then, when you're ready to move, you're not just reacting; you're moving from a deeper, more aligned place.

No matter your starting point, the Connect stage ensures that you're not embarking on this journey as a stranger to yourself or to those who can best support you. It will help you to root more deeply before you arrive at the Dream stage and imagine what's possible.

Dream

What could be possible if you gave yourself permission to imagine more? This is the stage where you turn to your imagination. But you are not dreaming for the sake of escape. Instead, you're daring to name what you really want—even if you're not sure how to get there yet.

In the Dream stage, you stretch. You explore. You allow hidden desires to surface. And, slowly, you begin to shape a vision that feels alive.

Navigators may realize their current plan needs to shift. Explorers will love the creativity here, but they will also learn to listen for what truly resonates, not just what's shiny.

The most important part of Dream is your willingness to explore what's possible. And although dreaming is powerful, dreams alone won't get you to where you want to go. That's why the Compose stage is next; it is a space to bridge your aspirations with action.

Compose

How do you turn a vision into something real and make a plan that can breathe? Compose is where ideas meet action, and you begin to sketch out your Opus, not rigidly, but like a musician discovering a melody. In this stage, you will create a first draft, test it, and refine it. You experiment. You begin. You ask yourself: What's one next step I can take?

You won't be figuring everything out at this stage. You're going to find cadence, coherence, and forward motion. Builders will be at home here; just be sure you're not playing it too safe. Catalysts, this is your invitation to slow down and imagine what your experience would be like if you pace yourself over the long haul.

The focus here is on creating a road map that reflects not just your goals, but also your capacity to achieve them over the near and long term. Then, map in hand, you'll move to the Embark stage, where your plans become reality.

Embark

What does it look like to truly live your dream—your Opus—and stay the course when it gets hard? This stage is where the rubber meets the road. You've dreamed, designed, and made a loose plan. Now it's time to Live Your Opus. And, yes, this is where resistance shows up. Old patterns. Fear. The temptation to go back to what feels familiar.

That's why the Embark stage is about more than just action. It's about more self-mastery and learning to stay with yourself when doubt creeps in. Learning to sustain your energy. Learning to trust that you can handle what comes next.

Hesitators will learn to take small, brave steps. Catalysts will learn how to sustain momentum over the long haul once and for all. Regardless of where you are, the Embark stage reminds you that progress doesn't have to be perfect; it just needs to begin.

This is the stage where you become the person who lives your Opus, not through perfection or overwork, but by showing up consistently with grace, intention, and self-compassion. You will learn to show up for yourself every day, especially on the days that are challenging.

YOUR BEGINNING, FROM HERE

You've now met the three essentials of the Opus Way: a way to understand where you are, how to cultivate your energy and direct it toward what matters, and a path to carry you forward toward your Opus life. I hope they've piqued your curiosity about what's truly possible for you and your life.

It's not important that you remember every aspect of the Opus Way at this point. You'll spend time with each part in the pages ahead, becoming deeply familiar with this framework. Today, you just need to take the next honest step.

Maybe that means pausing long enough to hear yourself think. Maybe it's naming the ache you've been ignoring in your heart. Maybe it's letting yourself hope that something different is possible. Or maybe you're already moving into action.

Wherever you are, *this* is your starting point.

For now, take a deep breath, and trust that today you are exactly where you need to be.

Part Two

TRANSFORM YOUR LIFE IN TWELVE WEEKS

This is a moment to pause—and to celebrate. You're here, standing on the edge of something new.

Maybe you're already asking new questions or have a new awareness of how to reclaim your energy. You may sense something stirring within you, perhaps something long buried or a dream that you didn't realize was still waiting for you. You may be coming alive in a way that feels unfamiliar, sensitive, or even a little thrilling.

Wherever you are, I want to acknowledge that you've already lived a rich, full life. You've likely written not one, but many Opuses. That's part of why this work matters so much; it honors all that you've been, while inviting you into all that you still can be.

These next twelve weeks, eighty-four days, are a sacred container. They are a space you create for yourself. A space to return to what's most essential: you. I invite you to begin the Live Your Opus transformation experience.

Chapter Two

GET THE MOST FROM *LIVE YOUR OPUS*

You've already explored the Opus Change Continuum and the Opus 8 Energy System. These are your guideposts, living tools that will help you stay rooted in your values, energized by your ambition, and steady in your transformation.

Now, in part two, you'll move through four distinct stages: Connect, Dream, Compose, and Embark. Each one will offer gentle—but direct—structure, tools, and practices to help you turn insight into action and action into alignment, directing your energy to what matters most.

Each stage comprises a main chapter and three sections labelled as weeks, beginning with week one in Connect. In weeks one through twelve, you'll find tools and exercises designed to support your transformation. You can move through the weeks and exercises at your own pace, but it is important to follow the stages in the order they're presented here.

Through this journey and these chapters, you will learn about yourself, how you define success and a meaningful life, and how energy and transformation can work together. Along the way, you'll explore the types of mindsets, energy, and habits of mind, body, heart, and spirit that propel and, ultimately, sustain a meaningful life and the ever-human tendency to self-sabotage. Finally, you will learn how to master yourself so that you can become the person you want or need to become to live your version of meaning and success.

For those of you who will complete the weekly exercises as you read, I recommend you continue reading the rest of this section before diving into Connect, the first stage. Here, I'll share a few more practices to help you prepare for and get the most out of your transformation journey.

Should you want to go deeper and access a wider range of practices and exercises that will enable you to further personalize and customize your journey, please take advantage of the *Live Your Opus Workbook* and the materials available at LiveYourOpus.com.

If you're here to learn how to Live Your Opus but prefer to reflect as you read rather than engage in the exercises, simply skip them for now and, instead, read these chapters as you've read the opening ones.

However you choose to engage with this experience, I'll be right here with you, each step of the way. I will offer stories, reflections, practices, and encouragement; nudge you when you need movement; and remind you to rest when you need to pause.

And because real transformation is rarely linear, let me say this: Like any intensive experience, there will be moments when you feel powerful and clear and moments when you feel less so.

If you find yourself overwhelmed, pause. Take five long, slow breaths. Step outside if you can. Take a walk. Then, reach out. Share what you're feeling with a trusted partner. Let someone in. And lean into the courage and strength that have already carried you through so much.

The path ahead is about becoming the person your dreams require of you so you can live them. It's about learning to listen to yourself, your energy, your longings. It's about letting your life become your greatest work.

Let's begin with the mindset that will carry you through.

THE OPUS MINDSET

Everyone brings, and builds, their own secret success sauce. But there are common ingredients, cross-cutting qualities, that make everyone's sauce richer, more resilient, more real. That's what lives inside the Opus Mindset.

The Opus Mindset is an inner stance and spirit. A way of seeing and being that infuses the journey ahead with clarity, compassion, and courage. It's about how you approach your life going forward, beginning with your work here.

Take a moment now to read through the following ideas slowly. Listen with your heart, not just your head. Let them land softly. Notice which ones feel familiar and which ones stretch you. You don't need to know how to live into them yet. Just begin by being open.

- **Your story matters.** I said it in the opening chapter, and I'll reiterate it here: every experience—every triumph, every stumble—has shaped you. Did you know that owning and narrating your life story increases your resilience and emotional well-being? So, embrace all of what you've lived through; don't minimize it. Even the chapters you've wanted to skip. Especially those. Don't hide from your story, share it; it's your greatest asset.

- **Curiosity ignites action.** Every meaningful change begins with a question: What if? Curiosity is the quiet force that moves us forward when we're unsure, overwhelmed, or afraid. It softens judgment and opens up possibility. Let your curiosity guide you here, even if the path ahead feels unclear. Especially then.

- **Action clarifies purpose.** You don't have to have certainty or all the information before you begin. Taking even the smallest step can generate clarity and momentum. That's because taking action activates the brain's reward system, creating a virtuous cycle. So, if you're stuck—don't wait. Move, even a baby step forward. Reflect. Then move again.

- **Joy and play are essential fuel.** Joy is not optional. It's not frivolous. It's a kind of wisdom. Play reconnects us to possibility and to each other. Studies show that even brief moments of joy can lower cortisol, increase focus, and strengthen relationships. So, invite delight. Let lightness in. Let yourself laugh. And enjoy this process.

- **Fear is a teacher, not a roadblock.** We all carry fear—of failure, of success, of being seen or not seen. And often we try to outrun it or avoid it. But fear, when met with curiosity, can become an incredible teacher. Instead of resisting it, ask yourself: What is fear here to show me? This shift rewires the brain, moving you into an inquiry state, making you more resilient and ready to learn.

- **Life is always changing.** You'll remember this from the opening chapter: Change is constant. Resistance is optional. Adaptability is one of the strongest predictors of well-being. Learning to ride the waves—rather than brace against them—is key to living your Opus. And it is something you can practice.

On this journey you'll work toward a new way of being that supports and fuels your energy and success from the inside out. These perspectives are your companions; when practiced, they'll help you to be intentional. Come back to them often, especially when you feel overwhelmed or uncertain. Let them remind you of who you are and what you came here to do. Pair them with the Opus 8 energy principles. Together, they'll support you in composing a life that is aligned, alive, and yours.

Remember, you are your greatest work. Your worth is not in your résumé, your productivity, or your performance; it's in who you're becoming each day. The self-actualized life is not a far-off destination; it's the one you create, choice by choice, by showing up as the most honest version of you and committing to master yourself.

CREATING THE CONDITIONS FOR GROWTH

When I teach the Live Your Opus four-stage transformation process as a course, I invite people to create what I call an Opus Bubble, a supportive space, both physical and emotional, that makes room for reflection, learning, and personal expansion. Think of these elements as a set of conditions, routines, structures, and tools that set you up to learn.

So now, it's your turn. You've already said yes to this work. Now it's time to become the person who not only begins the journey, but finishes it. To do that, we start by shaping your bubble. Your space. Your structure. Your commitment to yourself. Here are a few gentle ingredients that will help.

Time

Transformation asks for your presence. That's why I encourage you to block time in your calendar, an hour each week that belongs only to you. This is your sacred time; use it to read, reflect, complete exercises, recover your energy, or simply reconnect with yourself.

Gaining early momentum matters. When change has rhythm, it's easier to stay with it. This isn't pressure; it's flow. I've seen too many people start strong and lose steam because they never gave themselves the time to truly begin.

And I get it: We're all "too busy." Emails, meetings, errands, caregiving, social media scrolling—the list never ends. But I also know: *Busyness is often just disguised avoidance.*

As Dorie Clark says in her TED Talk, "The Real Reason We're All So Busy," busyness has become a status symbol. "When we say, 'Oh, I am so crazy busy,' what we're really saying is a societally accepted version of 'I am so important.' 'I am so popular.' 'I am so in demand.'"[6] But the cost is real. Chronic busyness chips away at our health, energy, clarity, and sense of meaning and control.

So, if you're struggling for time, ask yourself gently: What is my busyness costing me?

This isn't about discipline; it's about honesty and choosing to reclaim your time as an act of self-respect. Set a weekly schedule. Make an appointment with yourself. And if you miss it? Reschedule. No guilt. No shame. Just begin again.

Dedicated Space

If you can, choose a physical space that feels nourishing. It might be a favorite chair, a quiet corner, a park bench, or a corner table at your local café. Wherever it is, make it yours, if only for the time you set aside.

You might even create a small ritual to enter this space: light a candle, take three grounding breaths, close any open tabs on your computer, have a hot drink by your side, and silence your phone. In my workshops, we begin this way. The candlelight signals presence. The breath says, I'm here now.

Find your own way to mark your Opus time. Honor it.

Trusted Partner

Remember the old proverb: *If you want to go fast, go alone. If you want to go far, go together.*

This journey is personal, but it isn't meant to be solitary. So, find at least one person you trust, a friend, partner, coach, sibling, or community member, with whom you can share pieces of your process; someone who will listen without judgment, celebrate your insights, and hold space for your growth. If you don't have that person right now, you are warmly invited to connect with me and others through different mediums on LiveYourOpus.com. It's a space for people doing this work; you'll always be welcomed there.

Supplies: Journal and Three-Ring Binder

You're going to grow. A lot. Maybe more than you expect. You'll see things differently. You'll hear yourself in new ways. You'll return to old dreams or write new ones. And, as that happens, you'll want to remember. To track.

To catch glimpses of who you're becoming. So, take a dedicated journal or notes app along on your learning journey. And, unless you're using the *Live Your Opus Workbook*, keep a three-ring binder handy to collect and revisit anything you've written. You're composing your Opus. Treat this like a sacred archive.

CORE PRACTICES

There are three foundational practices I encourage you to engage in every week of the twelve-week journey: Activate Opus Mode, In-Service Actions, and the Opus Life Check-In.

I've shared more detail about each of these here so you can bring them into your practice, but they're not otherwise called out each week. (Note: If you're using the *Live Your Opus Workbook*, all of these activities are already included and customized for each week.)

1. **Activate Opus Mode.** Set your intention before you begin your work for the week. Enter the time you spend here with presence and give yourself a ritual to ensure you fully arrive. This is your creative space. Your inner studio. Your life lab.

2. **Weekly In-Service Actions.** Learning deepens when you share it. Teaching or articulating what you've learned cements it more firmly in your brain. You'll notice throughout this process that I don't often explicitly call out Service, an Opus 8 energy principle, as much as other principles. That's because Service is something you will practice regularly. At the end of each week, I encourage you to engage in **In-Service** Actions: Look for opportunities to talk about what you're discovering with a trusted partner. Share an insight. Spark a deeper conversation. Let the work ripple out from you as a way of rooting it more deeply within and watch your energy soar. Although working in isolation might feel safe, it can be lonely, and

beginning to live with Service is a key part of creating meaningful, sustainable success.

3. **Weekly Opus Life Check-Ins.** Pause. Reflect. Integrate. At the end of every week, take fifteen to thirty minutes to look back on what you've learned that week. Note the shifts—big or small. Jot down what moved you, what surprised you, where resistance showed up or something memorable happened. These reflections are your trail markers.

Use these three core practices each week to cement your Live Your Opus transformation learnings.

And now that you've got these practices packed with your other essentials, it's time to move into week one and Connect.

Chapter Three

CONNECT:
Setting Your Internal Compass

One evening, when I was living in a cottage in Kensington Palace Gardens, I invited a good friend over for dinner. The garden was small but private—a rare thing in central London. We sat outside, candles flickering, the quiet hum of the city just beyond the hedge. At some point, she looked around and asked, "Do you ever feel important sitting here?"

She didn't wait for me to answer. Instead, she nodded, as if answering her own question: "Because I can see how you could feel important sitting here. I do."

I paused. Then, to my surprise, I answered honestly. "Yes, I guess so."

I hadn't thought about it before she asked. Looking back, I can see why I felt that way. I started out my early career very poor, and I had worked incredibly hard to get to that moment. Moving from the academic sector to nonprofit to corporate, I had risen through the ranks, taken on bigger roles, earned promotions, moved to London, and created a life that, on paper, looked like success.

When I could finally afford to, with each step, I rewarded my hard work with material goods and experiences. Back then, the rewards included designer bags, jewelry, and prestigious home addresses, to name a few. There is nothing wrong with those things; I still enjoy many of them today, for different reasons. But back then, I believed that they, and things like them, including title, salary, and lifestyle, were proof that I mattered. They meant I had made it.

With reflection, I can clearly now see that, beyond building success, I spent most of my career striving to prove something. To whom, I wasn't sure. But I had spent years being driven by unconscious fears of not being enough, of losing what I had worked for, of failing. These fears likely came from my upbringing and from being financially and emotionally abandoned by my parents while I was in university. Somewhere, deep down, I worried the other shoe might drop again, and I could lose it all.

I even spent more time proving myself than *being* myself. As a survivor of childhood trauma, being myself was not something I was comfortable with. To be myself would have required a kind of safety and emotional energy I hadn't yet cultivated.

I now understand that, for much of my life, and mostly at work, I operated in what neuroscientists call "fear mode." Fear mode comes from the limbic system in our brain, that survival-driven place where stress, anxiety, and scarcity thinking take hold. For me that translated into a constant, unconscious striving to prove myself, to accumulate external markers of success, to regulate the anxiety that lived in my nervous system, to feel safe. The new title, a designer bag, a Michelin-star dinner, each one a temporary reassurance that I was doing well, that I was important.

The problem with fear mode is that it keeps us chasing, always looking for the next achievement, the next validation, the next thing that will make us feel like we are enough. But fear-driven striving pulls us off course and disconnects us from the very energy that fuels real fulfillment. Breaking free from this cycle doesn't happen overnight. It begins with reconnecting with yourself, and, more specifically, with your heart. With your energy, your body's signals, and your quiet inner voice, like I did during my burnout recovery.

Dr. James Doty, a neurosurgeon and researcher, offers an alternative to fear mode called "heart mode." While fear mode is about protection and performance, heart mode is about presence. It engages the parasympathetic nervous system, calming our stress response and allowing us to lead with compassion, clarity, and connection. It's a physiological and emotional shift from tension to trust, from reactivity to thoughtful response.[7]

I moved into heart mode during burnout recovery when I explored, for the first time, who I was without all of the external trappings. I experienced many painful realizations. But it was also the beginning of something much deeper: the work of reconnecting with who I was—with the source of my energy, my values, and my worth—beyond the titles, the paycheck, and the expectations. It was my first step to creating and living my Opus and becoming the person I am today. And that's where real transformation starts—within.

Living from heart mode doesn't just feel better; it strengthens our capacity to navigate life with steadiness and meaning, and it helps us build better relationships. And that's exactly what Vitality, Connection, and Grounding, the Opus 8 Stability principles, are designed to support. These three principles are truly foundational, especially here in the Connect stage. Without them, it's easy to keep running on autopilot, mistaking external success for internal fulfillment.

WHY CONNECTION MATTERS

So many of us live in an unconscious state of fear or depletion, running on autopilot, constantly pushing forward without ever pausing to ask ourselves a simple but hard-to-answer question: Is the life I'm building aligned with who I am and what I need today? Of course, to answer that question honestly assumes that we are in touch with who we are and what we need, which is not always the case.

That's why Connect is the first stage of the Live Your Opus transformation process. Before you can make any meaningful change—or direct your energy toward something new—you must first reconnect with yourself.

- Who are you beneath the titles, roles, and expectations?
- What do you love, value, and appreciate most about who you are? About your body? Your mind? Your heart? Your spirit? And about how you touch the lives of others?
- What do you truly need, not just from your career or business, but from your life, relationships, and yourself?

To get answers to these questions—and to renew your capacity for meaningful action—you must connect with yourself and, in time, with others. Most change models skip this step. They assume self-awareness and self-love are a given, jumping straight to goal-setting, productivity hacks, or big leaps. But you can't think clearly about the future you want without becoming fully aware and appreciative of who and where you are today, what matters to you, and what you need.

The Stability principles of the Opus 8 are essential to the Connect stage. When you begin cultivating your Vitality, you build the physical, emotional, mental, and spiritual energy required to move forward with clarity and steadiness.

When you've experienced positive Connection with yourself and others, you'll have support, emotional resilience, and further clarity to help you navigate transformation. When you use Grounding practices, you'll shift out of reactionary or fear modes so you can make decisions from a place of alignment.

Before you move forward, pause for a moment. Which of these energy principles feels strongest in your life today? Which one feels neglected and in need of practice?

As you move through this stage, keep these principles close. With practice, they become internal anchors that help you build your Opus from a place of wholeness, not depletion, from energy, not just effort.

Think of the Stability principles as roots beneath the surface. The deeper they go, the more resilient your growth above can become. As you connect inwardly, you're laying the energetic groundwork for the life you're about to grow.

DO CONNECT: THE FIRST STEP IN LIVING YOUR OPUS

You are here because you want to reclaim yourself and refine, change, or transform some part of your life, career, or business. You seek clarity on what exactly that change is, how to accomplish it, and, most importantly, how to sustain it over time. Before you can change the course of your life, you need to set your internal compass.

As high achievers, we often get caught up in external demands, our work, our goals, the expectations placed on us, and other people's opinions. But living your Opus requires a new approach: You have to make time to work *on* your life and career, not just be *in* them.

Working *in* your life means staying busy, managing tasks, reacting to deadlines, keeping up with daily responsibilities. Working *on* your life means regularly stepping back, recovering, reflecting, reconnecting, and taking time to check your energy levels, and make sure you are directing your energy to the right path. It's being more present—and awake—in your life. This is one of the fundamental changes you'll make here.

In Connect, you'll begin tuning in to your inner compass, appreciating things the way they are, getting clear on what truly matters, and learning to move forward with intention.

FOUR VITAL SHIFTS TO RECONNECT WITH YOURSELF

The moment you decide to make a change, your mind often leaps into action. What do you need to do first? What's the plan? But true transformation doesn't start with a to-do list; it starts with knowing and valuing who and where you are today.

Before you can move toward the future you want, you need to tune in—to your energy, your values, your rhythms, and your current state of being. In my experience, both personally and in working with others, there are four key shifts that separate those who make lasting transformations from those who get stuck.

These aren't steps or tasks to complete; they are shifts in how you see yourself, how you show up, and how you approach your life. Don't worry if these are new concepts to you. Over the next three weeks, the Connect process will prompt you to make these four shifts.

Shift One: Energy is Power—Own Yours (Vitality)

Most people don't fall short because they lack willpower or strategy. They fail because they're depleted in some way. Your energy, including your mental, physical, emotional, and spiritual energy, is the fuel for everything you do. Yet most of us treat it like an afterthought; we overcommit, multitask, push through exhaustion and burnout, miss appointments with ourselves, and hope for the best.

But you cannot create something new from a depleted state. When we are physically drained, our brain's prefrontal cortex, the area responsible for decision-making, focus, and long-term thinking, struggles to function. We make reactive choices instead of intentional ones. We lose sight of what truly matters, including ourselves.

That's why this shift comes first: Energy isn't just a resource—it's your root system.

Shift Two: You're Not Selfish; You're the CEO of Your Opus (Grounding)

If putting yourself first feels uncomfortable, you are not alone. Many of us have been conditioned to prioritize others' needs before our own. We say yes when we want to say no. We overextend ourselves, fearing we'll be seen as selfish if we don't. This is especially true for women, who are often socialized at home and school to prioritize the needs of others over themselves.

But when you constantly put yourself last, you don't just suffer; you become less effective for everyone around you. Dr. Neha Sangwan, a physician who studies stress and communication, found that chronic people-pleasing is a direct contributor to burnout, anxiety, and even physical illness. When you are always available to others, your nervous system is constantly activated, making it harder to think clearly, set boundaries, or make aligned decisions.[8] To stop the energy drain, you must learn to ground yourself in your own needs—without guilt or apology.

I like to ask: If you were the CEO of your own energy, what would you protect, prioritize, or stop doing entirely?

Shift Three: If You Lose Your "Why," You Lose Your Way (Connection + Vision + Service)

When was the last time you felt deeply connected to *why* you are doing what you are doing, pursuing the life or work you are pursuing, for example? Without a strong, personal reason behind a goal, it's easy to get distracted, discouraged, or abandon it altogether. There is neuroscience behind this: When we lack emotional investment in a goal, our motivation centers don't fully activate.

This is why developing practices to support Connection, Vision, and Service, three of the Opus 8 energy principles, matters so much. Connection ensures your dreams come from within, not from external expectations. Vision keeps you focused on what truly matters so that you don't lose yourself along the way. Service ensures you're impacting something bigger than just yourself.

But finding your way is so much more than just having a "why." You have to feel it. If your "why" is purely external (money, recognition, obligation), it won't sustain you or your progress over the long run. Your "why" needs to be personal, something that stirs emotional and spiritual energy, and brings you to life in new ways.

Don't worry about whether you are connected to your "why" now. That will happen over the next three weeks as you explore the Connect and Dream stages.

Shift Four: Your Identity is a Collection of Tiny Choices (Coherence + Present Focus)

We like to believe that big, life-changing decisions define who we are. But it's the small, daily choices that shape us. Psychologist Wendy Wood, an expert in habit formation, found that 40 percent of our daily actions are unconscious habits. That means nearly half of what you do isn't a decision—it's autopilot.[9]

The problem? You likely formed many of these habits unintentionally. These habits can reflect old identities, outdated priorities, or inherited patterns. If you want to create a new reality, you first need to become aware of the habits that define your current one.

This is where the energy principles of Coherence and Present Focus come alive, transforming your habits into expressions of who you are becoming. Practicing coherence ensures your actions align with your values. Present Focus practices help you stay engaged in the now, so that transformation happens not just in your mind, but also in your daily life.

Over the next three to six weeks, you will become increasingly conscious of the daily choices that shape you now, how those are enabling you to thrive, and whether anything might need to change to support your ambitions.

Each of these four vital shifts is a way of reawakening your energy and reconnecting with your whole self. You are the common denominator in everything you want to create. As you tune in to and replenish your energy, set boundaries, strengthen your "why," and align your habits with who you want to become, you'll become unstoppable.

The more connected you are to yourself and your energy, the more naturally your choices begin to align with your Opus. For the next three weeks, as you move through Connect, you'll begin a process that is deep, personal, and necessary. You'll reconnect with yourself—past, present, and future.

This is your moment. You have spent so much time pushing forward. Now, it's time to pause. To reconnect. To make sure the life you're building is one your energy can sustain and your soul can celebrate.

YOUR FIRST MISSION: A DAILY 1 PERCENT SHIFT

As you begin the Connect stage, your first mission is simple: Choose one small, intentional act that deepens your connection to yourself. Think of this as a 1 percent shift, a tiny but meaningful action that, over time, will transform how you show up for yourself.

Start by identifying the area where connection feels most needed right now:

- **If your energy feels low or scattered,** choose and commit to a micro-practice that helps you restore and protect it, like a short walk to start your day with fresh air and sunlight, a five-minute rest break, or a calming ritual before a meeting.

- **If you're used to putting yourself last,** practice one gentle boundary that reserves your energy for something you love. This might be saying no without guilt or apology, asking for what you need, or carving out a pocket of time that's just for you.

- **If your "why" feels distant,** give it voice. Spend two minutes each day to remind yourself why you're here and what matters, through journaling, quiet reflection, or a statement that anchors you in meaning. Write it down, say it out loud, and honor the fact that you showed up for yourself.

- **If old habits feel misaligned,** bring awareness to one automatic behavior. Observe without judgment and try a tiny shift, like preparing in advance if mornings feel frantic, or pausing before reacting.

Each micro-shift is a way to activate the Stability principles in your life. Consider them as guides, whispering reminders as you move through your day: Vitality asks: What helps me feel more energized today, physically, emotionally, spiritually? Connection asks: How can I show up for myself with kindness? Grounding asks: What simple acts help me return to center when the world pulls me away?

Choose one micro-shift and practice it daily for the next seven days. Notice how it feels—no judgment, just awareness. At week's end, reflect gently: Has anything softened, strengthened, or clarified? Then, decide whether you'll keep going with this shift, adapt it, or choose another. This is how your Opus begins: with one small, steady act of devotion to yourself.

WEEK ONE. CELEBRATING YOUR GROWTH AND RESILIENCE

Most of us think about change as something that starts today and moves forward, fueled by effort or willpower. But meaningful transformation begins with understanding where we've been. Your past holds clues to your resilience, strengths, and evolving sense of purpose. This week, you'll begin by connecting with your past self, exploring who you were at different stages of life, and how your experiences, dreams, and choices shaped who you are today.

By looking back, you'll uncover energetic patterns, rediscover passions and proud moments, and recognize strengths you may have forgotten or underestimated. More than anything, this week is about appreciating how far you have come; that knowledge will fuel your next steps.

Through the exercises this week, you will connect with your story in a way that empowers you. So, don't worry about getting mired in the past. My clients often describe feeling unexpectedly energized and affirmed after this week—a deep confidence boost. They own their story better, and that translates into excitement about what might be possible for them to create in their future.

So, let's look back to fully appreciate who and where you are today.

As we discussed in the opening of part two, each week you'll find one or two exercises that support the stage of the process you're in and the focus at hand, along with the recommended time to complete them. If you would like to access a wider range of additional exercises for each week, you'll want to use the companion *Live Your Opus Workbook* which you can access at LiveYourOpus.com.

Before you dive into the exercise below, remember to take a moment to get into Opus Mode, and be sure to engage in a weekly In-Service Action and Opus Life Check-In with yourself (see the "Core Practices" section in part two). If you're using the workbook, you'll find that these exercises are included each week and are customized for the work at hand.

EXERCISE: ME, IN DECADES (FIFTEEN MINUTES)

When my husband and I went on our first date, we shared snippets of our lives by decade, tiny portraits of who we were at ten, twenty, thirty, and beyond. It was a simple way to connect, to see each other more fully.

Over time, I turned that idea into a journaling exercise. I now use it in workshops and with clients as a way to reconnect with their personal timeline and their energy across it. Each time I teach it, this exercise offers something unexpectedly beautiful: not just a timeline, but a reminder of how far we've come, who we've been, and who we're still becoming.

This is your invitation to do the same.

Start from childhood and work your way to where you are now. You might choose to begin at age ten, or even earlier. If you're younger than twenty-five, five-year increments will work just as well. All you need is a quiet moment, a pen, and a willingness to remember.

For each decade, reflect on what defined that time in your life: your interests, your focus, your challenges, your dreams. Don't worry about getting everything down. Just notice what stands out. Who you were, what you cared about, what lit you up.

Here are a few gentle prompts to guide you along the way:

- **At ten.** Who were you as a child? What hobbies, interests, or qualities defined you? What did you love most about yourself back then?
- **At twenty.** Where were you as a young adult? What were your goals, your questions, your challenges? What were you learning about life?
- **At thirty.** How did your passions, career, or relationships evolve? Were you holding on to old dreams or letting new ones emerge?
- **At forty and beyond.** What shifted? What deepened? How did your sense of identity grow and change? And what has stayed beautifully the same?

Once you've jotted down your memories, take a moment to step back. Look for threads, themes, and turning points. Use these reflection questions to go deeper:

- What did you love about yourself in each stage?
- What experiences are you most grateful for?
- Were there foundational moments that shaped your identity or values?
- Did a past hobby or interest resurface? Could it hold meaning now?
- Have certain passions or values remained steady over time? How have they fueled your energy or where have they gone dim?
- Were there seasons of hardship or challenge? How did you persevere?
- Do you remember times when you felt deeply understood by people, place, or community? Do you have that now?
- When did you feel most energized, alive, or at ease? What was present in those moments, and is it present now?
- Are there patterns that reveal the person you are becoming?

And finally, bring it back to today. Where are you now in your journey? What do you love about yourself in this moment? What drew you to the Live Your Opus path? What kind of transformation are you longing for? If you set aside conventional definitions of success, such as job titles, promotions, and accolades, what does a meaningful life look like to you?

When you've finished this exercise, or if you find yourself feeling stuck, try looking at your life through a few different lenses. Sometimes a new angle brings unexpected clarity about who you've been and who you are becoming.

- Look at your life not by age, but by era. What title would you give each season? What was that version of you learning? And what chapter are you writing now?

- Set your achievements aside for a moment and focus on energy. When did you feel most alive? Most you? Look for patterns across the year. Energy is a powerful compass.
- Write a letter to your younger self. The one who was doing their best with what they knew. Thank them for getting you here. Let them know you see them now.

Reconnecting with Your Story

You've just completed the first week of your Opus journey; congratulations! By looking back, you've given your past self the attention, appreciation, and understanding they may not have received at the time. You've begun to remember who you are, not just what you've done.

In reconnecting with your story, you've also tapped into something powerful: your capacity to grow, to adapt, to restore your energy, and to begin again. Let that awareness stay with you this week. Let it shift how you speak to yourself and shape how you show up in the present.

Next week, we'll begin turning that inward connection outward, moving from memory to mindfulness and from story to intention. Then, in week three, you'll explore the life you're living today and begin to ask: Is this aligned with who I'm becoming?

But for now, pause and take this in: You've taken the first step. You've honored your past. And you're already becoming the person your future will thank you for.

WEEK TWO. NOTICING THE NOISE, RECLAIMING THE NARRATIVE

I remember standing at the bottom of a ladder; I was shivering, goggles propped up on my bathing cap. I was thirteen years old. My summer swim team practice had ended, the pool was mostly empty, my mom had gone to fetch my brother from camp, and I was alone with my fear. For weeks, I had watched others dive effortlessly from the highest board, but every time I climbed the ladder, my feet refused to move past the edge.

The lifeguard didn't say a word; he just watched. And in his silence, I could hear the loudest voice of all: my own.

"Come on, you should be able to do this. What's wrong with you?"

"I can't imagine what the lifeguard is thinking. He must think you're just stupid."

"You've done harder things before. Just jump."

"Never mind. Maybe you're not as brave as you thought."

Again and again, I would climb up, take a few steps toward the edge, and climb back down. Until one time, having finally made it out to the edge for more than a few seconds, my inner voice went quiet and something deeper stirred. For the first time, I stopped battling myself and just listened.

"Dive!" I heard my heart say.

I took a deep breath. And I jumped. It was one of the best days of my life.

That moment on the diving board stayed with me, not because it was brave, but because it was one of the first times I recall truly hearing myself. Not the anxious noise or the inner critic, but the quieter voice underneath. The one that said, simply, "Go."

That's the voice we're looking for this week. Not the loudest voice, but the truest one. This week, you become an active participant in your own energetic landscape.

Your Default Inner Dialogue and the Stories You Tell Yourself

By this point in your life, you've probably noticed the voice inside of you, the one that speaks up in moments of doubt, pressure, or uncertainty. It's quieter than the noise of your day, but far more powerful. Because it's not just any voice; it's the one shaping how you see yourself and what you believe is possible.

Most of us live with a steady stream of internal commentary, a kind of invisible narration that runs beneath the surface of our lives, shaping how we see ourselves and what we believe is possible. Arianna Huffington calls it the "obnoxious roommate" in her head.[10]

Neuroscience calls it the default mode network, which we touched on in chapter three. This is the part of the brain that lights up when you're not focused on a task, like when you're driving or walking. It's responsible for memory, identity, and reflection—but it can also trap your energy in old stories.

The thoughts you're having today? Most of them are the same ones you had yesterday and the day before that. Left unchecked, your inner voice can reinforce limiting beliefs and outdated narratives without you even realizing it. The good news is that, with awareness, you can reprogram it.

Start by noticing when your inner voice gets loud. Maybe it happens at work, when you're trying something new, or when your energy feels unsteady or exposed. What does that voice say? Is it kind? Is it helpful? Is it even true?

If the answer is no, pause and ask yourself: How would I say this to someone I love? Or better yet, how would someone who loves me say it to me?

Instead of saying, "I always mess this up," imagine, "I'm still learning. I can try again." Instead of saying, "I'm not good enough," try, "I'm doing my best, and that matters."

If it's hard to find that gentler tone at first, imagine someone who loves you—unconditionally—speaking on your behalf. Even if that someone is your dog.

You don't need to rewire your entire mind overnight. Just start with one thought. One rewrite. That's how the story begins to change.

Tuning In Versus Tuning Out: Grounding in the Present

When life feels overwhelming your energy scatters and it's easy to slip into autopilot, scrolling, snacking, overworking, numbing. We tune out not because we're lazy or careless, but because tuning in can feel vulnerable. It asks something of us.

But true transformation begins with presence. When we gently return to ourselves, our body, breath, thoughts, and emotions, we begin to hear the wisdom we've been too busy or too afraid to notice.

Grounding is the practice of coming home to yourself. It's how you shift from reacting to responding, from drifting to choosing. When you tune in instead of out, you begin to notice what you truly need. You strengthen your intuition. You rebuild self-trust.

One powerful way to begin is through a simple pause. Just three times a day (morning, midday, and evening), stop for a moment. Take three slow breaths. Ask yourself:

- **What is my body saying?** Am I tense? Energized? Tired?
- **What is my mind doing?** Is it focused? Spinning? Self-critical?
- **What am I feeling right now?** Am I feeling joy? Frustration? Disconnection?
- **What do I most value or appreciate about my energy in this moment?**

You don't need to fix or change anything. Simply notice. With practice, this kind of tuning in becomes a refuge. A way to stay connected to what matters, even when the world around you is moving fast or you feel overwhelmed.

You don't create your Opus by effort alone. Instead, you shape it in quiet moments like these, when you return to yourself and remember: You're already home.

This week, we turn inward, not to judge or fix, but to listen. Not to the noise outside you, but to the quiet inside: your energy, your emotions, your inner voice.

As you begin to listen more closely to your inner voice, the words you whisper to yourself in quiet moments, you're also tuning in to something deeper: your life force. This is the energy that fuels how you move through the world. It lives in your body, your thoughts, your emotions, your spirit.

The stories you tell yourself don't just affect your confidence; they shape your energy, how you eat, move, rest, love, and lead. That's why, before we shift the story, we take an honest inventory of where your energy is steady and where it's being drained. How are you really doing? Where do you feel strong? Where do you feel stretched thin? What's steady? What's wobbly? And what's asking for your care? That's where the Opus Life Force Check-In comes in.

And here's something to keep in mind: the patterns you'll notice in your energy often reflect how you move through change. If you're feeling scattered or depleted, you may be in a Catalyst season in an area of your life, driven, but stretched too thin. If you're feeling hesitant or uncertain, you might be in a Hesitator moment in an area of your life, yearning to move forward, but unsure where to begin. These archetypes, part of the Opus Change Continuum, offer gentle insight into where you are and what you most need. We'll keep exploring them throughout this process; for now, just notice what's true for you.

Exercise: Your Life Force Snapshot (Fifteen Minutes)

Your energy, health, and well-being are more than just background conditions—they're your life force. And they shape everything: how you show up, how you connect, and how you create meaningful change.

I designed this check-in to help you gently explore and honor the different dimensions of your well-being (physical, mental, emotional, and spiritual), so you can gain insight into what's supporting you and where you might need care or attention.

Although you will score yourself, what's most important is noticing how supported and aligned you feel right now, so you can move forward with more clarity and care. I've included a score so that it is easy for you to gauge which areas are going well and which need your attention. Other than that, ignore the score. Instead, listen to yourself with compassion and begin to understand the subtle signals your body, mind, heart, and spirit may be sending you.

Here's how it works:

- For each section, rate the items on a scale from 1 to 5 using the guide provided.
- Reflect using the prompts to better understand what's working, what's asking for support, and what small shifts might help you feel more aligned and energized.
- Use a notebook, journal, or your *Live Your Opus Workbook* to record your reflections. You'll return to this check-in throughout the journey, so think of it as a snapshot of your current inner landscape.

Please use the following scale to reflect honestly, not to judge yourself, but to gently notice where your energy is today and how supported or stretched you feel:

- **5: Thriving.** I feel deeply supported and aligned in this area. It energizes me, and I show up from a place of strength and clarity.
- **4: Steady.** Things are mostly strong here. I feel good in this area, even if there's still some room to grow.
- **3: Neutral.** I'm getting by. This area isn't necessarily causing stress, but it may not be offering energy or support either.
- **2: Struggling.** I'm aware this area could use some attention. It's functioning, but feels heavy, inconsistent, or out of sync.
- **1: Just surviving.** I feel depleted, disconnected, or unsupported here. It's asking for care, and maybe even some compassion.

SECTION ONE. PHYSICAL HEALTH AND ENERGY

	1	2	3	4	5
I feel well-rested and energized.					
I nourish my body with healthy food, movement, and rest that feels good.					
I am aware of how my body feels throughout the day, and I respond to discomfort rather than pushing through it.					
I appreciate how my body supports me every day.					
I actively set aside time to care for and restore my body (rest or sleep, checkups, exercise breaks).					

Total Score: ___ / 25

Reflection and Action:

- These habits sustain my physical health and energy:
- One thing I love about my body is:
- Here is one small action I can take to support my body this week (start/stop/continue):

SECTION TWO. MENTAL CLARITY AND ATTENTION

	1	2	3	4	5
I feel present and focused throughout my day.					
My mental energy is balanced between positive and negative thoughts.					
I am aware of my mental patterns or feelings and how they influence me.					
I appreciate my mind's ability to learn, solve problems, and grow.					
I set aside time to rest my mind (through meditation, stillness, or time offline).					

Total Score: ___ / 25

Reflection and Action:

- These habits support my mental clarity:
- One thing I love about how I think is:
- Here is one small shift to support my mind this week (start/stop/continue):

SECTION THREE. EMOTIONAL AWARENESS AND SELF-LOVE

	1	2	3	4	5
I listen to and express my emotions throughout the day honestly.					
I treat myself with compassion when I struggle.					
I notice and respond to draining situations or relationships, taking action to preserve my energy.					
I set and honor personal boundaries and feel comfortable saying no.					
I regularly experience moments of joy, play, or lightness in my day.					

Total Score: ___ / 25

Reflection and Action:

- These habits support my emotional well-being:
- One thing I love about my emotional self (or my heart) is:
- One small shift to support my emotional health (start/stop/continue):

SECTION FOUR. SPIRITUAL CONNECTION AND PURPOSE

	1	2	3	4	5
I feel a sense of meaning and purpose in my life.					
I feel connected to peace or something larger than myself.					
I nurture my spirit through rituals or reflection.					
I appreciate the unique way I bring meaning into the world.					
I take time to reflect on what truly matters.					

Total Score: ___ / 25

Reflection and Action:

- These practices support my sense of purpose or connect to my "why:"
- One thing I love about the way I connect with meaning or spirit:
- One small shift to deepen my connection this week (start/stop/continue):

Taking Stock

Now that you've moved through this check-in, take a breath. You've done something most people avoid: You've slowed down long enough to listen to yourself. So, what have you learned? What surprised you? What parts of you feel strong and steady? What's quietly asking for more care?

You might notice patterns. Or contradictions. You might feel proud. Or, even a bit emotional. Whatever emotion surfaced, honor it. It's all part of the truth of where you are right now.

Now gently ask yourself a few questions: Which area of my life force feels like it most needs my attention? What's one small shift, a "1 percent move," I can make to support myself this week? If a close friend had completed this same check-in, what kindness or encouragement would I offer them? Can I offer the same to myself?

Whatever your ratings, remember this: You are not a project to be fixed. Your energy isn't broken. You are already worthy, already enough.

This check-in isn't the end—it's a beginning. You're building your Opus not just through what you achieve, but through how you care for yourself along the way. So, keep going and keep listening. The masterpiece that is you is already unfolding.

Turning Inward

This week, you paused long enough to listen to your body, your mind, your emotions, and your spirit. That's no small thing. You noticed where your energy is flowing and where it may be blocked or sensitive and asking for care. You got honest about the voice inside your head. And you began to meet yourself with a little more compassion.

It's easy to move through life without ever tuning in. To keep going, producing, pushing. But this week, you chose a different way. You listened. You softened. You opened a new kind of dialogue—with yourself.

So, take a moment here. Before rushing on. What did you hear? What surprised you? What felt true? And maybe most importantly: What kind of voice is trying to emerge, and how can you let it speak more often?

This is about noticing who you already are, what you already know, and what you're ready to claim more fully. So, carry what you've discovered forward. Keep listening. And keep offering yourself the kind of encouragement you'd give someone you love.

Next week, you'll move deeper into who you are today as you understand your identity and explore your present Opus—the life you're living now—and who you may want to become in the future.

WEEK THREE. OWNING YOUR PRESENT OPUS

I can't count how many times a client has asked, "Should I answer this question from my work self or my personal self?" And I always offer the same question in return: "How many selves do you have?"

We've been taught to divide our lives into boxes: work over here, personal life over there. But the truth is, your energy and your life are not meant to be compartmentalized. You are one whole human. Every part of your life, the one that leads a meeting, cares for a loved one, pursues a passion project, or takes a holiday, is part of your Opus. One continuous composition. One life unfolding, moment by moment.

As Morten Albæk writes in *One Life*, the idea that we have separate selves is an illusion. We live one life, and everything we do contributes to our sense of meaning, fulfillment, and impact.[11]

When you create your Opus, you're not choosing between identities. You're choosing integration. You're making space for your full self, your energy, needs, desires, contradictions, and growth. You're honoring the truth that it all matters.

That means your present life, however messy, beautiful, or unfinished you may think it is, isn't separate from your Opus. It's already part of it. Even if it feels off course or energetically misaligned, you are already living a version of your Opus. And when you approach it with kindness, honesty, and respect, you gain the power to shape what comes next.

You've spent the last two weeks listening inward: tuning in to your past, your energy, your inner voice. Now, we meet your present. Where is your energy flowing with ease? Where is it feeling stuck or strained?

This week, looking across your whole life as it is today, we ask: If nothing changed, what kind of life would you be creating? Are the habits, energy, and patterns of your days shaping the life you want to live?

Don't worry if you don't have the answers yet. That's what this process is for. When you see your life as a whole, you can begin to lead it from the inside out—not just through goals or outcomes, but by embodying the person you're here to become.

Becoming the Person You're Here to Be

By tuning in to your inner voice and checking in with your energy last week, you began a different kind of listening, one rooted in compassion and curiosity. That reflection wasn't just about how you're doing; it was about how you're living. Now, we gently shift from insight to identity. Because the stories you tell yourself and the energy patterns you embody don't just shape how you feel—they shape *who you believe you are.*

Most of us were taught to pursue change through goals: lose ten pounds, write a book, get the promotion. But true, lasting transformation doesn't begin with what you achieve. It begins with *who you are becoming.*

This is what James Clear calls "identity-based change" in *Atomic Habits*. It is the idea that our habits and choices naturally shift when we begin acting in alignment with the person we want to be. (You may recall we discussed this in chapter three.)

- You're not just trying to exercise; you're becoming someone who replenishes and respects your energy.
- You're not just writing a book; you're becoming a writer.
- You're not just managing people; you're becoming a leader who makes others feel seen.

And that's the work of this week: You're not designing a whole new future (that's for the Dream stage) but gently noticing who you are right now and what Opus you're living.

With an appreciation for what you love about yourself, you can more easily identify the small shifts that may bring you closer to the identity you want to step into—the aspirational one.

So, pause here. Breathe. Let this be the week you meet yourself as you are and begin choosing, with intention, who you're ready to become.

Exercises: Reclaiming the Present You're Already Living

The following exercises will help you develop a deeper understanding of who and where you are now. Together, they'll support you in seeing your present Opus with fresh eyes: How are your work, relationships, personal growth, and well-being unfolding right now? What *is* the shape of your present Opus?

If you haven't already, take a few minutes to settle into Opus Mode, and, later this week, remember to teach someone something you've learned here (your In-Service Action) and check in with yourself (Opus Life Check-In). As this is your third week engaging in the work, I'll assume you've now got these weekly practices down, so you won't see any further reminders.

Who Am I? (Ten Minutes)

This might be one of the simplest and most revealing questions you'll ever ask: *Who am I*?

Not your job title. Not your role in your family or community. Not even what others see when they look at you. But you—beneath the labels, beneath the noise.

This question hit me like a wave after I burned out. At the time, it felt unsettling and scary. But it was also clarifying. Stripping everything else away and asking that question gave me back something essential: myself.

So today, I invite you to do the same.

Find a quiet place. Write the question "Who am I?" at the top of a blank page. Then answer it ten times.

Your first few answers might sound familiar: "I'm a parent." "I'm a leader." That's okay; they are part of your truth. Keep going. See what comes next.

By the seventh or eighth answer, you might start to surprise yourself: "I am someone learning to rest." "I am softer than I let on." "I am someone who wants to start my own business." "I am becoming."

You don't need to force it. Just stay open and curious. If you get to ten and nothing surprises you yet, write until something honest stirs.

When you're finished, circle the responses that feel most true—most honest—right now. Then, jot down five words that describe what you love most about who you are and how your energy shows up today.

Congratulations, you've just taken a deep breath inward, listening closely to the quiet truth of who you are, beneath the titles and roles. This is you today. And that's more than enough.

Now, let's step back and see how this self, the one you just met, shows up in the world you've created. The way you move through your days, where your energy flows, what brings you meaning; it's all a reflection of the identity you've been living. Let's take a look.

MY LIFE AS IT IS TODAY (FIFTEEN TO TWENTY MINUTES)

Grab a blank page. Write your name in the center, like it is the heart of a constellation. Around it, draw five or more orbits, each representing a meaningful part of your life today. You might include:

- Work and career (roles, responsibilities, goals).
- Relationships (family, friends, professional, romantic).
- Experiences (hobbies, travel, play, joy).
- Personal growth (learning, mindset, creativity, passions).
- Well-being (health, energy, rest, balance).

In each orbit, jot down what's true right now. What words, symbols, doodles, or feelings come to mind? What energizes you? What uplifts or restores you in that part of your life? You might even add hearts, stars, or other symbols to mark what feels especially joyful or meaningful.

Most of the time this exercise allows us to see our present circumstances in a new light, with more appreciation and respect—who we are and how we live today is often better than we initially thought.

Ask yourself: What feels full? What feels neglected? Where is joy? What deserves more of your love or attention?

Then step back and take it in. This is your present Opus. Let yourself see it with clarity and with care. There is no pressure to change anything. Just appreciate what's here. This is the life you've already composed. And it's beautiful in ways you may not always notice.

Already Becoming

Before you turn the page, take a quiet moment to acknowledge yourself, not just for completing this week, but for showing up with honesty, curiosity, and heart. You've completed the Connect stage, the first stage of the Live Your Opus transformation journey. Pause for a moment to notice: What has shifted?

You've done something rare. You've looked inward with compassion, then outward with clarity. You've listened to your inner voice, mapped the life you're already living, and gently asked yourself: Is this aligned with who I want to become?

That question alone is an energetic shift. Even without all the answers, you're seeing yourself and your life through a more aligned lens now. You're noticing patterns. You're spotting joy. You're beginning to trust yourself more.

That's what this week was really about, recognizing that you are already living a version of your Opus and that it's vital to honor it as is while still feeling called to create something more.

You may feel more rooted, more honest with yourself, or simply more awake. That's the energy of self-awareness activating. When we take the time to connect with who we really are, beneath the roles and expectations, something inside of us begins to soften and settle, and, at the same time, we feel stronger. We move from fragmentation to wholeness. From depletion to quiet power.

This energetic shift may be subtle, but it's profound. It's the feeling of coming home to yourself. And from this place of grounded clarity, a new current begins to rise: the energy of possibility. This might feel like a flicker of excitement, a renewed curiosity, or even a quiet question: What now?

This is the bridge to Dream. Don't rush it, just feel it. The stability you cultivated in Connect becomes the foundation from which your future self begins to stir.

So, appreciate the present Opus you've just explored. And know this: The person you are becoming is already here, awakening through your energy, choices, and care.

Next week, we begin Dream. For now, rest in the knowing that you've taken an essential step: You've come home to where you are. And that, truly, is where every transformation begins.

Chapter Four

DREAM:
Opening Yourself to the Future

Dreaming can feel exhilarating, but it can also leave you open to feeling vulnerable. When I asked a group of leaders to think beyond their current reality, to imagine the boldest, fullest expression of their lives, I could see the tension manifest immediately. Some people leaned in, their faces lighting up at the invitation to dream. Others hesitated.

One woman, Freya, sat with her arms crossed, eyes darting to her notebook as if hoping the words would appear on their own. Finally, she admitted, "I feel stuck. My body literally feels warm. It's like . . . I don't even know how to think this way."

I knew exactly what she meant. Sometimes, dreaming isn't exhilarating; it's uncomfortable. We spend so much time optimizing for the life we're in that the idea of envisioning something new feels foreign. While finding space to dream is hard, it doesn't mean you don't have dreams. It just means you may need to give yourself permission and space to listen to them. If you have ever felt uncertain about what's next, you are not alone. That is why we are doing this together.

As we step into Dream, you might notice a shift in energy. Connect asked you to root down, to turn inward, to stabilize, and to listen to what's true today. And, while it is essential that you keep doing that throughout this process, Dream now invites you to rise up. To stretch. To imagine. If Connect was about building a strong foundation, Dream is about opening the windows and letting the breeze in. The energy becomes more expansive, more creative, more spacious.

You may feel a lift in your chest, a hum of anticipation in your body, or even a moment of nervous energy. That's good. It means your system is responding. It means something is waking up. Let that sensation guide you. This is not about fantasy; it's about expanding into alignment with the life that wants to emerge from within you.

Now, before we go any further, take a breath. Remember the Opus Change Continuum in chapter two? Let yourself check in: Which archetype feels most true for you right now? It may not be the same one that brought you here, and that's okay. We shift. We grow. Even in the few weeks since you've started this process.

Some of us arrive here as Hesitators, unsure whether it's safe to want more; your courage is growing just by being here.

Navigators may feel unmoored without a clear plan, but this is your moment to explore, not to plan or execute.

Builders might hesitate to dream big, afraid it could unravel what's already working. Remember, dreams don't dismantle your foundation; they deepen it.

Explorers may light up with too many ideas; try listening for the one that keeps whispering back.

And Catalysts, like me, you might be tempted to race ahead—please don't. Pause here just long enough to ask what you truly want before you sprint toward it.

For me, dreaming feels like a soft, warm blanket or a star-filled night sky, comforting yet filled with awe. To get into the spirit, I'd like you to imagine that we're seated together in a cozy place, you, me, and anyone else you'd like to invite, perhaps around a fire. We're dreaming up what our lives and work might look like in the future. Grab a cup of tea or coffee and gather round then, because, before we begin, I'm going to tell you a story.

A dream can sit quietly in your heart for years, waiting for the right moment to surface. Sometimes, we don't even realize it is there until we make space to listen. That's what happened to me.

THE DREAM THAT WOULDN'T WAIT

In 2024, as I was preparing to teach Dream, I did what I always do: I used the tools myself before sharing them with others. I had already done many of these exercises before, but this time, something was different.

A particular dream kept surfacing, one that had been lingering in my journals, showing up in quiet moments, whispering in the back of my mind. Writing a book—this book.

Writing has always been a deep love of mine. When I was in grade school, I would self-publish my books, typing them on my mother's typewriter, designing their covers, and hand-stitching the binding. I submitted my stories to competitions at the public library, where they were recognized and proudly displayed. Although my parents appreciated my creativity, they made it clear that writing was not a "real" career path. And so, while writing has always been a big part of my professional work, I never pursued it fully.

When I engaged in the Dream exercises, my book refused to wait. In every version of my future, it appeared, not five or ten years from now, but immediately. And not just one book, but two! Alongside several other quiet ambitions that had been waiting for permission.

That was my wake-up call.

And, like many of you might feel when staring down a big dream, I felt a twinge of fear. A familiar voice crept in: Are you sure? Can you really do this?

This is the moment where we either step forward or step back. I chose to step forward. I even had the title of this book engraved inside my new glasses, a daily reminder that this dream was real, that it mattered, and that it was time. And the moment I fully committed—aligned not just in vision, but in energy—the right people, opportunities, and connections began to appear.

Maybe you have a dream like this, one that's been sitting quietly, waiting for its moment. Or maybe you are about to uncover something completely new. Either way, these next three weeks are your time to listen, explore, and give yourself permission to dream.

DO DREAM

"The Dream exercises have boosted my optimism and hope for the next five to six years. They've helped my Opus feel closer and less elusive than ever before," said an entrepreneur who participated in this work.

Another shared, "My biggest wow moment was the dream exercise. When I wrote my five-year and ten-year dreams without restrictions, no limits on cost, time, or resources, I realized I could tack the rest of my ten-year dream onto my current five-year plan and do both. Suddenly, I had a vision for my life that felt exciting, meaningful, and fully aligned. And the best part? I could involve my family in the journey. That realization has been incredibly inspiring."

These stories are powerful reminders that when you engage in the Dream stage, you are not just fantasizing; you are bringing your vision closer, making it feel possible, and perhaps even realizing that some dreams are ready to begin now.

You connected deeply with your past, your energy, your inner voice, and your present self in the Connect phase. You uncovered your strengths, patterns, and truths, and you gathered insights about who and what drive you, energize you, or might be holding you back. Now, it's time take what has been, imagine what else is possible, and step into your next chapter with intention.

Dream is the second stage of the Live Your Opus transformation process, a time to explore, imagine, and start shaping a life that aligns with your deepest values and desires. Because if you don't design your life intentionally, someone or something else will do it for you.

Think about it:

- What might you do if you could live or work in complete alignment with who you are? With your unique disposition, needs, and preferences out on full display.
- If no one were watching, you had no expectations to meet, no opinions to sway, what vision might you craft for your life or your career?
- What actions would you take if you trusted yourself fully?

At this moment, you stand at the threshold of something new—your future Opus. Through Dream, you won't just think about what you might do; you'll discover who you might become.

As you move through weeks four through six of this stage, you will open your mind, play, explore, and imagine freely. This is your opportunity to experiment, to dream without constraints, and to listen to what is calling you forward.

The path is simple, but profound. Open your heart, mind, and spirit to what is inside of you. Listen to your fears and ask yourself if you can handle them. You'll find that, more often than not, you can. Begin noticing and reprogramming your default mode, that internal voice that has shaped your beliefs, habits, and even the fear of other people's opinions. And, most importantly, step into the Dream stage with all the wisdom you have gathered about yourself over the past three weeks in Connect.

You have already built and lived several Opuses. You have overcome hurdles, shown resilience, fallen, and gotten back up. You have won whatever race you were running. And now you are here to become the person who intentionally creates an aligned life and fully lives their Opus.

So, over the next few weeks, I invite you to separate external influences from your truest voice as you excavate your dreams, bring them to the surface, and, with my support, compose a life that incorporates them into your Opus. Before you begin, let's consider the things that may hold you back, and how you can deal with them.

WHY DON'T WE LIVE OUR DREAMS?

If living our dreams were easy, we'd all be living in perfect alignment with who we are. But the truth is, most of us don't give ourselves full permission to live our dreams or, worse, we simply don't think it's possible.

What holds us back?

- **Fear:** Fear of failure, fear of judgment, fear of stepping outside the familiar or not getting it right.
- **External expectations**: The weight of what we should do, the pressures of achievement and approval.
- **The belief that it is too late:** That we missed our moment, that the path is already set.

The belief that the path we want is simply too unrealistic or radical: That we would upset the balance too much or need more time, money, and support than we would ever possibly be able to drum up.

And that's just the beginning of the list. This combination of fear and external influence drains our energy and creates a pull to stay safe, to avoid the discomfort of potential criticism or judgment. When we think of doing something that requires courage and stepping out of our comfort zone, our default mode tells us to play it safe, ignore our deeper desires, and avoid risks.

One person in a recent workshop almost skipped the Dream exercises altogether. When I asked why, she said, "I was afraid of failing at the dream itself." She wasn't worried about the logistics of making a change. She was afraid that if she let herself dream and it didn't happen, it would hurt too much.

I see this all the time. We avoid dreaming not because we lack ideas, but because we don't want to face the possibility of disappointment. The irony? Preventing yourself from knowing your dreams guarantees you will never live them.

What if, instead of avoiding your dreams, you let yourself explore them—without pressure, without expectation, just as an act of curiosity?

Here's what I want you to consider. Ask yourself:

- If I stay exactly where I am, what life am I building?
- If I keep making the same choices, where will I be in five years?
- Is that the Opus I came here to create?

SUCCESS: WHOSE DEFINITION?

For many of us, success was defined long before we ever had a say in it. Think about it: When and how did you first learn that achievement was rewarded? Can you recall the moment you realized that excelling—being the best, winning, getting it right—brought approval? And what about success itself? When did you first define it, or was it defined for you? Do you still agree with that definition today?

Growing up, I learned that success was about achievement, performance, and doing things "right." My family placed high expectations on excellence: grades, milestones, and external validation. My mother was an immigrant from Cuba, deeply committed to academics. My father was the first in his family to earn a university degree. Together, they instilled in me discipline, hard work, and an unshakable standard for high performance. In our home, emotions were not up for discussion. The focus was on succeeding—without hesitation, without mistakes, and never failure.

Success was tangible and transactional. My parents even paid me for getting good grades. An "A" meant a reward; anything less meant criticism and consequences. I pushed myself relentlessly, trying every sport, practicing longer than my friends, excelling in subjects beyond my grade level. I absorbed the message early: To be loved, accepted, and secure, I had to excel.

By high school, I had perfected the art of excellence. But I was crushed by the weight of expectations at home, so life outside of my home became my refuge. I buried myself in academics, extracurriculars, and friendships. I even got my first job at fourteen. I did anything and everything to minimize the time spent under the weight of those expectations.

My parents divorced soon after I left home for university at seventeen, and I was left to fend for myself financially and otherwise. And, yet, even though I had physically left their world behind and had always been independent and free-spirited, I unconsciously carried their definition of success and its energetic weight with me. Through university, I worked fifty hours a week to support myself so I could I stay enrolled full-time and, eventually, graduate on-time and with academic recognition.

I didn't realize it then, but I wasn't just pursuing excellence; I was maintaining a version of myself shaped by external expectations and definitions. And this strategy worked so well in university that I took it with me into the work world. I hit every milestone, surpassed every measure of success. But years later, in the depths of burnout, I finally questioned whether the framework I had been operating under was mine—or if it had been handed to me. That was the moment I saw the difference between the self I was told to be and the self I was choosing to become, between living life from a place of survival rather than as the sole creator of my life.

I once worked with a man who had built a highly successful career in finance. By every external measure, he had made it. He had the title, the income, and the credibility. But the more he thought about the future, the more he felt drawn to something completely different: social impact.

As he sat with this realization, he felt a strange mix of excitement and grief. "I feel like I'm mourning a version of myself," he admitted. He wasn't just considering a career pivot. He was reckoning with an identity shift. The version of him that had spent years climbing the ladder and proving himself wasn't the version of him that he wanted to bring into this next chapter.

This is the part no one talks about. To redefine success, you must not only choose a new path but also be willing to let go of an old one. And that? That takes courage.

THE FALSE SELF VERSUS THE TRUE SELF

We all carry a version of ourselves that we present to the world, a false self, shaped by roles, expectations, and early conditioning. It's the version of us that knows how to meet external demands, follow the rules, and gain approval. But often, it's not fully aligned with who we are.

Our true self, on the other hand, exists beyond pretense, ego, and external validation. It's the part of us that isn't defined by what we achieve but by what we value, what excites us, what feels inherently ours. The journey of personal transformation to Live Your Opus is, in part, about uncovering that true self and redefining success on your own terms.

Many of my clients reach a point where they realize the version of success they've been chasing no longer fits. It was shaped by family expectations, cultural influences, or societal norms—but it wasn't theirs.

How do you recognize when you're living from your false self?

The clues are there: Maybe you're meeting goals but still feeling empty. Maybe you've achieved what you set out to do, but something feels off, like you're running someone else's race. Maybe your version of success looks good on the outside but leaves your inner energy misaligned and depleted.

If the life you are building today is based on an outdated definition of success, what would happen if you redefined it? If you were living from your true self, what would success look like then?

You might be thinking: This sounds great, but if you live from your true self and build success your way, what will people think?

FEAR OF OTHER PEOPLE'S OPINIONS

One of the greatest barriers to dreaming is FOPO, fear of other people's opinions. What will they think? Am I qualified to do this? What if I fail—publicly? These are just a few of the questions that run through our heads sometimes when we're suffering from FOPO. I've experienced this myself.

For years, I held back on sharing my ideas publicly, not because I didn't believe in them, but because I worried about how they'd be received. I felt safe doing so when I was representing an established organization, like my employer or a volunteer organization. But, when I first struck out on my own, everything changed. I wondered: "What if my ideas weren't good enough? Or original enough? What if they shifted how people saw me, and drained my energy in the process?

I kept thinking that I just needed to find my voice. It wasn't until I recognized this as FOPO that I realized, once I silenced that fear, the only opinion that truly mattered was my own.

If you've got FOPO, you're not alone. It causes people to avoid applying for a promotion or asking for a raise, and it can prevent us from connecting with potential mentors or allies. Or, as in my case, FOPO can hold us back from voicing our ideas.

In his book, *The First Rule of Mastery: Stop Worrying about What People Think of You*, high-performance psychologist Michael Gervais describes FOPO as a protective mechanism, a way our brain tries to keep us safe from rejection. But, most of the time, the judgment we fear isn't even real.[12]

The next time FOPO creeps in, pause and ask: If the worst happened, if someone judged you, misunderstood you, or even dismissed you, could you handle it?[13] And, what's the best-case scenario? If you stepped forward anyway, what might be possible? Most of the time, the answer to these questions is going to be positive. When we recognize that we can handle discomfort, we take away fear's power.

If FOPO is holding you back, Gervais suggests that you start by:

- **Knowing what you stand for.** When you are clear on your values and principles, outside opinions lose their power. What truly matters to you, no matter what anyone else thinks?

- **Practicing being yourself.** Sometimes it's hard to be yourself around others. Start small by practicing authenticity in everyday, low-stakes interactions, like sharing your views with friends. Where can you start showing up as your authentic self, even in small ways?

- **Choosing whose opinions matter.** Feedback is important, but not all opinions are equal. You don't need to take in every opinion; instead, create a short list of trusted voices who support your growth. Who are the trusted voices you want to listen to?

- **Reframing FOPO as growth.** FOPO often shows up when you are stepping into something new; instead of seeing it as a stop sign, embrace it as growth. If you feel uncomfortable, is it a sign you are expanding?[14]

Practicing Present Focus, staying engaged with your own vision rather than anticipating others' reactions, can help quiet FOPO's grip. When you shift from worrying about what they will think to what feels right for you, fear loses its power.

By recognizing when FOPO is holding you back, and by shifting your response, you'll move forward with more confidence, freedom, and trust in yourself. The result is the ability to create and sustain a life that feels truly, deeply yours.

But, just in case it's not just FOPO holding you back, let's talk about something that nearly everyone—even the most successful people—suffer from: our upper limit.

MOVING PAST YOUR UPPER LIMIT

Have you ever noticed that just as you start to reach for something big, something inside you hesitates? Maybe you get excited about a new possibility, only to immediately think that this is too much. You wonder if you can handle it: Who am I to dream this big?

Almost everyone encounters this kind of inner resistance. Psychologist Gay Hendricks calls it the "Upper Limit Problem," an invisible ceiling we place on our own success, joy, and fulfillment. The Upper Limit Problem is a deeply ingrained belief about how much happiness or achievement we are allowed to have before something pulls us back into our comfort zone.[15] It often pops up when we try to go too fast or believe that success must feel difficult.

I first encountered my own Upper Limit Problem when I launched my first business. Finally, I had the freedom to structure my work in a way that energized me. I was pursuing something deeply meaningful, something that aligned with my purpose. But instead of embracing it fully, I found myself slipping into an old pattern: overwork and neglecting my well-being.

Even when things were going well, I filled every moment with tasks, convinced that I had to prove myself to justify this opportunity. I was just being diligent, I told myself. In hindsight, I can see that I was actually creating my own obstacles. Deep down, I was uncomfortable with the ease and joy I was experiencing. Some part of me believed success had to be hard-earned through depletion, that ease and joy couldn't coexist with high achievement.

That was my upper limit at work. And because I wasn't yet aware of it, I almost missed the deeper truth: While I was fixated on being a successful founder, I wasn't engaging in the work that aligned most with my true self. It wasn't until two of my cofounders left the business that I stepped back and saw what was really calling me. I count myself lucky to have recognized that moment for what it was.

Stepping beyond your upper limit doesn't mean pushing yourself into burnout; it means expanding with intention. Sustainable growth reminds us that big dreams unfold through steady, aligned progress. Instead of rushing toward an endpoint, trust that consistent steps forward will carry you beyond where your comfort zone says you should stop.

I once worked with a woman who had dreamed of launching a major initiative in her business for years. She had the skills, the funding, and a network ready to support her. But when it was time to take the next step, securing investors, she stalled.

At first, she told herself she was just refining her strategy. "I need more time to make sure it's right," she said. But the more we talked, the clearer it became: Instead of refining, she was retreating. "I realized I was using 'getting ready' as an excuse to stay safe," she admitted.

This is the Upper Limit Problem in action. We think we are stuck because we are unprepared. More often, we are stuck because we are afraid to step into something bigger. The only way through is action.

RECOGNIZING YOUR OWN UPPER LIMIT

Right now, as you begin stepping into your dreams, your Upper Limit Problem might show up in subtle ways:

- **Doubt.** You get excited about a dream but immediately question whether you are qualified to pursue it.
- **Worry.** Instead of imagining what is possible, your brain fixates on everything that could go wrong.
- **Self-sabotage.** You find ways to hold yourself back—procrastinating, overworking, or distracting yourself.

All of these thoughts drain your energy and momentum by emphasizing limitations over possibilities. So, if any of them show up as you dream, ask yourself if these are real limitations. Or is this your upper limit trying to keep you safe?

Chances are, these doubts are not a reflection of your dream's viability; they're a reflection of how much you are expanding beyond your current comfort zone. What if, instead of stopping at your upper limit, you stepped into it? What might happen if you imagined what went well?

As you work through the three weeks of the Dream stage, including the visualization exercises in week five, keep a sharp focus on your future self. What can you learn from them? What strengths do they possess? What advice do they have for you?

During one of my workshops, I asked participants to dream without limitations. No fear, no financial worries, just a vision of what they would do if nothing stood in their way. One woman hesitated at first, then started writing. When she finished, she looked up with surprise. "I thought my dream would be something completely different," she said. "But actually? It's not far from what I do now. I just need to stop holding myself back."

Sometimes, we assume that dreaming big means abandoning everything. But more often, the dream isn't so far away; it's just waiting for you to take the next step. And maybe your next step isn't about deserving success but simply allowing it.

Your upper limit is an invitation. It's a signal that you are on the edge of something big. And the more you step toward your dream, the more natural it will become. That is, unless you think it's too late. And it's never too late—until it is.

Have you ever thought that you should have started sooner? That your window has closed? That it's just too late?

I hear this all the time from people at every stage of life. Even from twenty-six-year-olds who already believe they have missed their chance. This belief, that it's too late, is one of the quietest, most persistent lies we tell ourselves. It keeps us safely within the boundaries of what's familiar, even when what's familiar no longer fulfills us.

Maybe you have also heard this voice: "I should have started when … " "Maybe I might have, if … " "I could have done this if only … " These stories that our voices tell us feel real because we have rehearsed them for so long. But they are just that—stories. And like any story, especially the ones your internal voice is narrating, they can be rewritten.

Most dreams take time to emerge and even longer to come to fruition. Some arrive late, not because we were slow to act, but because we needed to live a little first. To gather experiences. To grow into them.

Your timeline is your own. These stories prove that extraordinary things happen at every stage of life: Oprah Winfrey launched *The Oprah Winfrey Show* at thirty-two. Ray Kroc transformed McDonald's into a global franchise at fifty-two. Reed Hastings cofounded Netflix at thirty-seven. Julia Child published her first cookbook at forty-nine. Serena Williams won a Grand Slam at thirty-five while pregnant. Toni Morrison won the Nobel Prize at sixty-two. Harrison Ford didn't make it big as an actor until *Star Wars* when he was thirty-five and *Indiana Jones* when he was thirty-nine; he is still acting today at eighty-two. Shaquille O'Neal went from basketball to TV and a business empire in his forties.

So, whether you are twenty-six or sixty-six—whatever age you are—you are not behind. You are exactly where you're meant to be. The question isn't, "Is it too late?" The question is, "What do you want to create next?"

STEPPING INTO DREAM: THE MINDSETS THAT WILL GUIDE YOU

As you move into this next stage, here are five guiding mindsets to help you open your heart, mind, and to what's possible. You'll recognize the first three from the Opus 8 Alignment principles—each one a channel for activating and directing your energy:

- **Vision**. Stay open to what is possible, even if it feels out of reach.
- **Coherence**. Let your dreams align with who you are at your core.
- **Present Focus**. Start where you are. Dreaming is not about escaping today.
- **Curiosity**. Approach this with wonder, not pressure. Play, explore, imagine.
- **Small steps**. You don't need the whole plan. Just the next step.

The next few weeks are a chance to listen, explore, and start building what comes next. So, stay away from naysayers, and, if you choose to share your experiences, do so only with those you trust to support you. Think of this time and space to dream as a gift you are giving to yourself.

ACCEPTING YOUR DREAM MISSION

Grab a pen and paper or voice recorder. Take five minutes and write or dictate this sentence: "If I could live or work in full alignment with who I am—without any fears—what would my life look like?"

Write or speak freely. Let yourself dream. Nothing is off-limits! Not every dream will call to you in the same way. As you start writing, notice which dreams light you up. Those are often the ones most aligned with the Opus 8 energy principles. Whether it is energy, connection, or meaning, pay attention to what feels most like you.

This is your starting point, an early compass guiding you toward what really matters—because your Opus is waiting.

WEEK FOUR. CONNECTING WITH YOUR DREAMS

Welcome to the first week of Dream. For some of you, dreaming will feel like an energetic expansion; your mind might already be buzzing with possibilities. You may be here willingly, eager to explore what you may create next in your life.

For others, dreaming might feel unfamiliar or even uncomfortable. Maybe you have been so focused on responsibilities, stability, or meeting expectations that you haven't given your heart, mind, or energy system permission to dream freely in years. That's okay. This week, you won't spend time trying to force a dream to appear. Instead, you will reconnect with the part of you that knows how to dream and create energy and space for it to emerge.

Perhaps you picked up this book because your life has shifted unexpectedly, through loss, health challenges, new opportunities, or uncertainty. If that is you, know this: Dreaming isn't just for those who feel ready; it's also for those who are still finding their footing. In fact, dreaming can crack open the window of possibility, giving you permission to care for yourself in new ways and take action as you accept the new reality you find yourself in.

What happens to your energy when you dream? In the Dream stage, you will do more than set goals. You will activate and dive deep into Vision, one of the Alignment principles in the Opus 8 (see chapter one). You will let go of limits, think beyond what seems realistic, and allow yourself to explore possibilities. If you knew you couldn't fail, what would you do? If resources and timing weren't an issue, what would you create? You'll set your energy free.

I learned this lesson firsthand when I moved to Provence. It wasn't a move that fit any logical plan. My career was thriving, and my life in London had been established. And yet, there was a part of me that had always dreamed of something different: a richer way of living, closer to nature and creativity. When I finally allowed myself to take that dream seriously, as a unique opportunity instead of as giving up on my city life, everything began to shift. I changed my location, yes, but I also embraced a new way of being, a more expansive version of myself.

That's what this week is about: expanding your energetic capacity to dream. You don't need to take immediate action; just allow your dreams to take up space. If you're doing the exercises alongside the reading, get ready to activate your dream state now.

Exercise: Dream Activation (Twenty to Thirty Minutes)

Most of us carry dreams we rarely speak aloud. Sometimes they're quiet wishes we tuck away. Sometimes they're bold visions we talk ourselves out of before they have a chance to breathe. But dreaming is sacred work. To dream, you won't need spreadsheets or five-year plans. Instead, bring your wonder, imagination, and the deep knowing that life holds more for us.

This week invites you to explore three dream paths:

- **The purposeful dream.** If you already have a sense of what matters most but want to deepen your alignment, start here.
- **The sustainable growth dream.** If you are feeling restless and ready to grow, but want to do so in a balanced way, this is for you.
- **The inspired dream.** If you need to reignite joy, creativity, and wonder, this lens will help you dream beyond limits.

Each path offers a unique lens on what's possible in your life. They are here to stir your spirit, awaken your desires, and help you sketch a vision that feels honest, energizing, and deeply yours. You might choose one that resonates or dive into all three. There's no right way to do this—just your way.

Before you begin, set aside time. For some, these exercises will feel abstract. So, create structure by setting aside time to engage and have the necessary supplies on hand.

- **Set the mood.** Find a quiet space. Light a candle. Put on instrumental music. Let this time feel spacious and sacred.

- **Gather supplies.** A notebook, your *Live Your Opus Workbook*, or blank pages, some way to record your thoughts. You'll also need a pen (or colored ones, if you like), a timer, and an open heart. Please complete these exercises by hand. Doing so will help you keep it rough rather than perfect.

- **Set your timer.** Give yourself ten to fifteen minutes per dream. Enough to explore and energize you, not enough to overthink.

You'll want to consider how you will capture your ideas. I've seen people begin by journaling on each dream scenario and then create a table or a drawing. Others have reflected on the questions within each dream and then chosen to set their page horizontally capturing their ideas chronologically over the next few years. Reflect on the scenarios and you may find that the approach that works best for you soon emerges.

To get started or if you feel stuck, as you think of each dream scenario, close your eyes and imagine a day in your dream life. Ask yourself:

- Where am I? What do I see? Who's with me? What am I doing? And how do I feel?
- What does success look like, not just externally, but in how my life feels?
- What support surrounds me? Think about people, practices, and resources.
- What small challenges might grow me into the person I'm becoming?

Now, take a breath. And remember: You don't have to know everything. Dreams don't require certainty—just curiosity. So just begin.

The Purposeful Dream

A purposeful dream comes from the heart of who you are. Imagine living in complete alignment with your values and gifts. Your days reflect what matters most. Your energy goes where it truly belongs and wherever you want it to go.

This dream scenario is for you if you've been living by others' expectations or moving through life on autopilot. Choose this dream if you long to feel rooted in your own energy and values again, or if you're craving clarity, authenticity, and a deeper sense of meaning in the everyday. When your life feels scattered or performative, this is the dream that brings you back to center.

Ask yourself:

- If no one else's opinion mattered, what would I feel called to pursue?
- What kind of work or contribution feels most energizing and meaningful to me?
- What do I want to master or explore at a deeper level?
- What legacy or positive impact do I hope to leave, even in small, quiet ways?

Let this dream reflect the truest version of you, not who you think you should be, but who you already are underneath it all.

The Sustainable Growth Dream

The sustainable growth dream honors both your ambition and your well-being. Imagine expanding into new growth without feeling run down or risking burning out. You're stretching into possibility, but you're doing it on your own terms. You're thriving and not settling for a life that you just survive.

In this dream scenario, you balance your ambition with your well-being, inviting the Opus 8 energy principles of Pacing and Vitality into the design.

This dream asks: How can you grow, challenge yourself, and evolve in a way that energizes you and so that your physical, mental, emotional, and spiritual health are nurtured rather than extinguished?

Choose this dream if you've been pushing hard for a long time, and maybe it's even cost you. If you believe in your growth but want to find a way to pursue it without burning out, this dream is your invitation. It's for the part of you that has ambition but knows that overworking isn't sustainable. This dream helps you find a new rhythm: one that supports your success without sacrificing your well-being.

Ask yourself:

- Where do I feel ready for a stretch or the next level of growth? Where do I feel naturally drawn to expand, even gently?
- What would feel like an energizing, meaningful stretch, not a depleting one?
- What rhythms, habits, or communities would help me stay grounded?
- How would life feel if I moved at a manageable pace, one that actually supported me? How might that change my experience?

This dream invites balance. While it does invite momentum, it does so rooted in care, not pressure. With sustainable growth, you progress toward your goals at a pace that nurtures your relationship with yourself and others, ensures your well-being rises to meet your ambition, and allows you to fully enjoy the ride.

The Inspired Dream

This is the dream that gives you goosebumps. An inspired dream fills you with joy, wonder, and possibility, even if it seems impractical. These are the dreams that inspire you to action.

The inspired dream is where play, creativity, and joy live. Where you let go of "shoulds" and rediscover wonder. No limits. No filters. No expectations. Just pure possibility.

Here, welcome your most hidden—or biggest—dreams. The ones that you may have suppressed due to fear, impracticality, the needs of others, or because you thought you should play it safe. However, these dreams should align with your values and feel true to you and not be fueled by your ego or false self.

This is the dream scenario to choose if the idea of doing so scares you a little, or a lot. If it feels too big, too bold, too impractical, it might be exactly the one you need to explore within the safety of this exercise. The Inspired Dream helps you uncover the desires you've buried, the creativity you've quieted, and the joy you may have forgotten how to follow. Choose it if you want to stretch your heart and imagination beyond what feels safe, and especially if you're used to playing it safe.

Ask yourself:

- What makes me feel most alive?
- What would I love to try if I weren't worried about anything practical?
- What lights me up—even if I've never said it out loud? These may be experiences, environments, or creative pursuits, for example.
- Where in the world (places, people, or communities) would I love to immerse myself?
- If fear wasn't in the driver's seat, where would I go? What would I create? Who would I become?

Let this dream be wild, playful, and real. Even if it feels silly. Especially if it feels silly. That's where your soul starts to speak.

Lighting the Spark

You've just done something rare: you gave your heart and energy system a voice and listened. You've made space for something so many of us put off: imagining a life that calls to you, not just one that fits the mold.

This week invited you to notice what your inner self still hopes for. To step outside the lines of what's in motion or expected and into the open field of what's possible.

Whatever emerged during your dream activation exercise, whether it was bold, quiet, unfinished, or wildly unexpected—trust it. Dreams are invitations to listen more closely to what's stirring in your heart, not puzzles to solve.

Maybe your dream took the shape of a single image, a word, or a future you barely dared to sketch. Maybe it startled you. Maybe it moved you. Maybe you're still not sure what it all means. That's okay. Whether your dream felt silly, too big, just right, or long overdue, trust it. This is all part of the process. Some dreams arrive in full color. Others whisper their way in one brushstroke at a time.

What matters most is that you showed up. You gave yourself permission to imagine. You've just lit the spark. Let it flicker, grow, dance. Let it surprise you. And pause here. Honor the moment. Let yourself feel the shift: from constraint to possibility, from practicality to imagination, from silence to voice.

If you want to keep exploring, turn to the workbook. There, you'll find prompts and playful invitations to stretch a little further into your dreams.

Next week, we'll follow that spark. You'll begin to refine your dreams and listen more deeply for the one that burns brighter than the rest—your burning desire. But for now, breathe. Let yourself feel the energetic shift that comes from having said yes to yourself. And that, in itself, is a beautiful beginning.

WEEK FIVE. FINDING YOUR BURNING DESIRE

Last week, you opened yourself to your dreams. You imagined your future through different lenses, allowing possibilities to surface. Maybe the dreams came easily and felt vivid and exciting, or maybe they felt uncertain, unfinished. That is exactly as it should be. What matters most is that you have begun listening and attuning to the energy of what wants to emerge. Rest assured that wherever you are today, your dream will meet you there.

But how do you know which dreams are just passing thoughts and which ones are truly meant for you? The ones that will shape you, challenge you, bring you joy, and call you forward?

This week, you'll go deeper. You won't just be thinking about your dreams; you'll step inside them using your mind's eye to discover which ones truly resonate. Because dreaming is one thing. But finding your burning desire, the dream that won't let go of you—the one whose energy lingers, whispers, and keeps vibrating beneath the surface even when you try to set them aside—that is something more.

Experiences Waiting to Happen

We often think of dreams as distant aspirations. But what if our dreams aren't just possibilities? What if they are already a part of us, waiting to take shape?

One of the most powerful ways to connect with your dreams is to experience them as if they are already real, to inhabit the life you want to create, even if just for a moment. This is why visualization is so effective. Visualization gets a lot of bad press these days due to the amount of snake oil being peddled across the wellness industry. But the visualization I'm referring to here is based in neuroscience: It's a practice of mentally rehearsing your desired future, allowing your mind, heart, and energy system to experience what it's like to inhabit your dreams.[16]

Visualization works because it engages your brain much like real experience does. When you vividly imagine an experience, your brain treats it as if it's real. That's because when you visualize specific goals, you strengthen neural pathways and prime the brain for achievement, essentially "tricking" it into experiencing the future as if it's happening now. Athletes use visualization to improve performance. Leaders use it to prepare for big moments. We can also use it to connect with the future we most want to create.[17]

Effectively a form of mental and emotional rehearsal, visualization gives you the power of clarity and embodiment and prepares you to take real steps forward. Through it, you can:

- **Sense what truly excites you** and what might just be an expectation you have inherited.
- **Recognize resistance** so you can see where your mind tries to hold you back.
- **Create a strong emotional and energetic connection** to your dreams, making them feel more real and attainable.

Before we step into visualization, let's look at what separates dreams that remain ideas from those that become reality.

The Power of a Burning Desire

In a well-known study of five hundred high achievers, including Andrew Carnegie and Henry Ford, researcher Napoleon Hill found that they all had one thing in common: They had a clearly defined goal paired with an intense energy, an unwavering desire, to achieve it. Hill writes: "The starting point of all achievement is desire. Keep this constantly in mind. Weak desire brings weak results, just as a small fire makes a small amount of heat."[18]

Hill found that without a specific, passionate desire, people lack the motivation and persistence required to overcome obstacles. According to Hill, definite, burning desire acts as a force that fuels perseverance, creativity, and commitment, allowing individuals to stay focused on their goals until they achieve them.

With this kind of desire, you aren't chasing something just because it sounds impressive. You feel something deeper—a fire inside you that refuses to go out, even when obstacles arise. It is the dream you can't shake, the vision that keeps resurfacing no matter how many times life pulls you in other directions.

Beyond motivation, discovering your burning desire requires alignment. Hill found that those who succeeded weren't necessarily the most talented or the luckiest. They simply had a dream so clear, so deeply felt, that they were willing to pursue it through uncertainty, setbacks, and time.

Feeling a Burning Desire

Since recovering from burnout, my burning desire has become clear: to help ambitious people like you gain meaningful momentum while staying healthy and whole. More than just a wish for my career, this burning desire is the throughline that guides every step I take. Even in moments when I haven't known exactly how I would make something happen, my burning desire was there, pulling me forward—it still is.

Writing this book is part of that. So is every client or team I coach, every new idea I develop, every newsletter or conversation where I help someone see their potential more clearly. My burning desire sees beyond a single achievement and into my long-term commitment to serving others, a dream that evolves as I do.

Alongside that burning desire sits three others: the desire to maintain close friendships with my adult children, my love of living in Provence, and the pull of travel.

Now, your dream doesn't have to look like mine. But it does need to have one thing in common: It needs to be deeply connected to your true self, something that calls to you in a way that logic alone can't explain.

I know that might sound intimidating. Here's the thing: A burning desire will motivate you in the best of times and pull you through in the toughest of times. And your burning desire can fuel the long game: We often overestimate what we can achieve in a day, week, or month. But we underestimate what we can achieve in a decade or even in our lifetime. A burning desire can help us to attain meaningful success beyond what we can even dream today.

Don't worry; you don't need to have all the answers today or be ready to step into action. What you do need is a dream that interests you enough to stick with it for the long term.

So, before we move into visualization, answer a question: Which one of the dream scenarios that you explored last week pulls at you the strongest? Which one might you pursue even if success took ten years? Remember, attaining success doesn't require a full plan mapped out before you begin. Commitment, passion, and action usually come before clarity. They are the fuel.

Now, at the risk of contradicting myself, consider this: Not every dream is meant to be a burning desire. Some dreams are exciting in theory, but they don't hold up when you imagine committing to them long term. Others may be fulfilling for a season of your life, but not necessarily a defining pursuit. That's okay. You don't want to force every idea into a forever category, but you do want to start noticing which ones won't let go of you, even if only for a while. Which dreams energize you rather than drain you? Which ones feel like they already belong to you, even if you don't yet know how to make them happen?

Sometimes, the dream that sticks isn't the biggest or flashiest one. It's just the one that feels most right.

Your Future Self

If you think back across your life, as you did in the Connect stage, my guess is that there were many times when you weren't sure what was next or how to get from "here" to "there." However, a brief moment of deep clarity led you to leap anyway. Maybe it was a move, a new job, or a relationship you decided to pursue.

This was the case for me when my first husband and I decided to divorce. I didn't know what my future would look like: where I would live, where my children would go to school, or what the impact would be on my career.

But then, one day, when I was walking alone in my favorite woods, I stopped to sit on a rock. There, in the silence, I could hear the birds, the wind in the trees, and the train in the distance. I could also hear myself. And, in that moment, I got this wonderful feeling; it's hard to describe.

Although I didn't know what the future held, I had the realization, and I could nearly see myself in that future in my mind's eye, that I would be happy to explore whatever it had to offer. I got this firm sense that if I just leaped, everything would eventually fall into place: a home, my children's community, and even love. With that one deep glimmer of clarity and no details, no plan, no real certainty, everything suddenly seemed doable, positive. I stepped forward with newfound confidence.

Maybe you have had a moment like this, a time when you suddenly saw something with crystal clarity even before it became real. That is the power of visualization. Visualization connects you with the part of you that already knows the way. This week's exercises will help you to envision your dream scenarios and your burning desires. This is a powerful, but low stakes, way to step into the possibilities you're considering for your future today.

Preparing Before You Begin

Find a quiet spot where you won't be interrupted. Light a candle if that feels grounding. Or play gentle music in the background, something wordless that invites stillness or awe. Or engage in whatever else helps settle your energy.

Now decide how you want to explore the following visualization exercises:

- **Listen.** Visit LiveYourOpus.com for a guided audio version.
- **Imagine.** Close your eyes and journey inward.
- **Write.** Let the scene unfold on the page.
- **Embody.** Experiment with one element of your dream by acting it out or bringing it into your life somehow today.

Choose whichever path helps you *feel most connected* energetically, emotionally, and imaginatively. There's no right way, only your way.

Exercises: Living in the Future of Your Dreams (Ten to Twenty Minutes Each)

You've dreamed. You've explored what might be possible. Today, you'll meet your future self, the version of you who is fully living your Opus.

Think of this as more than just picturing possibilities. Think of it as a mental and emotional dress rehearsal. Today, you are giving your brain a real experience of what it feels like to live that future over the next five years, and that makes it easier to shape it and step toward it in reality.

If it feels hard to picture your future, that's okay. You don't need to have a bold vision, and you don't need to see everything clearly. Just start with one small image, one feeling of possibility, and see where it leads.

If picturing five years ahead feels too distant, that's okay too. Instead, imagine yourself six months from now, just far enough to feel some movement, but close enough to feel real. What would progress look like in that time? Who would you be becoming?

Arriving in Your Future

Close your eyes. Take several deep breaths. Inhale possibility, exhale and release any anxiety. Inhale hope, exhale and release any judgment.

Now, imagine it's the future, perhaps five years from today (or sooner if that feels more accessible). You've stepped into a future where you're already living the life or possibility you dreamed last week.

Whichever dream scenario you've chosen, purposeful, sustainable, or inspired, picture yourself living it now. If your burning desires are already clear, see yourself living in pursuit of them now. Take a moment to land in the future:

- **Where are you? Look around at your surroundings.** Are you in a city, by the ocean, in a creative studio? Then look beyond what you can see. How does it feel to stand here? Are you feeling energized, free, at home in your life?

- **What is the energetic signature of this place? Does it feel calm, expansive, exciting, fulfilling?**
- **What is different about you? Notice how you stand, breathe, move.** How are you carrying yourself? What is the unshakeable quality you now possess?

Let yourself fully land in this moment. Notice if your body feels different—lighter, stronger, softer. Energy often shifts before understanding arrives. Feel your emotions rising: Is it pride? Surprise? Meaning? This is real. Breathe into the joy, the calm, or even the awe. Let it rise.

Now, gently move into a day in your future life.

A Day in Your Dream Life

Imagine yourself moving through a day in that life, from the moment you wake up to the moment you rest again:

- **Morning.** What's the first thing you feel when you open your eyes? Peace? Purpose? Anticipation? What is different from how you wake up today?
- **Relationships.** Who shares this life with you? How do you feel in their presence? What kind of connection have you cultivated?
- **Vitality and well-being.** You feel strong, alive. What practices sustain you? What habits and rhythms have helped you stay grounded and vibrant?
- **Work or purpose.** How are you using your time and talents? What fills you up? How do you feel as you move through your day?
- **Evening.** What brings you a sense of satisfaction as the day winds down? What's your last thought before sleep?

There's no need to get every detail. Just be there. Let yourself fully feel this dream life, not just as the idea, but as a reality you are living right now.

What Did You Learn?

Take a few moments now to come back to yourself here in the present. Feel your body and the ground beneath your feet. Open your eyes and be present.

You have just experienced your future self. They are not separate from you; they are within. Reflect on what you learned from this visit to your future and ask yourself some questions:

- What stood out most from this experience?
- Did any dream feel more alive or compelling? Is that my burning desire revealing itself?
- Did I feel resistance, tightness, or energetic contraction? If so, what might that be asking me to explore?
- What guidance did my future self offer?

All dreams don't need to be big ones. And many big dreams don't require big leaps. The most powerful burning desire begins with small, steady steps. So, let it be simple; let it be yours.

A Glimpse Beyond: Other Ways to Visualize

There are other powerful ways to deepen this practice. You might explore spending time inside a future space, like your office, a creative studio, a sanctuary, or a meaningful place. Or you might imagine receiving advice from your future self, such as what your future self knows now that you might need to hear today.

Both of these visualizations are available in the *Live Your Opus Workbook* if you'd like to explore further. Each is an invitation to listen. To trust. To remember that your future self already holds the map.

Bringing a Bit of the Future Into Today

You don't need to wait five years to become the person you just met. Instead, think about any burning desires that revealed themselves to you. Then, choose one small way to embody your future self this week.

Maybe it's in how you carry yourself, your posture, your breath, your energy, or standing with the same confidence as your future self. Maybe it is a simple habit, something your future self does every day that you can start doing today. Maybe it is an energetic and mindset shift, believing that you are already becoming that person, that you have already succeeded.

Your Opus is not waiting for you six months, two years, or five years from now; it is unfolding within you, right here, right now. Can you feel it? The subtle shift in your energy, the resonance of what's already becoming real.

WEEK SIX. DREAMING YOUR OPUS

It's easy to think that dreams arrive with a burst of energy, demanding our attention. Although that certainly happens, more often than not, dreams, even important ones, begin quietly, sometimes as a whisper, a tug of curiosity, or a sense that something more is possible. Over the past two weeks, you've listened. You've let possibility speak. You've imagined futures that energize and inspire, ones that feel more aligned with who you are and what you're becoming. Maybe your dream arrived fully formed. Or maybe it's still unfolding, revealing itself in fragments. Both are perfectly right. What matters most is that you gave yourself space to begin.

Now, we move one step further. This is where your dream starts to take shape, not as a rigid plan, but as a living vision. Dreams, like people, evolve with time and attention. Your Opus isn't a single destination; it's an energetic direction. One guided by resonance, alignment, and vitality and which you'll refine, deepen, and walk toward again and again.

Right now, you might feel energized and clear or unsure and open-ended. That's exactly where you need to be. Embrace this moment as if you were standing before a blank canvas. Your Opus is yours to create—one brushstroke, one insight, one moment at a time.

This week, you'll begin shaping your Opus in a way that feels both expansive and grounded. You'll look across time in the near, mid, and long term and consider how your dreams might unfold in layers. You'll begin to sense the rhythm of your Opus and bring its pieces into focus. To support you, we'll return to a familiar energetic compass: the Opus 8, which will serve as a guide to help you discern what is most energizing, aligned, and enduring.

So, take a breath. Let this be playful. Trust what's coming into focus—and trust yourself to begin.

Reflection: A Conversation with Your Dreams (Fifteen Minutes)

By now, your dreams may feel vivid and energizing or a bit expansive and unfinished. That's to be expected. You started with two to three different dream scenarios. You reflected on any burning desires. Then, you visualized yourself in one or more of those scenarios. Now it's time to listen a little more closely. Which parts of those dreams are still echoing in your mind? Which ones feel undeniably yours?

This next step is about refinement. You won't be narrowing or restricting, but gently tuning in to what feels most true, most aligned. And to do that, we'll bring back the Opus 8 energy principles, this time as more of a conversation than as just a concept.

Think of it this way: You're sitting down with your dreams, asking them some thoughtful questions. Not to judge or evaluate, but to get to know them more intimately. Which ones are asking for more of you? Which ones energize you, and which ones ask more than they give?

Envision your dreams have a voice and try to listen carefully to how they respond to the prompts below. Use the questions to explore as many dream scenarios or burning desires as you like. Take your time. Let this exploration be relaxed and honest.

- **Energy (Vitality).** What parts of this dream light up my nervous system, making me feel energized? Which aspects feel draining? And which parts support my well-being, or, conversely, ask more than I can sustainably give?

- **Alignment with core values (Vision, Coherence).** Is this dream truly mine? Does it reflect my core values and identity, or is it something I think I should want? Do I feel any internal conflict about this dream? What may that be telling me?

- **Inspiration (Vision).** Does this dream light me up? Do I feel drawn toward it, naturally and eagerly?

- **True connection.** Will this dream deepen my connection to myself and others? Does it bring me closer to what matters most?

- **Sustainable growth.** Can I grow into this dream over time without burning out? Will it evolve with me and hold my interest and energy?

- **Present Focus.** Can I enjoy the path toward this dream, or does it feel like I need to "arrive" before I can feel fulfilled?

Spend a few minutes journaling your reflections or simply sit with the questions and notice what arises. Be honest with yourself; this is about gaining further clarity, not certainty. And about honoring what your inner self already knows.

Once you've had that conversation, you'll be ready to explore what it means to dream in time and to see how your Opus can unfold across the days, months, and years ahead.

Exercise: Dreaming in Time (Forty-Five Minutes)

Time can feel like a weight or a gift, depending on how you hold it.

Some people can see their dreams clearly ten years into the future. Others can only imagine the next few months. Neither is right nor wrong. Your Opus doesn't depend on how far ahead you can see; it depends on how open and honestly you're willing to dream from where you are.

I am one of those people who always cringed when someone would ask me, "Where do you see yourself in five or ten years?" First off, who can think that far ahead? Then, I'd get nervous, like I had to put the right stake in the ground, one that would make sense to someone else. So, for many years, I stopped asking those questions of others. And I stopped answering them.

But I've since learned is that time can be a creative tool. It allows us to pace ourselves. To expand. To move forward gently, with clarity and care. And most of all, it reminds us that we don't have to do it all at once.

Business strategist and author Dorie Clark calls this "playing the long game." It's about building a life that aligns with your values and goals over time, rather than chasing immediate results. She reminds us that long-term success often comes not from intensity, but from consistency. And that making peace with slow progress is what allows us to make *real* progress.[19]

For me, especially as a Catalyst, this shift has been freeing. I don't need to build everything, my business, my book, my personal life, right away. I just need to know what is calling me forward and then give each part of my dreams its place in time. This new awareness supported me in accepting the commitment and significance I attach to my work. The quality of it, my relationships with myself and those I serve, and its impact and longevity, are all critical. I am now very comfortable with a five and ten year view of my life and work.

To stay steady and on course, I use the Opus 8 energy principles as a guide. I now regularly cultivate Present Focus and Pacing through practices that, in turn, keep the quality and momentum of my work high. I engage daily in practices that support my Vitality and Connection. Together, these practices support and sustain my energy so I can more effectively direct it toward my work and the other vital elements of my life: travel, time with my family and friends, pets, hobbies, professional collaborations, my well-being.

That's how my Opus began to take shape, layer by layer, not overnight. You can do the same.

Instead of treating time as something to fear or chase, let it free you to dream and help you organize your vision. Some dreams might belong to this year. Others may take root slowly over five or ten years. Some may even surprise you by arriving sooner than you imagined. Because, of course, even if we consider time, we don't control it. Trust that your Opus will give you direction.

How to Begin

There's no one "right" way to map out your dreams. But giving your dreams space to stretch across time can be both clarifying and empowering.

This next practice invites you to map your Opus using three distinct time horizons:

- **Short term (the next twelve months).** What's close? What's already possible?
- **Medium term (three to five years).** What are you growing into?
- **Long term (ten years).** If your Opus were fully realized, what would life feel like?

You might find yourself naturally drawn to one of these more than the others. Start there. Or, if all three feel exciting, explore them all. Sketch, map, write; whatever makes it feel real to you. This is a creative process, and not a perfect one.

To begin, gather your insights from the past two weeks, your dream scenarios and any burning desires you've already identified, any visualizations that stuck with you, and reflections from the Conversation with Your Dreams that you completed last week.

Then, ask yourself: Which pieces feel essential? Which ones keep coming back? Which ones feel most like me, even if they scare me a little?

These are your burning desires, the ones you'll now shape into something more tangible.

You may find it helpful to identify a few pillars that matter most in your life and dreams. These might include:

- Career or meaningful work.
- Family and friendships.
- Travel or adventure.
- Creative expression.
- Home, health, community, or contribution.

Don't think of these as boxes to tick; they're pieces of the life you're building. Choose the ones that feel most alive for you right now. Then use them to imagine how your Opus might unfold across time.

Finally, grab a few sheets of paper and a pencil or pen. It's best to do this by hand to connect fully with yourself and avoid trying to make your dream perfect. Sketch, journal, or map. It doesn't need to be pretty or perfect. It just needs to make sense to you. Some people write in paragraphs. Others doodle or draw timelines. There's no format here, only freedom. I have seen people turn this exercise into very different-looking pieces of paper; mine is usually linear across the time horizons with doodles and a few words. Whatever you choose, let it reflect your unique energetic signature, what makes your presence felt in the world.

In the next section, I'll offer prompts to guide you through each time horizon so you can begin giving your Opus a shape that feels real and deeply right.

Mapping Your Opus Across Time Horizons

You've gathered your dream fragments. Now it's time to gently stretch them across time and to begin imagining how your Opus might unfold in thoughtful, spacious layers, not all at once.

As you explore each time horizon, let yourself move at your own pace. You might start with the short term to feel grounded. Or leap ahead to the long term to envision the full bloom. Trust your instincts. There's no pressure to map everything. Just see what emerges when you allow your dreams to breathe.

As you begin mapping your dreams, notice what thoughts arise. Do some feel easy and natural, while others feel out of reach? That's normal. You'll recall that we all have an upper limit, the place where we start to pull back, second-guess, or tell ourselves a dream is too much. Pay attention to where that happens, not as a reason to stop, but as a sign that you are stepping toward something important, something you care about deeply. See where you might stretch.

Use the prompts below to reflect, sketch, or journal. And remember: This is not a plan. It's a living vision. One that will evolve with you.

<table>
<tr><th>Time Horizon</th><th>What I Am Shaping</th></tr>
<tr><td>Short Term
(Next twelve months)</td><td>This is the season of stepping stones. What feels close enough to reach for? What might you begin—even in small, imperfect ways? You're not trying to do everything at once. You're just taking your first steps with clarity and care. Ask yourself:<ul><li>Where would I love to begin?</li><li>What feels energizing and essential to include now, something I need or want?</li><li>What is one small thing that feels exciting, even if it is slightly outside of my comfort zone?</li><li>What rhythms or habits could help me become the person I'm growing into?</li></ul></td></tr>
<tr><td>Medium Term
(Three to five years)</td><td>This is your expansion phase, where your Opus begins to take fuller shape. It's a time of building, learning, and becoming. What might be taking shape? Mark a few anchor points, milestones, or moments you hope to meet along the way. It's okay if they shift. This is a sketch, not a contract. Ask yourself:<ul><li>How have my dreams grown or deepened by this point?</li><li>Who am I becoming along the way?</li><li>What stories might I be telling myself that create hesitation? Can I name them and choose a gentler one?</li><li>What is inspiring me to continue forward?</li></ul></td></tr>
<tr><td>Long Term
(Ten years)</td><td>This is your Opus in full bloom. Let yourself feel the energy of this horizon. Ten years may feel far away, but it is a beautiful horizon to imagine. Let yourself go there—not to predict the future, but to dream without limits. Give yourself permission to dream expansively. Ask yourself:<ul><li>What am I building toward?</li><li>What dreams have found their way into reality?</li><li>Who have I become? And how does that feel?</li><li>What's different about my life now, compared to when I started?</li></ul>If you find yourself holding back here, gently ask yourself: What if I allowed myself to dream even bigger?</td></tr>
</table>

This type of thinking and exploration is about possibility. Some parts of your Opus may unfold quickly while others may take their time. That's the beauty of dreaming in time: You give each desire the space it needs to grow.

Witnessing Your Creation

Take a moment to step back and witness what you've created. You've just spent time not only imagining your future, but shaping it. That's no small thing.

Let's pause here. Instead of rushing ahead, let it all land. Ask yourself:

What part of my Opus excites me most right now?

Where do I feel a little hesitation? What kind of support, space, or encouragement might help me move through it?

If I send one message to my future self, what would it be?

You may not fully understand the weight of your dreams yet—and that's exactly as it should be. The dream you've envisioned is alive now. It may shift, expand, surprise you. Let it.

A Final Note Before We Compose

You've just completed the Dream stage and reached the halfway point of this transformation! That's worth celebrating.

Your Opus might still be forming. Some pieces might feel clear. Others may be floating just outside your reach. That's okay. You're not behind. You're in motion.

You aren't transforming yourself through this process to reach some perfect endpoint. Instead, revel in discovering more about yourself and daring to shape a life that feels like yours. Fully. Freely. Authentically. Trust the timing. Trust your voice. Trust the part of you that's dreaming something deeper into being.

The transition from Dream to Compose is a powerful one that often stirs something in us. Dream has asked you to open, stretch, and listen for what's possible. It invited your imagination, curiosity, and even a bit of courage, to the table. Now, something shifts.

Where Dream was spacious, Compose is grounding. You might feel that shift as a subtle change in energy, less like floating, and more like standing barefoot on the earth. There's still wonder here, but it's anchored now in direction. Your vision is no longer abstract. It wants to move and live in your actions, rhythms, relationships, and days. So, in Compose, you'll begin to help it come to life.

But for now? In this moment, just breathe. You've done something extraordinary: You've dreamed your Opus.

Chapter Five

COMPOSE:
Turning Vision Into Reality

Every great work, every piece of music, story, and life well-lived begins with a spark. A quiet idea. A glimpse of something. Over the past several weeks, you've been gathering those sparks, one by one.

You've listened deeply to yourself, allowed yourself to imagine, to feel, and connect with possibility. You explored new directions and even stepped into the lives you might lead. Some dreams you found felt clear. Some surprised you or felt exciting, even bold. And some you're still figuring out. And that's exactly how it should be. Because a vision—your Opus—isn't something you discover fully formed. It's something you compose.

According to anthropologist Mary Catherine Bateson, composing a life is a creative, improvisational act that requires continual adaptation and engagement with change.[20] And whether you've realized it or not, you've already been composing, every choice, every pivot, every small decision a note in your unfolding melody.

Yet most of us are unaware that we are engaged in a creative process; we simply live our lives. Even when we focus on achieving a specific goal, the truth is that we compose much of our lives through improvisation, shaping the arc of our days, choice by choice, rhythm by rhythm.

What if we did it on purpose? What if we approached our lives as a composition, one that is not rigid and linear, but fluid, responsive, and alive?

This approach suits the world we live in: Linear paths have faded. Ongoing rapid change demands flexibility, reinvention, and the ability to navigate shifting, often uncertain, landscapes. Composing your Opus—a life of intention—can help you retain a sense of control and steadiness. That's what this next stage is all about. Not rushing into action but iterating on your dreams, your Opus, step by thoughtful step.

As you make this shift from Dream, you may feel more rooted, clearer, or perhaps a little emotional, as if you've just touched something true that you're not quite ready to share.

That's because you have. You've dared to dream with heart and honesty. Now, the invitation is not to solve—but to shape. All of these feelings are welcome here. This transition marks a turning point: A move from asking "What if?" to gently considering, "What now?"

Over the next few weeks, you'll start composing by choosing a direction and taking the first step toward it. Like a musician discovering a new melody, you don't need to play every note perfectly. You just need to begin.

THE NATURE OF COMPOSING

Composing your life means stepping into a creative relationship with your future, one note at a time. Unlike rigid planning or reactive living, composing invites both intention and improvisation. You don't have to have every answer, but you do get to listen, to adjust, and to shape your life gently, in alignment with what matters most.

Too often, we think linearly: Choose a path, follow the steps, and arrive at the destination. But life rarely moves in straight lines. Our desires shift. Circumstances change. And so must we.

That's why in this stage, Compose, you're not going to set your future in stone. Instead, you'll engage with your dreams actively and with curiosity, letting them evolve through action. You will craft a life that's not only productive, but personal. Not just goal-driven, but soul-aligned.

In music, composition allows for movement, interpretation, and emotion. The same is true for your life. Think of a composer sitting down at the piano. They begin with a few notes, an idea, a feeling. The music doesn't usually arrive all at once. It builds, it bends, it grows. There's structure, yes, but also breath and space. So, while you're composing, turn also to the Opus 8 Energy System; with practice, these energy principles can provide a structure that holds your values, while making room for rhythm, joy, and unexpected turns.

As you go through the Compose stage, you will build a vision that resonates, something that feels both structured and spacious, with enough direction to move forward and enough flexibility to adapt as you grow.

When I moved from London to Provence, I didn't have a perfect plan. I was following something quieter, my intuition. I had a deep longing—a burning desire—for space, for beauty, and for new cadence to my life. I didn't know how all the pieces would fit. I followed the thread of that desire, not with rigid plans or certainty, but with curiosity. I first spent a few weeks in Provence, then a few months, and then a year. Slowly, the shape of my new life began to emerge: creative work, meaningful connections, a growing business, and deep energy and well-being. Each part strengthened the next.

My journey has been an ongoing act of intentionality, self-connection, exploration, and growth. It's still evolving—and never static.

That's what composing your Opus will be like. Less like checking off a to-do list and more like shaping something that's alive. You will begin where you are. You will build, reflect, adjust. You'll let your dream breathe.

I share this because your path may not appear all at once, either. It will emerge as you walk it, with curiosity, courage, and care.

This week, and in the weeks to come, give yourself permission to be a work in progress. You don't have to lock everything down. You just have to stay in the dance.

FROM INSPIRATION TO ACTION

Something shifts the moment we move from dreaming to doing. The energy changes. You might feel ready and eager one day, uncertain or overwhelmed the next. That's not failure—that's transformation at work.

This is the part of the process where many people hesitate. As long as your dream lives in your imagination, it's safe. But the moment you begin to act, doubts creep in. You start to overthink and ask yourself questions: What if I get it wrong? What if I don't have what it takes? What if I change my mind?

Let me reassure you: You *will* change your mind. Your vision *will* evolve. You'll try things that work beautifully and others that will fall flat. That's how the act of composing works. In this phase, instead of waiting for certainty, you're opening yourself up to learning.

So, when you start composing your Opus, expect to wobble. One week, you may feel unstoppable. The next, you may question everything. Trust me when I say: That's normal.

In a recent workshop, I asked people to name how they felt at this stage. "Hopeful." "Stretched." "Motivated but scattered." "Like I'm riding a roller coaster."

One person said, "I get energy from working on my Opus, but I still struggle to say no to everything that pulls me away from it." Another admitted, "I've barely begun, and already I feel like I'm losing sight of it."

You may fear the uncertainty from this emotional swirl, but view it instead as a sign that something important is underway; you are deep in the process of change.

When we stretch into a new way of being, it often feels like we're standing between two selves: the person we've been and the one we are becoming. That in-between space can feel messy and unsteady. But it's also where transformation lives.

This is another time when the Opus Change Continuum can help you. Each archetype reflects a different way we meet change; Compose is a moment when you might shift from one to the other. Take a breath, check in, and ask yourself: Which archetype feels most like you today? How might you support yourself with compassion from where you are?

Hesitators may feel unsure where to begin here, worried that if it's not perfect, it's not worth starting. Support yourself with a single, low-stakes action. Start small, then notice how your courage grows with each step.

Navigators, you may be reaching for your plan, looking for the perfect next move. But Compose asks for flexibility. Let your plan live, breathe, and evolve. It's okay not to have all the details noted or open questions answered yet.

Builders, you might be making slow, steady progress, but struggling to say yes to something that stretches you. Trust the foundation you've already laid. Let this be a time to take one bold step, even if it feels a little uncomfortable.

Explorers, your ideas may be flowing; it's hard to choose between them. Focus on just one. Give it room to live in the real world, even for a short while. You don't have to marry it; just take it out for coffee.

And, Catalysts, if you're charging ahead, filled with energy, pause. Breathe. Remember, pace *is* power. Composing isn't a sprint; it's a rhythm.

Wherever you are on the Continuum, know this: There's no wrong way to feel, no wrong place to begin. The invitation is simply to notice and then support yourself, with care, in moving forward.

So, if you're feeling a mix of excitement and resistance, stay with it. Keep returning to your Opus without forcing it and instead stay in relationship with it. However uncertain things feel, keep the dialogue with your dreams open.

You don't have to move in a straight line. You don't have to go fast. What matters is that you stay connected to what you're creating.

As you move forward, I invite you to hold this process lightly. Let it be playful and flexible, meeting you wherever you are today. Trust that the next step will reveal itself only when you take that first one. Because the moment you begin composing, you are no longer dreaming about your Opus; you are living it.

SHAPING WHAT'S NEXT

If Dream was about opening your mind and heart, Compose is where you begin to shape what's next. This is where your Opus begins to take form in small, steady movements that turn ideas into lived experience. Here, you'll combine vision with action and experimentation to start to create a life that feels deeply aligned with your values and dreams.

Composing isn't about rushing into productivity or intensive goal-setting. This is not about achievement for achievement's sake. Instead, ask yourself, again and again: What matters most? What feels true? What do I need today?

Composing often means *re*composing—tweaking, tuning, and even letting go. That's not indecision; that's craft. Over time, you'll begin to make choices that bring your Opus to life in a way that feels expansive, sustainable, and aligned.

Over the next few weeks, you'll:

- **Recompose your life or career.** Using all that you have learned and completed in Connect and Dream, you will take an honest look at where you are now and where you want to be. What fits? What no longer serves? What wants to emerge?
- **Test your Opus.** You'll try on your dreams through real-world action. No sweeping overhauls, just meaningful experiments that help you explore what aligns.
- **Refine your Opus.** As you test and experiment, you'll gather insights, clarifying what truly fits and what doesn't and adjusting your course accordingly. In this phase, you will integrate what you learn so that your Opus feels sustainable and real.

Throughout this process, the Opus 8 Energy System will serve as your compass, helping you check in with your energy, your alignment, your values, and your sense of presence. Each energy principle becomes a tuning fork, helping you stay grounded while you evolve.

Are you staying connected to your vision? Are your actions coherent with what truly matters? Are you present enough to adjust course as needed? Are you nurturing your Vitality? Practicing these energy principles can help you create with both intention and adaptability.

The end goal is an authentic and energizing alignment of the many pieces of your life. Think of it as if you were creating a symphony: Different movements, tempos, and instruments come together in harmony. This harmony grows through experimentation, reflection, and adjustment.

Let your dream shape you as much as you shape it. And trust that in this dance, both you and your Opus will grow wiser, stronger, and more whole.

MEETING FEAR WITH FORWARD MOTION

Many people arrive to this stage and realize they're carrying an invisible set of expectations shaped by others. One participant in a workshop described the relief she felt when she experienced that realization: "It's like I've been following someone else's map my entire life, and now I have to figure out what my map looks like." For her, that moment brought relief—and fear. What would it mean to create a map of her own?

This is common. Fear often signals that you're growing beyond your old stories, those beliefs that kept you safe but small. It might sound like: "What if I'm not ready?" or "What if I mess it up?" or "What if this isn't realistic?" Rather than barriers, think of those voices as invitations to reconnect with your deeper knowing. To explore what might be possible.

If that's where you are, pause and breathe. You're not doing this work wrong. You're simply human. Returning to practices that support you in living with Vision, Coherence, and Present Focus can help you recalibrate so that each step forward feels both intentional and grounded.

Just like my experience deciding to write this book, remember that fear doesn't need to be erased before you move forward. Susan Jeffers's advice to "feel the fear and do it anyway" reminds us that fear isn't a barrier; it's a companion on the journey.[21] Your task is not to eliminate it but to build trust in your ability to handle whatever comes next and take the first step.

As you begin composing your Opus, you will clarify what you do—and don't—want. Often, the greatest insights emerge when you test what your head says against what your heart feels. During this phase, you will listen to yourself, refining, releasing, and shaping what truly belongs.

The process can be exhilarating. It can also be jarring, especially as you come up against old habits or ways of being that once served you but now feel misaligned with the future you are envisioning. Recognizing and releasing them is another act of transformation.

Many people are looking for clarity before they take action. But clarity is the result of action. One participant shared, "I realized I don't need to have it all figured out before I start. Every step teaches me something, even if it's just what doesn't work."

One man I worked with had a beautiful and clear vision, but he found himself paralyzed by it. "It's too big," he said. "I don't know where to begin." Together, we scaled it back to the next small thing: one conversation, one hour on his calendar, one tiny experiment. And that changed everything. The dream didn't shrink—his sense of agency grew.

That's how you compose: by walking through fear, even with small, imperfect steps and by not overthinking or trying to leap over it.

Fear isn't your enemy; it's a signal that you're moving toward something meaningful. Let it ride beside you, but don't hand it the wheel.

And yes, you will make mistakes. They're not detours; they're part of the path. They help refine your direction. As Jeffers reminds us, "If you haven't made any mistakes lately, you must be doing something wrong."[22]

Composing your Opus is a creative process: You're starting with a sketch and shaping it layer by layer. Some parts will feel effortless. Others will ask you to stretch. Both are part of the masterpiece you are composing.

So, as you begin this stage, don't wait for certainty. Let action bring clarity. Let practice reveal the path. And, above all, stay in a relationship with your vision without rigidity and with love, curiosity, and trust.

YOUR FIRST MISSION: CREATING YOUR OPUS VISION STATEMENT

Every meaningful journey begins with a sense of direction, a guiding light. Your Opus Vision Statement is just that, a guiding light that helps you move with clarity, even when the path ahead isn't fully visible.

As you craft your statement, you'll begin to articulate your burning desire more clearly, what matters most to you, what calls you forward, what won't let you go. And, while your vision will evolve as you do, articulating it now gives you an anchor point for your dreams, allowing you to move them forward with intention and purpose.

This is a quick exercise that's meant to be an energizing experience, so spend no more than five minutes on it. This is a beginning, not a final declaration, and you'll have opportunities to revisit and refine your Opus Vision Statement in the coming weeks.

No matter where you are right now, whether you feel certain about your dreams or not, challenge yourself to put some stakes in the ground by getting as specific as possible with your Opus Vision Statement.

Think of it as a snapshot in time, a simple, heartfelt expression of the future you're beginning to create. Or, if you prefer, an inspiring big picture statement about what you are aiming to achieve or create or who you want to become in the next ten years (or whatever time horizon feels most comfortable).

Whatever you choose to write: Own it and make it yours.

To begin, take a few deep breaths. Find a quiet moment. Then write freely for no more than five minutes. The goal here isn't perfection—it's direction!

- **Name your vision.** What is the vision for your Opus over the next ten years? That is, what do you hope to accomplish? Write this in one to two simple sentences.
- **Clarify your "why."** In one to two simple sentences, write about why this vision matters to you.

- **Feel your vision.** Read your words aloud. How does your body respond? Do you feel a spark of excitement? A little nervous energy? A deep sense of knowing? These feelings are good signs. They mean your vision is alive.

If a single vision feels too narrow, give yourself permission to explore more than one possibility. Write down a few potential directions you could follow, and for each, consider what it might teach you.

There is no single right way forward, only the path you choose to walk. Every choice you make offers an opportunity to learn, grow, and move forward. Let this vision statement be your starting point. It will evolve as you do in the coming weeks and beyond.

For today, let it be enough to simply say to yourself: This is what I care about. This is where I want to begin. Tuck this statement somewhere visible. Return to it when you feel off course. Let it remind you of the life you're shaping.

AN ONGOING ACT OF CREATION

Your Opus is not a finish line. It is something you build, piece by piece, through the choices you make and the steps you take. That's why this stage of the transformation process is called Compose and not Complete. There is no final draft, no ultimate resolution. But there is joy in the act of shaping your life with care, curiosity, and courage.

In fact, there's a reason I chose the word "Compose" for this stage: My husband is a photographer and a musician, and I have watched him compose music for years. Here's what's fascinating: When he writes a song, he's not just thinking about the melody or the lyrics. He's composing for multiple instruments, most of which he doesn't play himself. And yet he can imagine how they'll sound together.

That's the beauty of composition: You don't need to have mastery over every piece of the puzzle. What you do need is a clear vision and, with time, the capacity to bring together the right elements and people to bring it to life. You're doing that right now.

Too often, we tell ourselves we need more time, more skills, more certainty before we can move forward. That we need to wait for the "right" moment when we feel completely ready, confident, and clear. But what if the opposite is true? You will gain certainty and momentum through action.

You don't have to be perfect. You don't have to know everything. You just have to start. Even small, intentional steps that keep us connected to what we care about most are effective at moving us forward. More than simple tasks or productivity hacks, these steps represent choices that reinforce who you are becoming.

So, as you step into this stage of your transformation, try asking yourself three simple questions:

- What's one small step I can take today that moves me closer to my Opus? This may be a way of stepping into who you are becoming.
- How can I shape my days to reflect the life I'm creating—not just someday, but now?
- What simple shift in habits, rituals, or focus would help me move with ease and gain momentum?

You're here to sketch the arc of your Opus rather than build a rigid plan. You're here to shape a life that feels real, rich, and deeply yours. There is no single right way forward. There's only your way. So, remember to love and appreciate yourself on this journey. Have patience with yourself as you learn, adapt, and evolve.

WEEK SEVEN. PREPARING TO COMPOSE YOUR OPUS

For the past six weeks, you've been dreaming, expanding your vision, stepping into possibility, and imagining what might be. Now, the energy begins to shift. It's time to ground that vision, to begin shaping your dream into something real and alive in your day-to-day life.

But before you act, you need a foundation, those first steps that will bring your dream to life.

This week, I invite you to consider which aspects of your Opus you'd like to explore in the next year. Let this be more than a mental exercise; notice what areas feel alive in your body, where your energy rises. These are signs of alignment. The idea is to get just a little more concrete about what you might create for yourself this year, leaving room for improvisation, and letting your energy and purpose lead the way. From now on I'll refer to this as the first year of your Opus, or Year One.

Maybe you're feeling ready to take this step, or maybe fear has just landed in the pit of your stomach. You may feel the tension between your vision and your current reality. That's normal. Big shifts require energy, and sometimes it feels scarce at the outset. Take a breath. This part of the process isn't about speed; it's about resonance. Take time each day to root into the Stability principles to ensure you maintain practices to support and boost your Vitality, Connection, and Grounding. And, remember, every creative process has a moment when the gap between where you are and where you want to be feels widest. You may be at that point today.

Thankfully, you don't need to close that gap all at once. This week is an opportunity to connect with your Opus and gather more insights about yourself and your future. To step back, get perspective, and trust that each small step you take moves you closer to the life you have envisioned.

You're playing the long game now. Trust me, with focus and effort, the progress you will make toward your Opus in this first year will be greater than you can imagine today.

The Space Between Dream and Action

Chances are, you have been here before, in the space between dreaming and action; the place where emotions stir and doubts arise. Maybe you have had a big idea simmering, like starting a newsletter, launching a business, or finally tackling that DIY house project. You tell yourself that you'll start when you have more time. You just need to feel ready. Months pass. Maybe even years. Then, one day, you finally take the first step. You write a few sentences, make the first call, try out a few moves from a YouTube video. And suddenly, you're off and running.

Your first newsletter is published. You have clarified the urgent problem your business will solve. You have built the bookshelf you once thought was beyond you. And you realize: The clarity you needed wasn't the first step after all—taking action was.

Something shifts when you move from dreaming to doing. One moment, you're full of possibility. The next, doubts creep in. You might feel excitement, hesitation, or even resistance—a roller coaster of emotions. That's not a problem. It's a sign you're waking up to something that matters.

The transition from vision to action is always an emotional one because it asks you to let go of who you have been and step into who you are becoming. This is why, before you start composing, it's important to pause and check in.

Take a few moments to ask yourself:

- What emotions are present for me right now as I prepare to step into action?
- What excites me? What, if anything, feels uncertain?
- How do I want to feel as I move forward?

Then try to visualize yourself feeling that way, bringing the full, positive emotion into your work.

As you check in, consider: Which energy principles feel most available to me right now? Do I feel clear in my Vision? Am I nurturing my Vitality? This awareness can gently guide your next step.

This week, you will explore these questions not by searching for a single answer, but by experimenting, trying different ways of stepping into your Opus in the first year. This is explorative, not definitive. It's about movement, momentum, and discovery. So step forward with an open mind, and let's see what you create.

Exercise: My First Opus Year (Fifteen to Twenty-Five Minutes)

You've dreamed it. You've seen what's possible. Now it's time to begin composing with your energy as much as with your goals by outlining the first year of your Opus. There's no pressure to know how you want it all to unfold. Instead, listen closely to the life you want to create and take your first few meaningful steps toward it.

Because this is a blueprint, not a sketch, you can think of this exercise like double-clicking on the notes and visions you created in Dream. You will consider what strengths and learning will support you in moving from where you are today to where you will be in a year.

So, grab a piece of paper, your journal, laptop, or workbook to take notes. To begin, return to the pillars and time horizons you shaped last week (in week six). What are the areas of your dream that feel closest, most ready to unfold? Those are your Year One priorities.

Take a moment to reflect and then write freely—just for you. Let this be rough, imperfect, and honest. One or two simple sentences per area is more than enough. If writing doesn't come easily today, a few bullet points or even symbols are just fine. Trust yourself. Use the prompts below to guide your vision:

- **Set focus areas.** What two to four key areas feel most essential to focus on this year? They might include work, creativity, relationships, well-being, or personal growth, for example. Which ones feel alive with energy and meaning?

- **Imagine yourself a year from now.** What would it feel like to say, "This year, I really showed up for myself"? What does success look and feel like in each of these areas? What matters most? And, beyond any achievements, how do you want to feel at the end of this year? What qualities, like confidence, curiosity, or trust, do you want to cultivate?

- **Understand your "why."** Ask yourself why these activities and goals matter to you. Not just the surface reasons. What's the deeper pull—the burning desire—that makes them meaningful?

- **Let your energy guide you.** Where do you feel natural momentum? Where do you feel resistance—and is that resistance fatigue, fear, or a signal to slow down? These are clues.

If you're wondering what kind of progress you might want to make this year, remember: You won't be finishing your Opus in Year One. You're beginning it with care, creativity, and consistency. (If you'd like additional practice, there are more exercises in the workbook to support you in further developing your first year.)

Here are a few invitations to help you imagine your journey:

- **Begin where you are (Present Focus).** Your year might begin this week with a single new habit, one honest conversation, or the courage to ask for help. That's composing.

- **Honor your capacity (Pacing + Vitality).** Not every season is for pushing. Sometimes composing your Opus means creating space, clearing time, energy, or old patterns that no longer serve, and that's making progress.

- **Create moments of alignment (Coherence + Vision).** Even five minutes a day devoted to something that feels purposeful and aligned with your Opus can transform how you feel and give you a sense of momentum.

Once you've finished, pause and read your notes back to yourself slowly. Let them sink in. What excites you most about this first year? Where do you feel a little tug of fear, and what might they be telling you? And can you handle it? What simple rhythms, rituals, or reminders might help you stay grounded in the weeks ahead?

And if you feel . . . nothing? That's okay too. Sometimes our system needs time to catch up. Energy comes in waves. Trust that the act of naming still has power.

You don't need to act on everything now. You've begun to name your plans for the first year of your Opus and that's powerful. This is your year to live into your dreams, one step, one note at a time. So, this week, let go of pressure and embrace presence. If all you do is listen to what matters and take one small step, you're already composing.

The Beginning of Becoming

You've crossed a quiet threshold this week—from dreaming into doing. You may or may not feel ready or certain; that's okay. What matters most is that you showed up for yourself, listened in, and started to shape the first notes of your Opus.

You'll soon make plans, yes, but also space. You'll take steps but also pauses. You'll grow steadily, gently, sometimes even unexpectedly. And as you do, remember this: Your Opus isn't something far off in the distance. It's already stirring in your daily choices, your mindset shifts, your willingness to try again.

So, move forward with kindness. Allow yourself to be both deliberate and light. Make space for joy. Each small action you take becomes part of the masterpiece you're creating.

And remember: You don't have to feel "on" all the time to be in motion. Stewarding your energy with care, resting when needed, choosing what matters, that *is* forward momentum.

WEEK EIGHT. TESTING YOUR OPUS

Testing your Opus is like trying on clothes. You won't know if something truly fits until you feel it on. The same is true for your dream. Rather than waiting to be ready, this week invites you into a courageous curiosity, experimenting with the pieces of your Opus to see what brings you to life, and then refining them as you learn what feels right.

Take my friend Greg, for example. He did not transition from corporate roles at IBM and Xerox to leading his own dance company in a single, dramatic leap; instead, he completed it in a series of small tests. While still working full time and completing his MBA at Harvard, Greg, who had danced when he was younger, began teaching dance classes on the side. He didn't know where it would lead, but each class, each conversation, each moment of stepping into movement was an experiment that revealed something new. Each step met him where he was—honoring his capacity, building energy gradually, and allowing his intuition to lead.

Over time, he saw a clearer path forward: "I had to create a viable infrastructure to do what I loved," he said, and he eventually created his own dance company.

Greg's story reminds us that transformation is rarely about a single moment of clarity. Clarity emerges after we take a series of small, meaningful steps.

Greg continues to experiment today. Beyond his dance company, he has created partnerships with schools and nonprofit entities; they began several years ago and are now a vital part of his business. Likewise, he has created a host of other offerings and collaborations, each of which began as a seed. What he discovered—and what you may find too—is that momentum builds not from perfect plans, but from engaged energy.

Many people wait for the perfect moment to begin, when they have more time, more clarity, or more confidence. But you can't think your way into your Opus. Resistance often arises not because you're on the wrong path, but because you've touched something true. That's why it's helpful to start by taking action and, this week, by trying things.

Experimentation is a way of thinking, a compass that can help you navigate. Sometimes, the urge to experiment is instinctive, like trying a new routine or approaching a problem differently. Other times, experimentation involves a bold move that shifts your path entirely. But whether big or small, every experiment you engage in related to your Opus reveals something: what excites you, what challenges you, and what hidden strengths or gaps exist. It's through testing—not planning alone—that you uncover what you truly want and how to move toward it.

And experimentation isn't just about external action. Inner shifts, like expressing an unspoken desire, listening with more compassion, or pausing before reacting, are equally potent. These internal tests deepen connection: to yourself, to others, and to what matters most.

Growth comes from stepping beyond the familiar, talking to new people, testing your ideas, engaging in different experiences. Small shifts often reveal opportunities already around you, waiting to be noticed. Experimentation also makes change feel manageable, breaking a big vision into steps you can actually take. And with each step, you gain momentum, confidence, and the energy to keep moving forward.

What if instead of trying to map out the perfect plan, you treated this next phase as an experiment? What if you approached your Opus with curiosity instead of pressure? You're still dreaming, only now, your dreams have legs. You're letting them walk into your life.

That's what you'll do this week. With the initial vision for the first year of your Opus in hand, it's time to step into action. But don't worry; you're not going to be making any irreversible commitments. Instead, I invite you to test elements of your Opus in small, but meaningful, ways. Try on different pieces of your dream, experiment with how they feel, and learn as you go.

Some things will click immediately. Others might need adjusting. As you move into this week, shift into a mindset of curiosity. Instead of asking whether this is the right step, ask what you might learn from this step. The more you experiment, the more your Opus will take shape in ways that feel real, exciting, and uniquely yours.

Exercise: Trying One Small Experiment, Your Opus Test (Time Allowance Varies)

This week, you'll investigate an aspect of your Opus. This is the only exercise in this chapter, and you will decide how you want to test your Opus and how many experiments you want to run.

Before you decide, take a breath. Close your eyes if you like. Ask yourself: Where am I feeling the most energy or curiosity? What's quietly calling for attention? Let this guide you.

There's no single way to test your Opus. Some people like to ease in; others prefer to dive straight in. The good news? You don't have to commit to one big, intimidating leap. Instead, conduct a series of experiments, each one giving you new insights, confidence, and clarity.

Some tests will be quiet and reflective; others will be active and hands-on. Some might feel like toe-dipping, others like cannonballing. All should feel playful. No matter where you start, every experiment moves you forward.

Although there's just one week here to run experiments, my suggestion is that you continue to run experiments on your Opus at least throughout the remainder of this process. The experimentation and insights gained will help you further crystallize your vision.

Here's how it works: Pick one element of your Year One Opus, preferably something that's been tugging at you with a bit of curiosity or energy. Then ask yourself: How might I try this out, even just a little?

You might start by observing. You could lightly engage, maybe shadow someone, take a class, or try a practice. Or you might feel ready to dive in more fully, immersing yourself in a small real-world experience that brings your dream to life, even if it's just for an hour.

Whatever approach you take, the goal is the same: *to learn.* What sparks something in you? What feels off? What gives you energy or clarity? What feels natural versus what feels forced?

Before you dive into the exercise, here are three simple approaches or ways to think about experimentation: observation, light engagement, and full immersion. I refer to them as levels because as you move from observation to full immersion you're more fully engaging in the act of experimentation. Use these approaches to guide how you ultimately test an aspect of your Opus.

If you're not sure where to start, choose the path of least resistance. The easiest or most fun step is often the best place to begin. You're not here to prove your dream to anyone, not even yourself, so approach this in the spirit of exploration, gently and with curiosity. Remember: Every experiment, no matter how small, brings your Opus into clearer focus.

Level One: Observation

If you're still gathering inspiration and not quite ready to take action, that's okay. Observation itself is a powerful experiment. Whether you're conducting research or engaging in a helpful conversation, observation also invites you to tune in to your energy patterns and notice where curiosity naturally gathers. Pay attention not only to what draws your mind, but also to how your body responds—a subtle spark, a surge of interest, a calm sense of resonance. If you choose this path, start with one of the following observational approaches and then challenge yourself to develop and run a light engagement test afterward.

- **Shadow or watch someone else doing what you want to do.** What do you notice about their approach?

- **Have a conversation with someone in your field of interest.** Ask about their path, what they wish they had known earlier, and what their typical day or week looks like.

- **Research or study a topic within your Opus that intrigues you.** Reading, listening, and learning can shift your thinking in unexpected ways. Listen in. Visit a bookstore. Attend a webinar, podcast, or Q&A session related to your Opus. Pay attention to how people talk about this field or experience. What resonates? What surprises you?

- **Experiment with small decisions.** If your Opus involves a lifestyle change, like moving to a new city or shifting how you work, start by immersing yourself mentally. Research neighborhoods, explore job postings, or map out what a typical day could look like.

At this level, you are going to pay attention to people, places, trends, and insights that can help you shape your Opus, and how you respond to these experiences.

Level Two: Light Engagement

If you're ready to dip your toes in and craft an experiment, but full immersion feels like too much, try a controlled, low-stakes experiment. Think of this level as a space for playful practice, where you begin to bring your Opus into form and gently build coherence between your inner vision and outer action. Even a small test can reveal great insights.

- **Take a five-minute test drive.** Choose something small and simple to test from your Opus: Write a first paragraph, sketch out a business idea, try out a new habit. Whatever you choose, take a brief initial step to investigate an aspect of your Opus.

- **Start with a hypothesis.** What's something you've been wondering about your Opus? Write it down as a simple statement and then test it.

- **Enjoy a dose of courage.** Choose one small action from your Year One plan that feels just slightly outside your comfort zone—and do it. It might be introducing yourself to someone new, asking for feedback, or sharing your ideas. What does this action teach you?

- **Change one routine.** If your Opus involves designing a new way of working or living, try shifting just one habit: experiment with a new morning routine, a different work setup, or a social habit.

At this level, you're just dipping your toe in—without any major risks.

Level Three: Full Immersion

Some of you might be ready to dive into the deep end. Full immersion is a bold step that activates both vitality and vulnerability. You'll likely feel a mix of excitement and fear—that's a good sign. It means your whole system is engaged, and you're stepping into alignment with something that matters deeply.

If you're feeling bold, immerse yourself in a rich experience that brings your Opus to life. This exercise is for you if you're ready to get your hands dirty and fully engage in an aspect of your Opus to see how it feels in practice.

- **Volunteer, apprentice, or take on a short-term project.** If your Opus involves a career shift, this is a great way to test if the reality matches your vision. Step into that new role in an impermanent way for a day, week, or longer.

- **Enjoy a one-day trial.** Choose one element of your Year One Opus to try on for a day. This might be a habit, a mindset, or a small action related to your goals. How does it feel? What do you learn?

- **Offer a prototype of your work.** Run a free class, share a piece of writing for feedback, or create a sample of your idea and share it with others. How does it feel to share your ideas with others?

- **Commit for a week.** If your Opus involves a significant personal change, like writing a book, launching a creative practice, moving to a new city, or improving an aspect of your well-being, design a seven-day experiment to live out fully. Write (or paint, compose, draft a business plan) for an hour a day, spend a week in your city of choice, give that well-being practice a week to take root.

So, which approaches will you take to test a part of your Opus this week? No test is too small, and none are final. The goal is movement, not mastery. Choose the experiment that excites (or scares) you the most and give it a try. You can always adjust, refine, pivot, or run more experiments. What matters most is that you begin.

Letting Your Experience Speak

Every experiment, whether energizing, awkward, surprising, or affirming, has something to teach you. So, when you've completed your first experiment, pause for a moment to get clear about what you've learned. Before you consider what the experience revealed mentally, let yourself feel what it revealed emotionally and somatically. Where did your body light up? Where did it contract? Your body can be a powerful guide to what matters most to you.

Then, tune in to what else the experience revealed and how it made you feel. Think of yourself as a scientist investigating the findings of your Opus experiment. If you have run multiple experiments, pause to reflect after each. Ask yourself:

- What surprised me about this experience?
- What parts felt natural, exciting, or easy? (Coherence)

- Did anything feel more energizing or more draining than expected? (Vitality)
- What did this experiment reveal about the pace of growth that feels right for me? (Pacing)
- Did I feel fully present in this experience, or was my mind elsewhere? (Present Focus)
- Did I feel any resistance, and what might that be pointing to? (Connection)
- What did I learn, not just about the dream, but about myself? (Connection)
- And perhaps the most important question: What do I want to try next?

Even if your experiment didn't go as expected, you've gained something valuable: insight. This is how we build clarity, not in our heads, but through action. The more you test, the more your Opus will come into focus.

So, honor what you've learned. Let it settle, without judgment. The fact that you took action this week, any action, means that you're now in motion. Trust that step by step, test by test, you're refining your dream and creating coherence between who you are and who you are becoming.

WEEK NINE. REFINING YOUR OPUS AND LIVING IT

You're now ready to cross the bridge from composing your Opus to living it.

Over the past eight weeks, you've shaped a vision for the life you most want to live.

You've sketched dreams, tested possibilities, and begun to align with what matters most, not just in thought, but in how you feel and move through your day. This week marks a turning point: It's where your Opus moves from the page into your daily life.

Like a musician who's spent months refining a composition note by note and phrase by phrase, there comes a moment when the music must move beyond the sheet to be played, felt, and lived. That's where you are now.

Rather than creating a rigid plan, you're laying the foundation for a new way of being, one shaped by clarity, intention, and energy. As you refine the first year of your Opus, you'll begin to define the habits and rhythms that will support you as you step more fully into this life you're creating.

For this week, beyond preparing to act, you will be making a quiet, powerful declaration: I'm in. I'm all in on my Opus.

Let that commitment settle within you, not as pressure, but as possibility. You are stepping into the life you are meant to create. And you already have everything it takes to begin to do so.

But before you take your next steps, there's something essential to consider: how you'll sustain yourself along the way. Living your Opus isn't just about clarity or courage, it's about energy. And now is the moment to make sure yours is replenished, aligned, and ready to carry you forward.

Fueling What You Create

You've spent the past eight weeks dreaming, refining, and composing your Opus. But now comes the deeper challenge: embodying it. Learning to live your Opus in a way that nourishes your energy, rhythm, and spirit.

To do that, you'll need something even more essential than discipline or willpower: You'll need energy. Not just the kind that gets you through the day, but the kind that that allows you to stay grounded in the face of change, aware and connected to what matters, and open to the growth your dreams will ask of you.

This is what Tony Schwartz and Jim Loehr taught in their pioneering work: high performers don't break down from stress—they break down from a lack of recovery. It's not the demands of our lives that undo us, but the absence of rhythm. Without cycles of rest and renewal, we can't sustain growth.[23]

Which is why your well-being—your energy—isn't a side note. More than talent, timing, or even strategy, your energy is the number one predictor of success; your Opus thrives when you do.

We don't often think about energy; we might think about well-being. And, more often than not, we think of it as basic self-care: sleep, nutrition, movement. These are vital, yes, but, as we've discussed, true well-being is about cultivating and replenishing the energy that fuels your clarity, creativity, resilience, and joy. When you focus on your energy, you tend to your whole self, physically, mentally, emotionally, and spiritually, so you have the capacity to live the life you are creating.

To Live Your Opus, even in this first year asks that you be well-resourced and rooted. Your energy is not just fuel—it's your signal of alignment. When it's flowing, you're more able to act with intention, clarity, and joy. Before you take off into the first year of your Opus, check in on your energy and the practices you're using to renew it regularly. Begin by noticing what replenishes you and what doesn't. (You can refer to Tool 2 in Tools to Live Your Opus.) Then, try small, intentional shifts in the areas that most impact your energy:

- **Physical.** What best supports your body right now: sleep, movement, exercise, hydration, nourishment, strategic breaks? And, are you making space to play, explore, and wonder, even five minutes at a time? Notice when you feel physically buoyant or heavy; that's data. Energy starts with the body.

- **Emotional.** What is supporting your capacity to feel, connect, and regulate? What relationships, experiences or restorative practices bring joy and meaning? What needs clearing or healing? Notice when your heart feels open or constricted. These cues guide where attention and healing may be needed.

- **Mental.** What is supporting you to focus your attention where it most needs to be? How are you managing distraction or overwhelm? Can you simplify, set a boundary, or give yourself a true break before exhaustion sets in? When your thoughts align with your values, energy flows. That's coherence.

- **Spiritual.** What reminds you that your life has meaning? What are you connected to that is larger than yourself? This may be achieved by spending time in nature, prayer, meditation, or in connection with or service to others. Even small spiritual experiences like a moment of awe, a deep breath, or a sense of meaning can recalibrate your entire day.

When all four dimensions are nourished, you operate from wholeness. Your ideas take root with more ease. Your leadership becomes resonant. Your presence becomes magnetic. You move from surviving to thriving.

Each small choice is an act of self-respect and possibility. A way of saying to yourself: I matter. My energy matters. The life I'm creating matters. And I deserve to feel alive inside it.

Imagine trying to launch something as meaningful as your Opus life without the fuel to sustain it. No matter how inspiring your dream, it won't achieve liftoff unless your energy supports it.

That's why this week isn't just about planning your next steps; it's about making sure you have the inner resources to carry them through. So, before you leap forward, pause and ask:

- Where is my energy strongest? Identify what fuels your energy, such as certain activities, people, environments, or habits.
- Where am I running on empty? Notice what consistently depletes you and make deliberate choices to minimize its impact.
- What practices truly restore me? Build time for restoration, not just numbing or escaping, but renewing. This may be through rest, movement, creativity, stillness, or something else.

Then, begin to build your rhythm through practices. Maybe it's a fifteen-minute walk outside at lunch, screen-free Sunday mornings, a standing desk to work at, music that lifts your spirits, or journaling. Maybe it is making space for the joy that used to get left behind. Your practices don't have to be dramatic; they do have to replenish your energy on more than one level.

This is how you'll sustain your Opus. Not through force, but through flow. Not through pushing harder when you've got nothing to give, but through creating systems that allow you to replenish your energy and return to yourself, again and again.

Your energy is the soil in which your Opus will grow. Tend to it with care and reverence. What you nurture, thrives.

Exercise: Refining Your First Opus Year

Now that you've reconnected with your energy—the vital fuel that will sustain your Opus—you're ready to shape the path ahead. Let this next step be guided by how you want to feel and live, not just by what you want to achieve.

By now, you've tested elements of your dream, taken small steps, and listened deeply to when you feel most alive. This week is about weaving those insights into a shape, a rhythm for your year ahead that's both clear and supportive.

But let's be clear: You're not building a rigid plan. You're composing a living framework, one that allows structure without suffocation, progress without pressure.

Some people love plans. Others need space. Both can work beautifully. Whether you thrive on quarterly milestones or loose rhythms, the invitation is the same: Shape the first year of your Opus in a way that honors your energy, your values, your needs, and the life you're growing into.

This week, as you refine Year One of your Opus, focus on creating a way forward that feels natural and motivating to you. And, before you plan, pause. Let your current energy be your compass. What rhythms, rituals, or practices would make this feel sustainable? That's your foundation.

Step One: Going All-In and Committing to Your Opus (Fifteen Minutes)

Revisit your Opus Vision Statement from week seven, and the priorities for your first year that you named last week. Let them rise back into focus.

Now, write a short statement, a personal commitment or promise to yourself for this first year of your Opus. Let it inspire and ground you. Don't aim for clever or perfect; it just needs to feel true.

Examples might sound like: "This year I will create space for what truly matters, trusting that every step I take, no matter how small, moves me closer to my vision." Or: "Over the next year, I will build my business and life in a way that reflects who I really am, honoring deep work, family time, and rest."

This commitment is for you. It should be short and simple enough for you to remember it clearly throughout your daily life. When you are finished, place it somewhere visible as a resonance check and a reminder that you are already living your Opus. When your energy drifts, this is the commitment you'll return to.

Step Two: Shaping the Year Ahead

Now that you've set a clear intention, choose how you want to shape the first year of your Opus. Of the two simple paths, choose one or blend both:

- **Option A, mapping key milestones.** This is best if you love clarity and goals. It can be helpful for putting specific stakes in the ground to work toward, knowing they may change.
- **Option B, building a strong foundation.** This works best if you prefer setting rhythms and habits to support the bigger picture.

Option A: Mapping Key Milestones

Look back at your Year One Opus sketch. Based on the focus areas you chose and what you're learning through experimentation, name three to five key milestones that define meaningful progress. These could be external, such as launching a new offering, finishing a course, or shifting careers. They could also be internal, such as deepening a relationship, building confidence, or rewiring a core belief, mindset, or behavior.

For each milestone, ask yourself:

- Why does this matter to me? What do I love about it?
- What will success look and feel like? Where is the joy?
- Who am I becoming along the way? And what do I appreciate most about that?
- What habits, daily practices, or ways of being (think of the Opus 8 energy principles in practice) will help me sustain my energy and momentum along the way?
- What energy shifts (small or large) will support each milestone?

These stakes don't need to be big or permanent. Think of them as waypoints, helpful markers on a dynamic path. If you feel stuck, start small.

Even one clear milestone for one focus area of your Opus vision can generate momentum.

Option B: Building a Strong Foundation

Begin by naming three to five focus areas from your Year One Opus sketch that matter most to you. These might come from your pillars in Dream, your visualizations, or your experimentation.

Then ask yourself:

- What practices will keep me energized, grounded, and growing in each area?
- Which daily or weekly rhythms will help me to show up fully?
- What mindset do I want to carry into the year ahead?

These might include creative rituals, morning and evening routines, ways of working, journaling, or time off. Think of these as the inner scaffolding, quiet supports that help you grow your future with intention and care. Look for moments where you feel most energized and most at peace. Those are clues. Energy is your compass; let it shape your routines.

Bringing It Together: Your Year One Vision

Whether you prefer milestones or rhythms, or a little of both, the invitation here is the same: to get clarity about what matters most this year and how you will create and sustain your momentum.

With that clarity in hand, pause and take a step back. Ask yourself:

- What excites me most about the year ahead?
- Do I feel any hesitation? If so, about what? And what might help?
- How do I want to feel at the end of this first year of my Opus? Have I left space to engage in the practices I'll need to ensure that I have a good chance at feeling like that?

Let this be your guide as you move forward. This is your Opus—and you are shaping it, one step at a time. And if you begin to drift, return to energy. How does this step feel in your body, heart, and spirit? Your answer is there.

Already Living Your Opus

This is the moment where imagining turns into becoming. Not tomorrow. Now.

You've spent weeks connecting, dreaming, and composing. You've listened to yourself, stepped into your vision, tried it on for size, and shaped a Year One that reflects a way to live your burning desires. And, while maybe you don't feel finished (you're not supposed to), you've already done something profound: You've begun.

This is what it means to Live Your Opus. Not waiting for some perfect moment when everything is clear or you finally feel ready, but choosing to move with intention, curiosity, and courage in the direction of what matters most.

You still don't need to know every step ahead; you never have. What you need is trust—in yourself, the vision you're crafting, and in your ability to respond to what unfolds. So let go of any pressure. Trade perfection for presence. Trade control for creativity. And take the next step, any step.

Remember, transformation is not always loud. Sometimes it's a quiet moment of energy aligning with intention. And in that instance, you are already living your Opus.

This moment also marks a powerful transition, not just in your plan, but in your way of being. You are moving from Compose to Embark, from shaping your vision to inhabiting it. This next phase isn't about getting the plan right; it's about choosing to show up, day after day, in the life you've imagined.

Your Opus is here, alive in your choices. Let this be your moment to say yes to a new way of being. To living in alignment. To creating with intention. To becoming the person you've already started to be.

Take a breath. Feel your feet on the ground. You are already living your Opus. Now, you are ready to Embark!

Chapter Six

EMBARK: Becoming the Person Who Lives Your Opus

The music score is ready. You've recorded the song. Now it's time to step onto the stage. In Embark, you will carry the vision you've composed into the world. It won't be a finished piece, but it will become a living practice. One you'll nurture with the energy, insight, and clarity you shaped in the Connect, Dream, and Compose stages, translating it into real moments, lived choices, and embodied presence.

This step looks different for each person, as the shape of it depends on your goals, approach, and what's important to you. For some, it might look like talking about your Opus with friends, connecting with people working in your space, getting to know potential or live customers, sharing your ideas on social media, traveling to try out a new city to live in, or otherwise stepping into your life with new energy, clarity, mindsets, and ways of handling yourself.

And, as you start to move forward, Embark is also about preparing to stay the course, keeping yourself well, thriving in the ways you've promised yourself you would, not just through discipline, but through sustained energy and compassion. It's about recognizing that your energy is your compass. It determines whether you walk your path with vitality or depletion, joy or resignation. It determines how you respond when you start to get in your own way, which you will do. Because we all do.

You'll need practices that nourish all four energetic dimensions of your being: physical, emotional, mental, and spiritual. Here, the Endurance energy principles from the Opus 8 rise to the surface as your anchors: Pacing, to help you move with steadiness rather than urgency; Service, which reminds you that your Opus isn't just for you; Connection, to keep your heart engaged; and Present Focus, to help you return to the moment when the future feels overwhelming. These principles are energetic tools to help you sustain the life you're now living.

Many of my clients arrive at this stage excited to "begin" and, at the same time, feel surprised and frustrated at how much time they're spending managing themselves, as though they are spending more time working on themselves than working on their Opus. But, working on yourself *is* working on your Opus; it means you're focused on who you are becoming, which is vital to achieving your goals. Any internal tension you're feeling, and the effort it may take to manage it, is to be expected. This is where Present Focus practices become essential. Instead of trying to manage everything at once, you return to what's needed now. And by honoring your energetic capacity each day, you begin to pace yourself for the long haul, rather than burning out before you truly begin.

Up until now, you've been refining, testing, and shaping your Opus. But the shift from talking about something to doing it challenges the "way it is" and the "way it has been," the hardwired parts of you. So, it's normal for fears, judgment, blocks, and especially your own behaviors to get in your way. You are nine weeks into a change process; your mind thinks this is downright scary.

That's what happened to Emma after she had made a strategic decision to leave her job and grow her side hustle into full-time work. She had spent several months dreaming about her business, mapping out her services, defining her ideal clients, even designing a website. But instead of launching, after leaving her job, she found herself scrolling job boards late at night, updating her resume, and submitting applications just in case.

"I kept telling myself I needed more financial security before I went all in," she said. "But when I was really honest with myself, I realized it wasn't about money at all—I was afraid. Afraid of failing, but also afraid of succeeding—because what if it actually worked? What if I got too busy, couldn't handle it, or had to tell my family I wasn't available in the same way anymore?" In the meantime, Emma was exhausted and hadn't yet connected with any new future clients.

Emma wasn't applying for jobs because she needed the money; she had saved for this transition. She was building an escape hatch, a way to feel like she wasn't risking too much. But staying halfway in and halfway out drained more energy than committing. "Once I recognized what I was doing, I told myself, 'I can always get a job later. But, for now, I have to at least give this a real shot.'"

Emma's hesitation wasn't a flaw; it was a signal. Her energy was fragmented, stuck in a place of half-commitment. Once she named it and chose full alignment, she reclaimed her power.

Without training, all of our minds work like this: We crave what we know best, what keeps us safe, even if that's not what we really need or want.

When you introduce new habits and new paradigms, like starting a business, changing the way you take care of yourself, or transitioning to a new career, there is a part of you that wants to protect you from the change and get you back to the way things were.

The solution is to challenge your beliefs, adopt new habits, change your mindsets, and have compassion.

Be kind to yourself and understand that, if you're facing fears or getting in your own way somehow, managing yourself is key. And, yes, it may take time, especially at first. But this work isn't just about you; it's also about engaging in Service. When you choose to grow, you expand your capacity to offer your gifts more fully to others.

Depending on the nature of your Opus, how much you're stretching yourself, and where you are in your personal development, managing yourself could take upward of 50 to 75 percent of your time right now.

As you face and master yourself and your Opus, you will become comfortable and confident with the direction you are heading and the ways of being required to get there and stay the course. With that confidence, your effort to manage yourself will go down, and you will step into the dreams you have for yourself.

In the Embark phase and through part three, we're going to talk about how to stay the course as you begin to Live Your Opus. If you don't stay the course, you'll never launch your business, change careers, free your creativity, become the person you want to become, or live a created life, no matter how much you want to. And, if you don't stay the course, you won't realize your Opus. And that is how dreams die.

To be sure that's not what happens, this week, we're going to dive back into fears and how to resolve them while you begin to live the dreams you have created for yourself. And just like every part of this journey, you don't have to feel fully ready yet; you just have to be willing to take the next step.

STAYING THE COURSE

A plan is just a plan. And then there is reality. You set out with a clear plan. A vision. You thought you knew the steps. But then reality shows up—messy, unpredictable, and full of detours. Suddenly, you wonder if you were wrong. Can you really do this?

Most people assume that once they have a plan, everything will fall into place. But plans, no matter how well-designed, are just starting points. They don't account for the unexpected twists, the days when motivation dips, or the inner resistance that rises when you start stepping into the unknown. They also don't capture the depth of personal transformation that happens as you evolve into the person who lives your Opus.

This is why staying the course is about much more than executing your Year One plan. To stay the course, you have to develop the resilience, flexibility, and self-trust to keep going, especially when things don't unfold exactly as you expect.

THE BIGGEST BARRIER

The biggest threats to your Opus won't come from external obstacles; they will come from within. Even the most brilliant, accomplished people hesitate when stepping into something new. Not because they lack drive, but because stepping into something bigger is uncharted territory. It happens in small, insidious ways: procrastinating on something that matters, second-guessing decisions, or slowly deprioritizing dreams and allowing other demands to take over.

The difference between those who bring their Opus to life and those who don't isn't luck, talent, or even the quality of their plan. It's the ability to recognize and overcome the natural resistance that comes with change and to keep doing so time and time again. It's consistency.

If you've ever started something important like a business, a creative project, or a major life change, only to get stuck, you know what this feels like. The initial excitement gives way to hesitation, self-doubt, or even avoidance. It's not because your Opus isn't meant for you. It's because stepping into something bigger requires you to confront the habits, fears, and beliefs that have kept you where you are. That's what happened to Jason.

Jason had rewritten the announcement email for his new accounting firm six times. Each time, he found a new reason to tweak it: The wording wasn't quite right, the offer could be clearer, the timing wasn't perfect.

"I kept telling myself I was 'refining' my message," he admitted. "But, in reality, I was just avoiding putting myself out there. As long as I was still tweaking, I couldn't fail."

It wasn't until a mentor asked him a simple question that Jason realized the fear holding him back: "What's the worst thing that happens if you send it today, right now?"

"I laughed because the answer was . . . nothing. The worst thing that could happen was that no one would respond. And then I could send a follow-up."

Jason finally hit send. Within twenty-four hours, three potential corporate tax clients had booked calls with him. "I lost months to perfectionism. But the clarity I was waiting for? It only came after I took action."

Instead of rushing forward, return to Coherence: Why did this matter to you in the first place? Who are you doing it for? And then root yourself in Present Focus: What's one meaningful thing you can do today, not someday?

How do you stay the course? By understanding why dreams die—and what it takes to keep them alive.

HOW DREAMS DIE, AND HOW THEY THRIVE

Most dreams don't fail in dramatic moments. They don't go up in flames or crash in some spectacular failure.

They fade. They get buried under responsibilities, quietly pushed aside for later, or lost in the noise of everyday life. They dissolve in hesitation: the email that never gets sent, the idea that stays in draft mode, the opportunity that lingers on the edges but is never fully seized. They shrink under self-doubt: the quiet voice whispering, "Who do you think you are?" Or the endless loop of, "I'll start when I'm ready. I just need more time. More clarity. More certainty." They weaken when energy runs low, when exhaustion replaces inspiration, when rhythms disappear, and when recovery isn't built into the cycle of effort. And, perhaps most painfully, they stall when normal, expected, inevitable setbacks are mistaken for signs to quit.

But the people who bring their Opus to life don't have more time, fewer responsibilities, or an easier path. They aren't luckier, more talented, or immune to fear. They just keep going.

They stay connected to the dream, returning to it again and again, anchoring themselves in the vision of what they're creating. They notice when resistance shows up, but they don't let it drive them. They recognize perfectionism for what it is: fear in disguise. They see procrastination as a warning sign, not a stop sign.

Using practices, habits, and rituals, they build rhythms that regulate and replenish their energy. They know that endurance isn't just about bursts of effort; it's about consistent, grounded renewal. Trusting in themselves, others, and the universe, they release the need for certainty, embrace new paths that appear.

And, let's not forget another vital mindset: They take the long view. They remind themselves that real success isn't built in a day, a week, or even a year, but over time, with steady, imperfect, and committed steps.

If you feel resistance, if you feel self-doubt, if you are tempted to pause and wait for the right moment, know this: You don't have to do this perfectly. You just have to keep going. And every step you take—every imperfect, messy, real step—through any resistance, self-doubt, or unexpected challenges is proof that your Opus is alive.

Living your Opus isn't a sprint; it's an act of endurance. Pacing practices become your ally, reminding you that slow, steady steps accumulate into real transformation.

MASTERING YOURSELF: THE BIGGEST CHALLENGE

By now, you might have guessed that, at this stage, the hardest part of living your Opus isn't about strategy or logistics—it's about you. Not because you are doing something wrong, but because doing so requires stepping into a new version of yourself. And that takes courage. Self-mastery isn't just emotional; it's energetic. As you move into new terrain, you are learning to metabolize uncertainty and stay grounded even when your nervous system screams retreat. This is what allows you to keep going with grace.

No matter how well you plan, obstacles will arise, and, often, the greatest resistance comes from within. Learning to navigate your own patterns, fears, and habits is what will determine whether you stay the course or slowly drift away from your Opus. This is where the real work begins, the work of mastering yourself even more than you have in the past nine weeks, so you can move forward with clarity, resilience, and consistency.

Vanessa's Story: The Value of Mastering Yourself

Vanessa assumed most of her time would be spent building her business: writing, marketing, and serving clients. Instead, she found herself spending more time managing herself.

"I thought I'd be working on my website," she said. "But I was actually working on my procrastination. I thought I'd be pitching clients, but I was working on my fear of rejection. I thought I'd be refining my offer, but I was working on believing in my own worth."

At first, she felt frustrated, like she was wasting time on inner work instead of making progress. But then she realized: This *was* the progress. "Managing myself is the work right now," she said. "Because if I don't learn how to stay focused, how to work through fear, how to trust myself and take action—then no amount of strategy is going to matter."

To work with, and not against, yourself, you'll need to recognize when resistance shows up, not as a sign that you should quit or as an opportunity to judge yourself, but as a natural part of stepping into something bigger. It also means aligning your Opus with what energizes you most, so that your work fuels instead of depletes you.

Neuroplasticity, the brain's ability to change and adapt, means that the discomfort you feel stepping into your Opus is a sign that you are rewiring your brain. Dr. Joe Dispenza, a *New York Times* bestselling author and leading authority on the brain, mind, and consciousness, teaches that when we consciously direct our thoughts toward our desired future, we create new neural pathways that reinforce that reality.[24] This is self-mastery: learning to guide your mind toward possibility instead of fear, resilience instead of hesitation. The more you practice stepping into your Opus, the more natural it becomes.

This is where self-Connection matters most. Not just knowing your why, but feeling it, embodying it, and letting it pull you forward even when the path feels steep.

RECOGNIZING AND DEFEATING SELF-SABOTAGE

You've done the work. You've clarified your vision, tested your Opus, refined your Year One plan. So why—now that it's time to truly step forward—does part of you hesitate?

This is where self-sabotage enters the picture.

One of the biggest obstacles to mastering yourself is self-sabotage. And this isn't just procrastination or fear; it's a protective mechanism. Your mind resists change because change, even positive change, is unfamiliar. And the unfamiliar can be perceived as a threat.

Even the most capable, driven people fall into patterns that hold them back: procrastination, perfectionism, hesitation, or avoidance. Sometimes these patterns are subtle, disguising themselves as rational justifications. But when left unchecked, they quietly erode our progress. Understanding how self-sabotage shows up—and how to dismantle it—is critical to stepping fully into your Opus.

Jennifer's Story: Internal Resistance Preventing Action

Jennifer knew exactly what she wanted: to save $10,000 to fund her Opus. She made a plan, did the math, and even found ways to cut expenses. She had it all mapped out.

And then? The doubts crept in.

"Maybe I should start with $5,000," she thought. "Or maybe I should invest in that course instead. Or wait—should I get a side gig first?"

Before she knew it, her goal had shifted so many times that she had no real plan at all.

"I realized I kept shifting my goal so I wouldn't have to start," she said. "As long as the goal was changing, I had an excuse not to take action."

Jennifer's shifting goals weren't just mental; they were energetic. Unacknowledged fear leaks energy. Clarity, even imperfect, gathers it.

That's the tricky thing about self-sabotage: It rarely looks like destruction. More often, it looks like hesitation, overcomplication, or waiting for the perfect time. It wears a disguise, pretending to be responsible planning or smart caution. Underneath it all? It's just resistance keeping you stuck.

Maybe you've felt it too. That moment when you tell yourself you just need one more certification, one more book, one more month to get everything perfectly lined up. That moment when you say yes to everything except your Opus, filling your days with obligations that make you feel productive and busy, but not purposeful. That moment when you downplay your own dreams, convincing yourself they don't matter that much or that now isn't the right time. Or when you delay sharing your work, not because you aren't ready, but because the idea of being seen, of putting yourself out there, makes you hesitate.

If any of this sounds familiar, you're not alone. These patterns are part of stepping into something new. They don't mean you're not ready. They don't mean your dream isn't worth pursuing. They just mean your brain is doing what it's designed to do—protect you from uncertainty.

But the only way through uncertainty? You guessed it. Action. Not perfect action. Not fearless action. Just action. If you find yourself overthinking, hesitating, or waiting for the perfect time, pause. Breathe. And then, take one small, imperfect step forward, even if it is reaching out to someone who loves you but will challenge you firmly, so you keep moving.

Your Opus isn't waiting for you to be perfect. It's waiting for you to begin.

Why We Do It: The Upper Limit Problem

Your brain is wired for efficiency. It seeks to conserve energy, minimize risk, and maintain the status quo. By now you understand that when you start making bold moves toward your Opus, your subconscious mind reacts as though you are stepping into danger, even if the danger is simply stepping slightly outside your comfort zone.

Self-sabotage is essentially a misfired survival instinct. It's not that you don't want success. It's that part of you equates change with uncertainty, and uncertainty with potential failure—that's human nature.

What's behind this? Often, it's the Upper Limit Problem, which we discussed in the Dream stage. This is the hidden tendency to pull back just as you're expanding into a new level of success, joy, or fulfillment.

Psychologist Gay Hendricks coined this term to describe the way we unconsciously self-regulate our success. Maybe you have experienced this before: You start gaining traction toward a goal, and, suddenly, you get sick, pick a fight with a loved one, or convince yourself you don't really want it after all. These may feel like coincidences, but, in reality, they're defense mechanisms that keep you in familiar territory.

Why? Because stepping into your Opus means stepping into the unknown. Even when it's what we want, it can feel unsettling to grow beyond the identity we have always known.

The secret is that just beyond your upper limit lies your Zone of Genius, the space where your natural talents, passions, and highest contribution align. "The Zone of Genius is the set of activities you are uniquely suited to do. They draw upon your special gifts and strengths," writes author Gay Hendricks, who coined this term in his book, *The Big Leap*.[25] This zone is where you feel in flow, energized, and deeply connected to your work. But stepping into it requires trusting yourself enough to stay with the discomfort of expansion, rather than retreating to what feels safe.

The Zone of Genius and Staying in Your Lane

"Liberating and expressing your natural genius is your ultimate path to success and life satisfaction," author Hendricks explains about the Zone of Genius.[26] That's why one of the most powerful shifts you can make as you Live Your Opus is recognizing that you don't have to be everything to everyone. Your Zone of Genius is the space where:

- You do your best, most impactful work.
- You feel energized rather than drained.
- Your skills, strengths, and natural inclinations align.[27]

We often sabotage ourselves by doing too much, overcomplicating, or refusing to delegate, not because we have to, but because we think we should. To help yourself out of the self-sabotage quagmire, ask yourself a few questions: Where do I do my best work, the work that feels effortless and deeply aligned? Where am I making things harder than they need to be? What could I let go of, delegate, or simplify to stay in my lane?

Rahul's story is a perfect example of how this concept plays out in real time.

Rahul's Story: The Fear of Stepping Fully Into Success

When Rahul's first client signed a big contract with him, he didn't feel excited—he felt terrified.

"I should have been celebrating," he said. "But instead, I panicked. I started thinking, 'What if I can't deliver? What if they realize I'm not as good as they think?'"

Without realizing it, Rahul started sabotaging himself. He delayed responding to the client's emails, overcomplicated his onboarding process, and found reasons why the client wasn't the right fit.

"I was doing everything I could to push success away," he confided in me.

At first, he thought he was just being cautious. But then, a conversation with a coach shifted everything.

"They asked me, 'What part of this work feels effortless for you? What lights you up?'"

Rahul thought about it. Strategy. He thrived when mapping out big-picture ideas and creating a clear road map for others. But he had spent so much time proving himself that he was stuck doing work that drained him, the small, tactical tasks that weren't aligned with his strengths.

That's when it clicked: Rahul wasn't afraid of failure. He was afraid of success.

Up until that point, Rahul had been operating under an old identity, the idea that he had to do everything himself to prove his worth. But success at the next level required something different: trusting his expertise and stepping fully into his Zone of Genius.

Instead of pulling back, he redesigned his approach and started doing more of what he did best, high-level strategic work, while delegating the smaller details to a collaborator.

The shift changed everything. He began working with his client. His confidence grew, his energy increased, and suddenly, work felt expansive rather than heavy.

"The fear didn't disappear overnight," Rahul admitted. "But I realized something: I was never 'not enough.' I was just stuck in the wrong lane. Once I stepped fully into what I was best at, everything opened up, including finding more big contract clients."

Once Rahul broke through his upper limit by moving into alignment with his Zone of Genius, energy followed. His confidence didn't just grow; his energy expanded, his creativity flowed, and resistance softened. Alignment is an energetic event.

Using Your Zone of Genius to Break Through Your Upper Limit

When self-sabotage creeps in, pause and ask yourself a few questions:

Am I hitting an upper limit? Am I holding myself back because I am afraid of what might happen if I fully step into this next version of myself?

Am I avoiding my Zone of Genius by staying in work that feels comfortable instead of work that truly excites and challenges me?

Where am I making things harder than they need to be? Am I overcomplicating or delaying success because I feel like I haven't earned it yet?

Self-sabotage is not a sign that you're not capable; it's a sign that you are outgrowing old patterns. Like Rahul, rather than fighting against yourself, trust that you are ready to step into something bigger.

OVERCOMING SELF-SABOTAGE: PRACTICAL STRATEGIES TO STAY ON COURSE

Willpower won't help you overcome self-sabotage. You will need awareness and intentional action (Present Focus). When you notice the patterns, you can pause, reassess, and choose differently. Instead of seeing fear or resistance as a stop sign, you can recognize it for what it is: A sign that you're on the edge of something important.

Here's how to move through it:

- **Name it when it shows up**. When you notice yourself delaying, overthinking, or avoiding, pause and name it: "This is self-sabotage showing up." Naming it takes away some of its power.

- **Reframe the fear.** Instead of asking, "What if I fail?" ask, "What will I learn?" Shift from a fear-based mindset to a growth-based one.

- **Start before you feel ready.** As we've seen, clarity doesn't come before action; it comes from action. Take one small, imperfect step. Momentum follows.

- **Simplify and commit to tiny wins.** If a task feels overwhelming, break it down. Instead of "launching a business," commit to writing a single paragraph about your idea. Instead of "getting in shape," commit to a five-minute walk.

- **Create accountability and support.** Share your commitment with someone you trust. Knowing that someone is witnessing your progress can help keep you moving.

- **Use self-compassion, not self-criticism.** When self-sabotage happens, because it will, don't shame yourself. Instead, ask what led you here. What's one small shift you can make? And how much wiser are you now from the experience? Growth isn't linear; what matters is continuing to move forward.

- **Stay connected to your "why."** Self-sabotage loses power when your commitment is stronger than your fear. Revisit your burning desire daily. Visualize yourself living your Opus.

Letting Go of the Outcome

One of the biggest triggers for self-sabotage is attachment to a specific outcome. We fixate on how things should unfold, believing there is only one right way for our Opus to take shape. And when things don't go as expected, we panic.

We second-guess ourselves, trying to control every detail, fearing that if we let go, things might fall apart. But what if letting go is exactly what allows it to come together?

Self-mastery involves discipline and emotional flexibility. Dr. James Doty, a leading neuroscientist, has shown that when we learn to navigate fear with self-compassion, we develop the resilience to keep going.[28]

Instead of resisting uncertainty, what if you welcomed it? Rather than fixating on a single outcome, what if you trusted that each step is shaping you? Learning to embrace this mindset allows you to stay committed to your Opus without being rigid about how it unfolds.

Jessie's story shows us that our job isn't to force an outcome; it's to create the conditions for our Opus to thrive.

Jessie's Story: A Story of Letting Go

When Jessie launched her first business, she had a clear vision: She wanted to build a marketing consultancy for small businesses. She spent months refining her message, setting up systems, and crafting offers. But despite her careful planning, something felt off.

"The more I pushed to make it work, the more drained I felt," she admitted. "I wasn't loving the work I was doing—it felt like I was forcing something that wasn't quite right."

One day, during a casual conversation, an old colleague asked, "Why are you limiting yourself to just marketing? You light up when you talk about leadership and personal growth."

That single comment changed everything.

Jessie took a step back and let go of the need for her business to look a certain way. Instead of clinging to her original idea, she followed her energy. She started offering executive coaching and blended her expertise in marketing with leadership development. Within months, she felt alive in her work, and her business took off in a way she never expected.

Her biggest lesson? The success she imagined was smaller than what was actually possible. By letting go of a rigid outcome, she stepped fully into her Zone of Genius, the place where her talents, passions, and highest contribution aligned.

Just like Jessie, when you release the need to control every step, or do things the way you think you're "supposed to," you create space for something bigger than you imagined. Your Opus is so much more than one fixed achievement—it represents the larger life you are building, the person you are becoming, and the meaning you create along the way.

Let go. Trust. And allow the path to unfold.

THE MOST IMPORTANT STEP: STAYING CONNECTED

You don't have to force your Opus to happen. You just have to keep showing up for yourself.

When people feel disconnected from their Opus, it's often because they're measuring success in the wrong way, that is, by immediate progress rather than ongoing commitment. Some days, the path forward will be obvious. On other days, it will feel like you're wandering in the dark. This is normal.

The key is staying connected to your Opus, even when you're having an off day, dealing with competing priorities, or when clarity feels distant. One way to do this is through the Opus Visualization, a daily practice designed to help you reconnect with your purpose, realign your energy, and remind yourself why you're doing this.

This visualization practice will help you embody your Opus so that you don't just chase success, but live it, feel it, and, in time, become it. By mentally stepping into your future each day, ideally first thing in the morning or at another time when your energy is naturally quiet, you create a path toward it. You can find the Opus Visualization in "Tools to Live Your Opus" at the end of this book; you may also access an audio recording of the visualization at LiveYourOpus.com.

At the end of each day, check in with yourself:

- Did I take one step, big or small, toward my Opus today? What did I learn?
- What was I doing when I felt most aligned with my path, and who am I becoming?
- Was there a moment where I felt misaligned or disconnected? What did I do then? What might I do next time I feel this way so that I can better reflect the person I am becoming?
- Where are things feeling easy, joyful, or in flow? Where do they feel forced?

Stay with it. Keep showing up. Your Opus unfolds in the process.

Staying the Course: Energy, Rhythm, and Resilience

Some days you'll move forward with momentum and clarity. Other days, the next step will feel murky or just hard to take. That's normal. The key isn't to force progress, but to stay in a relationship with your Opus, even when you feel unsure, unmotivated, distracted, or tired. This is where rhythm, energy, and resilience meet. Resilience is not just grit. It's the result of tending to your energy like a living system. When energy is low, even small obstacles feel insurmountable. When energy is aligned, even setbacks can become stepping stones.

The most important commitment you can make now isn't to your progress or productivity; it's to your energy. Remember, the absence of sustainable rhythms is what knocks you off course. So, start with your energy. Always.

So, put this question to everyday use and, before you push forward, ask yourself: Am I fueled for the journey today? If not, use the guidance in week nine and in chapter three, to support yourself in replenishing your energy across four dimensions: physical, mental, emotional, and spiritual. Your Opus depends on it.

Next, build rhythms that sustain you. Think of your Opus as a garden. It doesn't flourish because you worked on it once. It grows because you tend to it regularly. Some days, that will mean taking bold action. On others, it will mean stepping back, giving everything a break, and reassessing. Motivation may come and go, but structure, habits, and pause buttons keep you anchored.

Check in with yourself regularly:

- What daily or weekly rituals help me stay aligned?
- What's my personal pause button, my reboot practice? This could be a walk, a reset playlist, a phone call to someone who knows you well.
- What can I put in place now to pace myself so that I don't live in cycles of intense exhaustion and recovery?

Discipline doesn't mean rigid hustle. I like to think of it as devotion, showing up for myself and what matters most to me with presence and care.

And when resistance shows up? Bring it to the mat.

I once had a yoga teacher who would say, "When you don't feel like practicing, that's when you need to show up the most—in those moments, bring your resistance to the mat." She didn't mean force the practice. She meant bring the resistance itself to the mat. Acknowledge it. Name it. Explore it. And move through it with curiosity instead of judgment.

You can do the same with your Opus. When you feel stuck, unmotivated, or hesitant, don't fight it. Bring it to the mat.

Here are a few practices that can help:

- **Movement-based practice.** Step away from your work and engage in movement. A walk, a few stretches, even pacing around the room can help shift stagnant energy.
- **Journaling prompt**. Instead of avoiding the discomfort, write to it: "Resistance, what are you here to teach me?" See what comes up.

- **Mindfulness exercise.** Close your eyes and sit with the discomfort for two minutes. Instead of pushing it away, get curious. Where do you feel it in your body? What thoughts arise? Is there something beneath the resistance: fear, self-doubt, perfectionism?

Many of my clients, especially founders and creatives, struggle when early momentum fades. What they don't always realize is that this is where self-mastery matters most.

Momentum often fades. But that doesn't mean something is wrong. It just means that it's time to return to yourself, not to force things, but to align. This is where self-mastery begins.

You don't need to power through. You need to stay connected. Each time you realign, you strengthen your resilience. Each time you return to your practices, your energy, your purpose, you reinforce the foundation of your Opus. This isn't about willpower—it's about awareness.

So, ask yourself: What sustains me? What drains me? What helps me return to the version of me that I'm becoming?

You don't have to Live Your Opus perfectly; in fact, striving for perfection is a fast way to drain your energy. You just have to stay connected. Keep showing up. Tune in to your energy daily, like a musician returning to their instrument, adjusting gently, intentionally. This is how your Opus grows: from energy into expression. Because Endurance isn't about force; it's about devotion. The steady rhythm of returning to yourself, your vision, and the energy that allows it all to unfold.

YOUR FIRST MISSION IN EMBARK: A PROMISE TO YOURSELF

When you embark on your Opus, you show up for yourself through every high and low. How will you return to yourself and your Opus dreams when challenges arise? How will you come back to center? This week, your first mission in Embark is to write a personal commitment to yourself about just that.

This commitment is different from those you have written so far. This is a promise not just to your Opus, but to yourself: When doubt creeps in, when things get hard, how will you respond? This might become your compass, your anchor, or, on the hardest days, when doubt sets in, your lifeline. Consider this your Opus Reboot practice.

Remember, this is where Present Focus practices anchor you. If something isn't going right, you don't need to fix everything; just return to one breath, one practice, one moment. And use Pacing practices to remind you that regrouping is not a delay; it's an act of alignment.

On challenging days, days when I feel disconnected or stressed, or when I witness old patterns of thinking in myself, I head to my yoga platform. Alone, I use yoga, meditation, and breathing exercises to face myself. Sometimes it's the exercise that does it, other times meditation, and, on a really tough day, a good cry. Whatever happens there, I stay there until I've reconnected with myself, my Opus, and moved myself into a state of creation, rather than survival. From there, I can move on with my day, usually as planned. And, when that's not an option, I cut myself some slack and take the day to do something else I love. This practice saves me every time, and, more often than not, it saves me in just minutes; it's my Opus Reboot practice. So, let's find yours.

Start by relaxing your gaze or closing your eyes and taking a deep breath. Think about the inevitable moments when you will feel lost, uncertain, or discouraged. How do you want to respond in those moments? What will bring you back to yourself and your Opus? Is it something physical like swimming or running? It is stillness? Or a connection with a trusted partner?

Then, in two to three sentences, craft your promise. This should be a simple statement with an actionable step you can take to come back to yourself and your Opus. Here are a few examples:

- "When I feel doubt creeping in, I will pause, breathe, and reconnect with my Opus by looking at my dreams (on paper) before making any decisions."
- "When I feel overwhelmed, I will take one small, intentional step forward, however small, even if that is simply calling a friend to ask for help rather than shutting down."
- "I will not measure my Opus by speed or what other people think. I will measure it by alignment with who I am and who I am becoming."

Write your promise on a note card, in your journal, or as a phone reminder, somewhere you can return to whenever you need to reset. Your journey won't always be linear. But with this commitment, you'll always have a way back to yourself and your Opus.

WEEK TEN. STEPPING IN AND GETTING OUT OF YOUR OWN WAY

Here you are, stepping into the first real weeks of living your Opus. But, before you move forward, ask yourself where you are right now. Not where you think you should be or where you wish you were, but where you actually are in this moment.

Right now, as you move from vision to action, you may feel different than you did in earlier stages. Maybe you're energized, eager to dive in. Maybe you feel stuck, hesitant, or unsure. Maybe you're somewhere in between. There is no right way to experience this moment; there is only your way. And by recognizing where you are, you gain the power to move forward with intention.

Back in chapter two, you explored the five archetypes of the Opus Change Continuum: Hesitators, Navigators, Builders, Explorers, and Catalysts. At the time, you used the Continuum to understand how you typically move through change and found your starting point for this work. You've also used it to check in with yourself throughout this process.

Now, before you begin your work for this week, revisit the Continuum again and ask yourself which archetype best describes how you feel as you begin Embark. Once you identify the archetype, reflect a bit on its significance today:

- What's one strength from this archetype that will serve me well in this transition?
- What's one challenge from this archetype that I'll need to be mindful of?
- Which of the Opus 8 energy principles can I put into practice to help me navigate this moment?

Maybe you're still moving with Catalyst energy but starting to feel the signs of burnout. Or maybe you've shifted into Hesitator mode, unsure whether to fully commit. Perhaps you're considering multiple paths like an Explorer or craving structure like a Navigator.

Wherever you are—that's okay. These shifts don't mean something's wrong. They mean you're alive in the process of change, and that's exactly right.

Embark is about Endurance, and that's less about pushing or forcing progress and more about Pacing. It's the part of your journey where your energy becomes the compass you follow. Are you fueled? Are you clear? Are you connected? This is where the Opus 8 principles guide you: Pace yourself gently, reconnect intentionally, and stay present. Endurance isn't about brute strength; it's about staying lovingly aligned with your purpose, especially when the path stretches long or winding, which it usually does.

Exercises: Staying Connected

How you show up for yourself is how you will Live Your Opus. The exercises this week focus on staying connected to your Opus and yourself. You'll do this through visualization, observing your thought patterns and habits, and experimenting with new ways of thinking, acting, and making decisions. There are three suggested exercises here, and more in the *Live Your Opus Workbook*. Each one is a step toward greater self-awareness, trust, and momentum, so have fun with them!

Opus Visualization

Visualization allows you to imagine the future—and shape it. By consistently stepping into the life you're creating, you strengthen the path toward it. You calibrate your energy to it and to yourself.

Use the Opus Visualization this week to support you in envisioning yourself living your Opus so you can then step into it fully, living, feeling, and becoming the person you're meant to be. Embark isn't about intensity; it's about returning to your inner rhythm, letting your vision stir gently to life through daily, nurturing presence. It's about engaging in practices that build Endurance. The Opus Visualization will help you to do this. You will find it in the "Tools to Live Your Opus" section at the end of this book.

Challenge yourself this week to engage in the visualization every day, not just on days when you work on the exercises. Visualization isn't an exercise; it's an energy recalibration. So, choose times of day when your energy is most quiet or available. The best times might be when you first wake in the morning or just before bed. By visualizing your Opus each day, you'll establish an even stronger connection to yourself and your dreams, making your journey more loving, open, and joyful. Start today.

Meeting Your Inner Champion (Ten to Fifteen Minutes)

In chapter four we talked about our inner dialogue and the power of the stories we tell ourselves. In challenging moments, it's easy to hear the voice of self-doubt, but there's another voice within you, too, one that believes in you, sees your strengths, and knows you are capable of living your Opus. This is your inner champion. Your inner champion is the voice of your strengths, the parts of you that have faced hard things before and come through stronger. It's the voice that says, "You've got this. Keep going."

This week, your mission is to catch your inner champion in action. Begin by remembering your strengths:

- When in your life have you overcome something difficult? (You might want to turn back to the Me, in Decades exercise in week one for ideas.)
- What qualities (such as resilience, creativity, kindness, adaptability, focus) helped you do that?
- If someone close to you were describing what makes you strong, what would they say? If you're not sure, go ask someone!

Write down three strengths that have carried you through past challenges. Then, spot your inner champions in real time. Over the next few days, pay attention to when your inner champion shows up. It may sound like: "I don't know how yet, but I'll figure it out," or "This is hard, but I've done hard things before," or "I don't need to be perfect; I just need to keep moving," or "I see that you're scared. Remember when … yes, we'll face that together here too."

Each time you notice your inner champion, write it down. Keep a small list in a notebook or your phone and refer to it in any moments of doubt, asking yourself what your inner champion would say to you right now.

Each time you connect with your inner champion, you renew your internal energy field. Think of this voice as a power source. One that helps you reconnect to your purpose and reminds you why you began. Your Opus will ask for courage, but it also offers replenishment through connection to your core truth.

Catching Your Internal Villains (Fifteen-Minute Daily Self-Check)

Your mind has a cast of characters, some helpful, some not so much. This week, pay attention to the voices that pop up as you move through your Opus. Each evening, jot down quick notes about your thoughts that day. Especially look out for:

- **The Critic.** "You're not ready." "Why did you do that?" "This isn't good enough."
- **The Excuse-Maker.** "Now's not the right time," "Maybe later." "If only [this] would happen . . ."
- **The Overachiever.** "Do more, work harder, let's just push through; you can take care of yourself later."
- **The Avoider.** "Let's check email one more time." "I should clean the kitchen first." "I can't do this for myself because someone else needs me to do something first."

When you notice one of these voices, gently challenge it. Write down a response from your wise future self or your present internal champions. What would they say to your internal villain?

Living Your Opus: One Week In

You've just spent your first week in motion. And this is a big step forward. Maybe you visualized your future every morning. Maybe you only managed it once. Maybe you were processing what you learned in the opening of this chapter. Or maybe you caught your internal villains or met your inner champion in a single powerful moment. Maybe your insights came late at night, or in the middle of an ordinary conversation.

Whatever your experience, pause here and ask yourself:

- What did I learn about myself this week?
- What surprised me?
- What felt harder than expected?
- What felt easier?
- And what felt true?

If there's one idea, one phrase, or one new feeling you want to carry with you into next week, write it down now and let it guide you into the week ahead.

And remember: This is just the beginning. With each step forward, you are becoming the person your vision requires and your life is already beginning to change.

So, take a breath. Keep going. You are pacing yourself now, building the steady rhythms that will sustain your energy and deepen your alignment. This is the pulse of Endurance. Learning to stay, instead of rushing or retreating. Staying connected. Staying present. Next week, we'll explore how to Live Your Opus even when life gets complicated.

WEEK ELEVEN. FALLING AND GETTING BACK UP

What do you do when life intervenes? You've spent the past week stepping more fully into your Opus, recognizing where you hold yourself back, noticing patterns of self-sabotage, and learning how to move forward using your energy as a force despite any fear. But now comes the real test: What happens when life throws you off course?

Because it will. No matter how much you prepare, life has a way of stepping in with its own agenda. A project stalls. A key opportunity disappears. A personal crisis shifts your priorities. You feel overwhelmed. You lose momentum. Doubt creeps in. The vision that once felt clear now feels fragile.

This is where Endurance is vital. It's not about pushing harder, but in learning how to *stay*. Stay with yourself. Stay with your Opus. And stay present, even when everything in you wants to retreat. This week, we turn toward energy, the steady flame kind that helps you keep going, even when you hit a rough patch.

This is the part most people aren't ready for, not because they're incapable, but because setbacks feel personal. A detour gets mistaken for a dead end. A challenge gets mistaken for a sign to stop.

Setbacks aren't signs that you should stop. They're not endings, but part of the rhythm of any meaningful journey, part of your pacing. You are not off course; you are on a new or longer course. This is where Present Focus becomes your anchor: being with what is, not what should have been.

John's story is a great example of recalibrating when life intervenes.

John's Detour

John had spent years working toward a leadership role in his company, and when the promotion finally came, it felt like everything was falling into place. He had a seat on the executive board, the opportunity to shape strategy beyond his division, and the chance to impact the success of the company—work that truly energized him.

And then, life happened.

Just two months into his new role, his wife was offered the opportunity of a lifetime: a chance to lead an international project in another city. It was exactly the kind of career-defining move she had been working toward, and John knew how much it meant to her. But the logistics were daunting. He had just stepped into his dream position. Could he really walk away? Could they make it work?

For a few weeks, they were paralyzed in indecision. Would he have to quit? Could they manage a long-distance setup? Was this the end of the vision they had each worked so hard to create? The uncertainty made John question everything.

Then, instead of forcing an all-or-nothing decision, John and his wife started looking at it differently. What if this wasn't a setback, but a chance to expand?

He proposed a hybrid solution to his company, splitting his time between remote leadership and periodic travel back to headquarters. It was unconventional, but to his surprise, they were open to it. Meanwhile, he and his wife created a new rhythm for their family life, one that required more support, intention, and communication, but one that also made them more conscious of what truly mattered.

His Opus didn't disappear, and neither did hers; they evolved. And when he looked back, he realized something: What had felt like a disruption at the time had actually been an expansion, giving him license to define success on his own terms.

What John learned—and what you're learning—is that endurance often asks us to *redefine momentum*. Not by speed, but by staying oriented to what matters, even as the terrain changes. That's how endurance leads to expansion.

Exercises: Getting Back Up

The difference between those who live their Opus and those who don't isn't that setbacks don't happen; it's that they've learned how to get back up.

So, this week, as you move forward, you're also going to prepare for the inevitable moments when things don't go as planned. How might you navigate them with more grace, resilience, and trust?

You tackle them not just by pushing through, but by listening to your energy so you are sure to steady yourself when the ground beneath you shifts. Can you hear what's needed now?

This week you build emotional endurance through rhythm, small steady resets that help keep you connected and resilient. Because the only thing you can truly control is how you respond. You will need to cultivate trust in yourself to keep going, no matter what's happening.

The following exercises provide a fun, light way for you to consider how to shift your response when things don't go as planned and help you regain momentum in a way that feels steady and sustainable.

Changing the Channel (Ten Minutes)

When a song you don't like comes on the radio, you change the station. When a show isn't resonating, you pick something else to watch. You can do the same with your thoughts. One of the fastest ways to shift your energy is to shift your story.

For this exercise, you will reframe setbacks in real time. This will teach you how to recognize when you're stuck in an unhelpful thought loop and practice how to switch to a new, more empowering narrative. You can use this for a setback you encounter this week or practice by workshopping a recent setback.

Begin by writing down that negative or discouraging thought that is running through your mind about a recent setback. Here are a few examples: "I messed up." "This isn't working, and maybe it just won't." "I should have known better." "I didn't expect this."

Once you've written it down, follow these steps to reframe the situation:

- **Name the station.** Give this thought pattern a radio station name. Make it fun or ridiculous. Here are a few examples: "Failure FM," "The Self-Doubt Network," "24/7 Imposter Syndrome Hour."

- **Change the station.** Now, rewrite the thought in a way that reframes it as a learning moment or a step forward. What would "Growth FM" or "Opus Radio" play instead?

- **Say it out loud.** Read your new statement and notice how it shifts your energy. Here's an example: "I should have known better" changes to the new station, "Learning in Progress," which plays, "I didn't know then, but I do now. And that means I'm growing."

As an extra challenge, make a sticky note of your new station and put it somewhere visible for the week. When doubt creeps in, remind yourself that you control the remote.

The Service Reset (Five Minutes)

This is the heart of the Opus 8 principle of Service. When energy collapses inward or fear creeps in, we don't force ourselves outward, instead we *offer*. A breath, a gesture, a contribution. These small moments restore our rhythm and remind us: We are not alone in this work. Try it.

Wherever you are, pause. Take a slow breath in. Exhale. Then ask yourself:

- Who benefits when I show up fully?
- What impact does my work have, big or small?
- Am I being selfish by keeping my talents to myself?
- How can I contribute right now, without needing to be perfect?

Now, take one small step—just a tiny act of service to reconnect with your purpose, your "why." Maybe it's sending a note of encouragement to someone, sharing an insight, offering a helping hand, or simply showing up for others with enhanced presence and care. How does that single act change how you feel?

As an extra challenge, write this down somewhere you'll see it and repeat it when you're feeling stuck: "Living my Opus is not about being perfect. It's about being present for what I'm here to create."

More Ways to Reset When Life Gets Hard

When things don't go as planned, you don't need more pressure; you need energy practices that return you to yourself, ground you, and get you moving in time.

In the *Live Your Opus Workbook*, you'll find simple reset practices like:

- Let Go of the Rush, a short breath-based reset.
- Presence Practice, for when your thoughts spiral.
- Ground and Go, a sixty-second recovery ritual.
- Resilience Playlist, because sometimes music is the best medicine.

Choose what you need. Ignore the rest. Just know: You are not stuck. You have tools at the ready. They are rituals for endurance designed to realign you with your body, breath, and purpose.

Steady On Your Path

Setbacks, when they happen, are not the end of your story. They are part of your unfolding. They don't pull you off your path; they show you how strong your footing really is. Each one is an invitation to slow down, listen inward more closely, and find your rhythm again. To remember who you are and why you began, so you can rise with more energy and courage. This is Pacing. This is self-trust. This is Endurance.

As you move forward, carry this truth with you: You are not here to avoid the fall. You are here to rise again and again, stronger, wiser, and more yourself than ever before.

Your Opus is still unfolding. And you are still becoming. Endurance may not be glamorous, or easy. Yet, the daily, imperfect act of showing up for yourself and your Opus, with presence, care, courage, and, dare I say, joy, is the one of the most fulfilling you'll ever experience.

WEEK TWELVE. THE REAL BEGINNING

Welcome to week twelve, the final week of your journey in this transformation. And congratulations on completing the entire twelve-week Live Your Opus transformation process! You arrived here with a dream whispering in your heart, and you leave having taken steps, some small and some bold, to bring your dream to life. I'm curious: What are you most proud of in this journey?

As you stand at this threshold, remember: this final stretch isn't about speed or achievement. It's about energy and Endurance—about living into your Opus with renewed connection, clear pacing, and the kind of quiet presence that sustains you beyond the page.

Think back to the very beginning, eleven weeks ago, when you first put pen to paper and began imagining your Opus. Think about the version of you who sat down and traveled through the weeks of the Connect stage. You didn't just reflect on your life; you gained a glimpse of all that you have and will create. That person was looking ahead, wondering who they might become.

Now, here you are, standing at the beginning of the next decade, as more than just a dreamer, as the composer of your Opus. What once felt abstract is now something you are stepping into with clarity, intention, and momentum, a vision with real movement behind it.

This is the week where you fully claim the life you have been designing. You have tested, refined, and adjusted along the way. You have confronted internal barriers, navigated setbacks, and strengthened your ability to stay the course. These are the muscles of endurance: learning to pace yourself through change, reconnect when you're stretched thin, and return to presence when clarity wavers. Now, the work shifts—not from action to completion, but from preparation to full embodiment. And, guess what? You still don't need to have all of the information. Remember, the key to living your Opus is learning how to stay connected to yourself and to it, even as things shift and change.

Living your Opus is a commitment to yourself that you renew each day through your actions, mindset, and presence. It's a commitment to pacing rather than pushing, to small acts of presence that accumulate into a powerful life.

There are no set exercises this week. Instead, we'll focus on vital tools you can use to remain focused, as well as advice and learnings from those who are living their Opus.

Vital Tools to Stay the Course

Throughout this book, you've encountered and used many tools. Here, we're going to focus on two of them that will help you to stay on track, especially as you move into the coming month. These include:

- **My Opus Life, a living framework where you can further shape how you want to live, not just what you want to achieve.** Here, you'll incorporate the thinking you did about your key habits and your well-being throughout the process, as well as the commitments to yourself you set in Compose and Embark. (You will find this framework in the "Tools to Live Your Opus" section at the end of this book.)
- **The Opus 8 Compass, also found in "Tools to Live Your Opus."**

My Opus Life

Over the past weeks, you have shaped a vision, taken first steps, faced obstacles, and built momentum. Your Opus now infuses how you move through your days, the rhythm you live to, the energy you bring, and the habits and practices that sustain it all.

Now, it's time to integrate all of that into a living framework, one that will evolve with you, the My Opus Life framework. For the full benefit and to guide your work, use the complete version of this tool included in the "Tools to Live Your Opus" section at the end of this book.

This is your Opus Life you're creating—a way of being, a way of moving through the world with clarity, purpose, and presence. Let it be alive. Let it evolve. This version of your life is built not by perfect plans or goals that are set in stone, but through presence, one breath, one choice, one realignment at a time. Today, you will refine it as needed and fully commit to yourself.

Take a deep breath and settle in. Pull out your notes, your reflections, your past exercises. Trust what you already know. Now is when you weave together the threads you've been gathering over the past eleven weeks.

To begin, look at the Opus Vision Statement and the Year One sketch of your Opus, both of which you created in chapter six (Compose). Read them slowly. Notice how you feel when you read them. Do they still excite you? Do any parts of them need to shift? What, if anything, has changed?

Take a few moments to refine them if needed, adding anything that feels truer today. Write it down. Let your words be simple, clear, and energizing. This is your North Star for the year ahead.

Your Energy, Well-Being, and Health Goals

Your Opus is only as strong as the energy that fuels it. By now, you appreciate that you can't just push harder to achieve sustainable success. You have to take care of yourself and regularly replenish your energy so you can show up fully, day after day. This goes beyond sleep, nutrition, and movement, although those are important.

We've talked a lot about investing in practices to support the renewal of your energy and, therefore, your well-being. But you may not have yet set specific practices and goals for how you will do this. This is the time. What kind of energy do you want or need to bring to your Opus? How will you generate and replenish it regularly? This is the Endurance tier of the Opus 8 in action: choosing the daily rhythms that keep your inner fire burning.

For example, maybe you want to bring more calm into your life or live less frantically. Or perhaps you want to focus on increasing your energy, beginning with your physical energy. Or maybe you want to begin by having a bit more headspace each day.

What does well-being look like for you? Not in an idealized, perfect way, but in a way that is doable and possible in your real, daily life. What does it mean for you to renew your energy? What goals do you have for your well-being as you Live Your Opus?

Consider the following:

- What keeps you grounded when life gets busy?
- What small, consistent habits help you feel your best physically, mentally, emotionally, and spiritually? How will you hold yourself accountable for engaging in these habits?
- What's one shift you can make to better cultivate or replenish your energy?

Write down a few practices you'll commit to. This could be a specific morning or evening routine, movement, mindfulness, meditation, prayer, nourishing food, or simply more time in nature. Let these be things you want to do, not things you should do, because it is the joy of engaging in them that contributes significantly to your well-being. Remember, you and your needs change over time, so expect to adjust the ways in which you support your well-being.

Your Key Habits and Rhythms for Alignment

Big dreams are built through small, daily actions. Every choice, every habit, every small decision adds up to the life you are building.

It's easy to get caught up in tasks, measuring your progress, and focusing on what needs to get done next. But the real magic happens when you take time to connect with and work on your Opus and step back, reflect, and refine your course. This is the difference between living *in* and working *on* yourself, your life, and your Opus, the perspective shift we discussed in chapter four at the beginning of the Connect stage.

Connecting with the bigger picture will move you beyond productivity and into becoming the person who can sustain the vision you've set in motion. That means creating rhythms that help you stay connected to your Opus, not just in moments of inspiration, but making adjustments as needed in the ebb and flow of daily life.

So, as you reconfirm your vision, consider what daily habits will anchor you in your Opus. Maybe it's a morning intention-setting practice, the Opus Visualization, five minutes of journaling, an evening gratitude practice, or simply reminding yourself of your "why" each day.

What weekly ritual will help you reflect, reset, and realign? Perhaps it's a dedicated check-in once a week or month, a walk where you think about the big picture, a weekly call with a friend or mentor, or a Sunday evening ritual to set the tone for the week ahead. Keep your rituals simple, achievable, and meaningful.

These rhythms are your roots. They keep you grounded when life sways. Think of them as your return points, as spaces of stability, presence, and self-respect.

Your Commitments to Yourself

Finally, what promises are you making to yourself as you step fully into this life? These are your internal commitments, how you will show up for yourself, no matter what, not external goals or achievements.

You've written a few statements already, in chapter five (Compose) and in this chapter. You can use those as they are or take a moment now to refine them. Your commitments to yourself can be as simple as the following:

- "I commit to trusting myself and my vision."
- "I commit to showing up for my Opus, even on the messy days."
- "I commit to caring for my energy, knowing that sustainability is success."

- "I commit to using my Opus Reboot practice to get through tough days."
- "I commit to pacing myself and protecting the joy of my journey."

Whatever statement you choose, let it be your foundation. Your Opus Life is within you; live it one choice at a time.

The Opus 8 Compass: Using It to Stay Aligned

Prioritizing yourself and making regular choices in favor of your Opus takes practice. The energy principles in the Opus 8 offer a natural way to build practices into your life that will support you in sustaining healthy, meaningful success over time.

You have already used the Opus 8 Compass to assess how you were doing across each of the three energy tiers: Stability, Alignment, and Endurance. But the Compass doesn't just support direction; it supports endurance. It's a quiet system of self-checks that brings you back into rhythm.

Regular use of this tool each week, month, or quarter can help you stay aligned, grounded, and energized as you move forward. It can support you in pinpointing what's happening below the surface when something feels off, and it can help you remember to invest in your well-being in periods of great momentum. When something doesn't feel right, don't default to fixing. Instead, use the Compass to check your energy. Where have you disconnected? What needs replenishing? What would Service look like here?

If you haven't used the Opus 8 Compass lately, take a few minutes to revisit it now, or soon, and incorporate it into your regular routines for working on your Opus. Let it guide you back to center, ensuring that the way you Live Your Opus is as fulfilling as the vision itself.

What You've Gained

Over the past twelve weeks, something in you has shifted. Maybe you dared to trust yourself or reconnected with what lights you up. Maybe you're taking better care of yourself and connecting more with others. Maybe you're going after a big dream you thought you'd never dare to attempt. Or maybe you recognized your capacity to live or lead with more calm.

From hundreds of conversations with others who have taken a similar journey, including those who have taken my Opus courses or worked with me on their Opus, five key growth areas emerged. I think they may resonate with you: well-being and putting yourself first, moments of self-trust, overcoming self-sabotage, letting go of the outcome, and leaning into what you love. The following stories represent some of the inner shifts and realizations people have had along the way. Let's explore them briefly to see whether they align with your experience here.

Caring for Yourself as You Grow

At some point, you may have believed that living a more meaningful, successful life meant pushing harder, sacrificing sleep, skipping meals, or working until you were running on empty. Maybe, like I used to think, you thought success would come if only you tried harder.

But something shifted over the past twelve weeks, didn't it? You started to realize that you are the instrument of your Opus—and if you don't take care of yourself, nothing else works.

Jeff shared this realization: "I used to power through, thinking I'd rest when I was done. But I was never done. I was always chasing the next thing. The biggest shift for me wasn't in my work—it was in how I take care of myself. I finally started treating rest as part of the process, not a luxury."

Gina shared that now, when she's feeling stressed or demotivated during the week, she knows that it is because she skipped swimming too many mornings. Once she gets back in the water, she relaxes, her perspective shifts, and she's back to feeling like her optimal self.

Frances had a similar experience, but with meditation. If she's feeling disconnected or antsy about the pace of her progress, she can usually point to missing her meditation time. That's the time that she uses to reconnect with herself and her Opus; when she misses it too many days, she loses steam.

Think about the moments when you felt your best during this journey, when you felt clear-headed, steady, energized. What supported you? Was it:

- Morning walks that helped you think?
- Going to bed earlier so you could wake up refreshed?
- Stepping away from screens to reset your mind?
- Time alone? Time with friends?

You've grown so much. You know this isn't about self-care as a checklist; it's about what actually helps you feel strong, centered, and capable of showing up fully for your Opus, the way you've been doing for the past twelve weeks. Because you know that you are not only your greatest work, but also your greatest resource. And your Opus can only thrive if you do.

Moving Forward Anyway

Think back to the beginning. Maybe you felt uncertain, maybe even a little foolish as you dared to claim your Opus. But look at yourself now. You've taken steps of all sizes toward something that once existed only in your imagination.

Dania shared something familiar: "I kept thinking, 'Who am I to do this?' I wanted someone else to confirm I was ready to launch my own consultancy. But I decided to take the first step anyway with one initial conversation with a potential client. And over time, I started trusting myself more." Do you remember a time when you didn't think you could do this? And yet, here you are. You are someone who has moved forward despite the doubt.

Or maybe, like David, you almost talked yourself out of trying to create your Opus, to bring your dreams to life. Maybe you convinced yourself you weren't ready. Maybe you got stuck in perfectionism or overthinking.

Maybe you started doubting whether your Opus was even worth pursuing. But here you are. You kept going.

David shared: "Every time I made progress, I noticed I'd find a way to slow myself down—overcomplicating things, waiting for more clarity, suddenly deciding I needed another certification before I could start. I didn't realize it at first, but I was making sure I never actually had to take the leap. Now I know better."

Self-sabotage rarely looks like outright quitting. It's subtle. It shows up as procrastination, unnecessary perfectionism, staying in your comfort zone, or getting too busy for what really matters. At some point, you probably caught yourself doing something like this. And instead of stopping, you kept going. That's the real breakthrough. You've learned to notice when you're holding yourself back, and, more importantly, you've learned how to move forward anyway.

Letting Go of the Outcome

There was a time when the unknown might have stopped you. A time when you thought you had to know before you could begin.

Daniel realized this along the way: "I used to think I needed a clear road map before I could begin. I thought if I didn't know exactly where I was going or what the right next step was, I would get it all wrong. But now I realize that every step reveals the next. I'm learning to trust the process instead of forcing a specific outcome."

What if you didn't have to force anything? What if your Opus unfolds at exactly the right speed for you, revealing itself as you walk the path? Now you understand to trust yourself and the process.

Leaning Into What You Love

Something else has shifted, hasn't it? You're no longer just working toward something; you are discovering what lights you up, where you feel most at ease, where your best work flows effortlessly.

Maria had this realization: "I spent so much time doing what I thought I should do. I was filling my days with tasks that drained me, thinking that was just how work should feel. But when I shifted to focus more of my energy and time on what I love—what lights me up—I realized that's where I do my best work. Work doesn't have to be draining. I don't need to force myself into a mold that doesn't fit."

Where do you feel most alive in your Opus? Where does time disappear, and you feel like this, this right here, is what you're meant to be doing? Whatever that is—do more of it.

A Final Reflection

You've done something remarkable. You haven't just imagined your Opus. You've begun to live it. Instead of an ending, you've reached a new beginning.

Be proud. You have come so far! And the best part? You are just getting started because living your Opus is the journey of a lifetime.

So, here's what I want to offer you as you continue: Choose your rhythm. Return to what grounds you. Let your energy, not urgency, carry you forward. Take one small action each day. And when things inevitably get messy or uncertain, stay connected to your Opus. Remember: This is an entirely new way of living; it takes practice.

Share what you've discovered. Reflect aloud. Send a note to someone who's inspired you. Say your dreams out loud. Let someone witness this version of you.

And above all else, trust that the version of you who began this journey is now becoming the person who lives their Opus.

A meaningful life isn't rushed. It's composed daily, lovingly, and with the energy to keep saying yes.

You don't need anyone's permission anymore. You already have everything you need to Live Your Opus. Go live it.

Part Three

TAKE THE JOURNEY OF A LIFETIME

By the time you read this, I'll have been on the journey to live my Opus for nearly six years. I'd like to tell you that my Catalyst ways have subsided a little, or that my life is now always smooth sailing. But I'd be lying if I said that. What has changed is my relationship to the rhythm of it all. Through the Opus 8, I've learned to pace myself with more care, to reconnect through Service, and to meet each moment with more presence and compassion. I'm a work in progress for sure, but this continues to be the most joyful, honest, and rewarding life I've lived.

The truth is that life is full of bumps and bruises, no matter how wonderful it is. What's different is the lens by which I experience it all, that of my Opus, and the tools I use to keep me steady, to reconnect, to revive myself and to keep moving forward with a sense of joy no matter what happens.

As I was writing this book my Labrador, Toby, was diagnosed with lymphoma at the age of nine. We'd just had a lovely rainy weekend filled with wet walks and writing; the next day he refused to eat for the first time in his life.

I was unprepared for his diagnosis, which we received a few weeks later, and for the chemotherapy and treatment plan we quickly found ourselves in. And, since he responded well to treatment, I was unprepared when he suddenly spiraled into the sickness just before Christmas, and, over the course of just a few days, we found ourselves with no choice but to lovingly end his suffering.

Everyone has a different relationship with their dog, but Toby was a kindred soul to me, a best friend who had seen me through everything you've read about in this book and more. His death knocked me off-track. And it came at a time where life had also thrown me some health challenges of my own.

I took a month off from writing this book and focused on restoring myself. I traveled, spent the holidays with loved ones who cared for me and let me lean on them, and then I came home to get some semblance of rhythm back.

Although it took weeks to reestablish a writing rhythm and my personal routines, I am grateful my Opus Reboot practices were very well established. Unlike times when I've been knocked down before, I had a solid foundation to return to, a formula, if you will, which included a clear understanding of myself, where I was on the Opus Change Continuum, set practices to cultivate and replenish my energy, near and long-term plans to support my dreams, and a burning desire to get back to writing this book, among other things. It was my Endurance practices—Pacing, Present Focus, and Connection—that helped me rebuild.

It wasn't easy, and it took intention and effort, but focusing first on my energy, and that which sustains it, letting others love me, and continuing to connect with and act on my Opus all helped me regain momentum with time.

As I write this, it's been five months since Toby's death. I'm still not back to normal, but I understand that time has passed. The new normal is different. And it's brought many wonderful surprises: Through a fluke outreach to a wonderful breeder in Italy, the universe brought us in touch with Toby's Labrador family. Suddenly we had the opportunity to adopt his second cousin, who we named Soleil (the French word for Sun); she is now six months old and brings lots of silliness and joy into our home.

Perhaps most importantly, I've been reminded again that we each have one chance at life, one that I intend to continue to live fully. For this, living my Opus, and you living yours, is the journey of a lifetime.

Chapter Seven

WALK THE PATH

Five years ago, while recovering from burnout, I discovered Julia Cameron's Morning Pages, a simple but powerful daily practice of writing three pages of stream-of-consciousness longhand first thing in the morning. No editing. No judgment. Just write.

At first, I didn't quite grasp what it would do for me. But, over time, I came to rely on it as a way to clear mental clutter, unlock creativity, and hear myself more clearly. Morning Pages gave me a direct line to the thoughts and feelings I had buried beneath the noise of daily life.

Since then, my journaling has ebbed and flowed with life's rhythms. But one thing hasn't changed: I always return to my journal when I need to refine my Opus. In fact, the Opus Way was born in those pages. First, as scattered thoughts. Then, as sketches on letter-sized paper, and later, in flip charts and slides. Eventually, it became something I could shape and share. Each version brought greater clarity, each step an evolution of the one before.

Looking back at those journals, I'm often struck by how wise, clear, and honest they feel. Sometimes I forget how much the person who wrote those words has to teach me—even now.

The gift of reflection is that we get to trace the path we've taken: see when inspiration struck, when we hesitated, when we nearly gave up, and, importantly, remember how we kept going.

Through those journal pages, I can track the origins of my ideas. I can see the moments when inspiration struck, the times I hesitated, the places where I nearly abandoned the vision, before coming back to it, refining and recommitting.

Those pages are more than words. They're artifacts of becoming; hopes and dreams written earnestly, honestly. And the power isn't just in writing them; it's in returning to them later. It's in looking back, not just at our dreams, but at the things we say we are willing to do to achieve them. Then, the moment of truth comes: We check in with ourselves to see whether we've actually done what we set out to do.

These artifacts are a literary sense of accountability. They're also a window into your energy: what nourished you, what drained you, and what helped you endure. Reflection reveals not just what you did, but how you sustained yourself in doing it. Kristen's story is a beautiful example of this.

KRISTEN'S STORY: RETURNING TO A DREAM SKETCH ONE YEAR LATER

Before joining one of my programs, Kristen had never thought of her life as an Opus. She had built a successful career in education and edtech, where she was widely respected. She knew her domain deeply, and she was confident in it.

But when she took the leap to launch a community for female entrepreneurs, everything changed. She felt like a beginner again. Sometimes she questioned her right to be in the room. She had spent years as an expert in her field. But now, in this new world of startups and founders, she wondered: "Who am I to guide others?"

Through the Opus process, that inner narrative began to shift. Kristen started to see how everything she had done before had led her here. Her experience wasn't a mismatch; it was a foundation. She realized that rather than an outsider, she was right where she was meant to be.

At the end of the year, she returned to the plan she'd created during the Dream stage: her map for the next ten years. She expected to check in, take stock, refine her direction.

But instead, she had a realization: She had already achieved everything she'd written down for Year One. And not just Year One; some of what she thought would take two or three years had already come to life.

Almost without her noticing, her efforts had led her to grow into her new identity, and she had become the person who lives her dreams.

How often do we rush forward, feeling like we haven't done enough, without stopping to consider how far we have already come?

For Kristen, this changed everything. That moment of recognition was powerful. It reminded her she wasn't behind. She was right on time. It softened her self-judgment and gave her permission to trust the path she was on.

So, she revised her dream. She extended the vision. And she committed to checking in with herself every year, using those early sketches not as pressure, but as proof of progress.

"It's very easy to get caught up in the day-to-day," she said, "and think that you haven't done anything."

But she had. She was a year in and most certainly living her Opus.

Like Kristen, my dreams guide me, day by day, season by season. And I'm always surprised, when I check in with them, by how on track I am, even when life has gotten messy or progress feels slow.

Even in the quiet seasons, the ones that feel stagnant or heavy, I can still feel the thread. I know where I'm headed. My North Star is steady. What I am building is clear. How I need to show up in this work is clear. And as I walk this path, I learn. I stretch. I grow. I have become the person who lives their dreams—the person who lives their Opus.

The same is true for you.

Through this journey, you've connected deeply with yourself and with others. You've dreamed boldly, composed a vision that feels true, and taken real steps to live it. You've learned to pace yourself, to listen inwardly, and to course-correct with intention.

Live Your Opus isn't just a book, and it's not just a process. It's a mindset. A way of living. A promise to care for your life and yourself as though you are your greatest work.

Because you are.

WHERE THE REAL WORK BEGINS

Living your Opus is a practice, a choice you make again and again, showing up for yourself, in the best of times and in the worst of times. There will be days when you feel crystal clear and wildly confident. And there will be days when resistance shows up disguised as doubt, fatigue, or even success.

Sometimes, doubt will whisper, "Can you really keep this up?" Other times, your ego will say, "You've got this; you don't need to do the work anymore."

And this is where most people stop. But not you. You know that self-doubt isn't a stop sign. It's a signpost. And ego? It's just a signal to pause, get grounded, and reconnect to what matters.

Even a life that feels aligned and purpose-driven includes struggle. That's part of the deal. The difference is: Now you know how to return to yourself. And that makes all the difference.

LETTING GO OF OLD IDENTITIES TO STEP INTO YOUR OPUS

Sometimes the hardest part of change isn't building something new; it's letting go of who we used to be. If you have built an identity around a past career, title, role, or achievement, it can feel disorienting—maybe even painful—to realize that it no longer defines you.

Maybe you were once the high-powered executive, the award-winning artist, the respected expert in a particular field. That identity came with social proof: external validation, recognition, and a sense of certainty.

But something in you is shifting. You're evolving. And yet, part of you wants to hold on to what you know. Why? Because the world praises certainty over evolution. Because it's easier to stay with what others recognize than to become someone new.

Sometimes, it is doubt that keeps us clinging to the past: "What if I am nothing without this? What if I fail at what's next?" But just as often, it's ego: "I've already proven myself. I am successful. I've done enough work. I've got this."

This is where people get stuck. But not you. Because you're practicing Presence, honoring Connection, and learning how to pace your growth with intention. You understand that your Opus lives in who you're becoming, not just in who you've been.

The most fulfilled people I know are the ones who allowed themselves to change. To grow. To reinvent. Again, and again.

So, what do you do when an old identity no longer fits?

- **Honor where you've been.** Be grateful for the version of you that got you here.
- **Recognize that identity is fluid.** You're not meant to stay the same.
- **Watch for the ego trap.** "I've already mastered this." Have you? Or is it just comfortable to be seen a certain way?
- **Give yourself permission to evolve.** Even if no one else fully understands.
- **Anchor in your Opus.** Don't ask "Who am I without this title, affiliation … ?" Ask "Who am I becoming?"

Letting go is hard. But holding on to something that no longer serves you? Or settling for something that no longer feels right just to have it? That creates a quiet tension—a misalignment—that keeps you from a life of joy, of thriving.

Trust that what lies ahead is more aligned than what you're leaving behind. Letting go of who you used to be is only part of the journey. The real work begins when you start fully living your Opus, and then, slowly, the old patterns start to tug at you again.

Maybe it's the tendency to overwork, to measure your worth through productivity and approval.

Maybe it's the impulse to play small, to shrink into what feels safe.

Maybe it's the tension of feeling that you've changed, while others around you may not have.

Or maybe it's your ego that flares up when you choose to say no to something shiny but misaligned.

This is why the Opus Way isn't just about creating change or success; it's about *sustaining* it. Because Alignment isn't something you reach once; it's something you choose again and again. And when life gets messy, when resistance, doubt, or uncertainty resurface, you don't have to start over. You just have to reconnect.

HOW TO STAY ENGAGED WITH YOUR OPUS OVER TIME

You already have the tools. You've practiced them. You know how to listen inwardly. Now you just have to stay in relationship with yourself and your Opus.

Here's how to reengage when life pulls you off course:

- **When you feel lost or stuck, use the Opus Change Continuum to locate where you are.** Are you hesitating? Navigating? Building? Let that awareness guide what you need next. Then, bring in the Opus 8 Energy System: What principle could you practice to support yourself now?

- **When you're evaluating an opportunity, run it through the lens of the Opus 8 and your energy.** Does this align with your Vitality? Your Vision? Does it support your Coherence or stretch it? Alignment is about resonance.

- **When you need clarity, use the four-stage process to Connect, Dream, Compose, and Embark as a reset.** Sometimes, a quick pass through the steps is all you need to remember your promises to yourself and see clearly again.

You don't need to take weeks to re-ground yourself. You can do it in moments by reconnecting to your energy, your vision and your pace. This is a way to gain clarity and confidence more quickly, strengthen your resilience, and stay true to the promises you've made to yourself. Here's how:

- **In one minute: Pause**. Breathe. Ask yourself: Am I in alignment? Connect: Tune in. Dream: Recall what matters. Compose: Ask what this moment is asking of you. Embark: Move forward with intention.

- **In twenty minutes: Reflect and ask yourself a few questions.** Where am I on the Opus Change Continuum? What am I resisting or craving? What wants my attention?

- **In a few days or a week (or when things feel off): Take yourself through the full four-stage process.** Don't rush it. Let yourself see clearly again. Refine what matters.

- **Once a quarter or once a year: Return to your Dream phase sketches or your My Opus Life framework.** Check in and ask yourself: What's working? What needs to evolve? Who am I becoming now?

Use the Opus 8 Compass (see Tools to Live Your Opus) to assess which energy principles you're practicing that are supporting you well and which ones need tending. Often, it's the Stability ones (like Vitality or Connection) that are asking for your attention.

You don't need constant discipline to stay engaged. You need intention. You need presence. And you need a North Star that allows for recalibration. Because without that, it's easy to drift. And drifting is what leads to regret.

WHAT REALLY MATTERS IN THE END

We live in a world that moves fast, one that often tells us success is about more. More output. More accolades. More achievement. However, when we slow down and ask deeper questions, a different truth emerges.

I was recovering from burnout when I first encountered Bronnie Ware's *The Top Five Regrets of the Dying.* A palliative care worker, she had spent years sitting beside people in their final days, listening. What surfaced repeatedly wasn't regret about unfinished projects or missed promotions. It was far more personal. Far more human.

The regrets touched upon being more genuine, not working so hard, having the courage to express and live in line with one's true feelings, staying in touch with friends, and seeking more joy in life.[29]

Are these regrets familiar to you? Or foreign?

The first time I came across them, I didn't feel surprised; I felt like I was meeting familiar friends. I felt seen. I had already met these feelings during the quiet reckoning that followed personal loss, burnout, and deep inner work. That's why I now consider myself privileged to have faced them early—before it was too late to do something about them.

You might not expect the word "privileged" here. But I'm being honest. I was privileged to have had the opportunity to start over: to design a life with (mostly) no regrets, a deliberate life, my Opus. A life where I respect my Vitality, stay rooted in Connection with myself and others, where I live with Present Focus grounded in my Vision.

When you look closely at those regrets, they map right back to the Opus 8 energy principles.

- **Vitality:** I wish I hadn't worked so hard.
- **Connection:** I wish I had possessed the courage to express my feelings and had stayed in touch with friends.
- **Present Focus:** I wish I had allowed myself to experience more happiness.

- **Coherence:** I wish I had lived a life that was truer to my authentic self.

The same patterns emerge in the "Harvard Study of Adult Development." Decades of research revealed that the deepest fulfillment comes not from what we *achieve*, but from how we *live*, when we do so with meaning, connection, and alignment to what matters.

And we see the same themes in the Blue Zones, those rare regions where people live longer and healthier lives. These communities aren't defined by ambition alone. They're built around purpose, deep relationships, and sustainable rhythms of work and rest.

The message is clear: The way you live today shapes how you will feel at the end of your life. So, when things get busy, when resistance whispers, when the ego tries to take the wheel, come back to the deeper questions and ask yourself:

- Am I living true to myself, or am I being shaped by someone else's version of me?
- Am I working so hard that I am missing the life I am building?
- Are there unspoken truths or overdue conversations waiting for me?
- Am I allowing myself joy?
- And most of all: Am I focused or just busy?

Because you can't go back and rewrite your life at the end. But you can choose today to live a life with fewer regrets.

KEEPING YOUR OPUS CLOSE

Sustaining your Opus is about staying in relationship with yourself, your work, and what truly matters to you. Like any meaningful relationship, it takes intention. Attention. And care.

You won't always feel in flow. You won't always know the next step. That's okay. The Opus Way was never designed to be a straight line. It's a compass, not a treasure map where X marks the spot.

So, how do you stay connected to your Opus when life inevitably pulls at you?

- **Revisit your vision regularly.** Just like Kristen did when she returned to her dream sketch, carve out time to reflect. What did you once hope for? What have you already brought to life? Sometimes we're further along than we realize.

- **Notice when you've drifted.** Disconnection, frustration, exhaustion—these aren't failures. They're invitations to come back to center. To begin again. To realign. Often, the quickest way back is to nurture your Vitality and to reconnect with yourself.

- **Trust the rhythm of growth.** Progress doesn't always look like forward motion. Some seasons are meant for reflection. Others for momentum. Either way, you're still in the process. Stay in the dance.

- **Lean on your people.** You don't have to do this alone. Surround yourself with those who believe in your potential, even when you momentarily forget it. Kristen didn't build her Opus in isolation. Neither will you.

- **Let your Opus evolve.** You're changing. Let your vision change with you. What felt right two years ago may feel like an old jacket now. That's growth, not failure. Let go of what no longer serves you and Dream again.

And if you find yourself slipping back into autopilot or losing sight of what matters, remember: You don't need to overhaul your life to realign.

Often, all it takes is a pause. A breath. A check-in. Or coming back to the tools here to reset.

I know I keep repeating this, but it's because I want you to remember it well: Your journey doesn't require perfect discipline or a life without doubts. It just requires you to return to and choose yourself and your Opus, over and over again. Because that's what makes this a journey worth staying on.

JUST THE BEGINNING

Your Opus is never finished.

It will stretch and shift, contract and expand, right alongside you. Some seasons will be filled with powerful momentum. Others will ask for stillness, for recalibration. This is the rhythm of a meaningful life. A return to center again and again.

And through it all, your Opus remains:

- A North Star to guide you.
- A framework to hold you.
- A way of living that helps you stay grounded in what matters most.

This journey—this commitment to build a life that is meaningful, sustainable, and true—is not a one-time transformation. Reclaiming your energy, redefining success, and building a life that truly matters, it takes daily practice. A series of small, intentional choices that, over time, shape not just what you do, but who you become.

But here's the most important part: You are not alone. There is an entire community of people walking this path, people who are choosing intention over inertia, alignment over achievement alone, meaning over just momentum. People who, like you, are learning to return to themselves again and again. Who are choosing to live their Opus.

So, if today feels clear and focused, Live Your Opus.

If tomorrow feels messy and uncertain, Live Your Opus anyway.

If resistance shows up, or doubt creeps in, return to the work. Come home to yourself. Live Your Opus with presence, purpose, and the energy you've learned to protect.

This book is not an ending. It's an invitation. To continue. To refine. To trust your process. To know that you don't need to rush. That staying in relationship with yourself is enough.

So, stay with it. Keep going—Live Your Opus! And above all, be kind to yourself along the way.

Because you are your greatest work. And today? Today is just the beginning.

Epilogue

FOLLOW A NEW MODEL OF SUCCESS

We were taught that if we worked hard, chose the right path, and checked the right boxes, success would follow. And for a while, maybe it did. But something deeper is stirring now, something we can't ignore. We're beginning to realize that achievement alone isn't enough—not if it comes at the cost of our energy, our presence, or our sense of purpose. In a world that moves faster than ever, it's not just outcomes we're craving; it's energy, alignment, and endurance. The kind of success that lasts isn't built on pressure, but on meaning and presence.

Yet, today, people are working harder and feeling less connected than ever. They're achieving more yet wondering what it's all for. They're staying in jobs, launching businesses, leading teams, yet feeling disconnected from the very things they've built, both at work and at home.

More than an individual experience, this is a cultural shift. We saw it in The Great Resignation, The Great Breakup, Quiet Quitting, and, more recently, The Great Detachment. What all of these have in common is a silent, collective questioning of the old model of success.

More than half of workers say they're disengaged. Some are walking away. Others are staying but showing up in body, not in spirit. And the world around us isn't slowing down. It keeps shifting. From AI and automation to political and economic upheaval and climate disruption, the future has arrived. And, with it, people are feeling a growing ache to feel healthy, steady, and purposeful.

Beneath it all, one quiet question keeps rising: What does success really mean, and is it still working?

SUCCESS IS NO LONGER ENOUGH

We've long measured success by what's visible: promotions, productivity, titles, and paychecks. From early on, we're taught to chase outcomes: get the grades, land the job, earn the accolades. We're told that these are the things that will make us happy. And for a while, they do.

But, today, as people move through their careers, whether starting out, pivoting, or stepping back, they're asking themselves new, deeper questions:

- What does all of this add up to?
- Does my work align with what matters to me? What impact am I actually making?
- Am I building something that matters or just playing a role that I fell into?

These are not surface-level questions. They're existential. And most of us were never taught to ask them, let alone answer them.

We were taught how to perform, how to achieve, how to succeed. We weren't taught how to pace ourselves. How to stay connected to what matters. How to honor our inner compass when the path ahead isn't clear. And, most of all, we weren't taught how to define success in a way that renews our energy rather than depletes it.

So, we built workplaces around output, not meaning. We optimized for speed and scale, not sustainability. And as people step back to reassess, the cracks are starting to show:

- **Leaders** are stretched thin, expected to drive performance while also creating cultures of meaning and belonging, often without the tools or support to do so.

- **Entrepreneurs** are caught in the relentless pressure to scale, innovate, and stay relevant, often realizing that success has come at the cost of their own well-being or that of their loved ones.

- **Teams** are operating in a constant state of urgency, struggling to keep up with demands in workplaces that measure efficiency, but rarely endurance.

- **Entire industries** are experiencing record levels of disengagement, as employees at every level question whether their work aligns with what truly matters to them.

This is more than just an individual or personal issue; it's cultural. If the future of work is going to be sustainable, it can't just be about productivity, efficiency, performance, or even adaptation.

Adaptation will help you survive, but if you want to thrive, the real levers are well-being and meaning. And that starts with rewriting what we expect—not just from work, but from ourselves and from success itself.

If meaning and well-being have been missing from the equation, then how do we bring them in?

THE OPUS WAY: A BLUEPRINT FOR LASTING SUCCESS

The Opus Way is more than just a guide for personal growth. It's a blueprint for building success that's meaningful, healthy, and sustainable by supporting people to reclaim their energy, redefine success on their terms, and build a life that truly matters. And this is exactly what people and workplaces are craving.

When people are engaged in work that fuels them, they perform better. And when people perform better, organizations thrive. But organizations don't change through another engagement survey or corporate wellness program; they change when people change. When people learn to live and lead from vitality, from coherence, from a place of sustainable alignment with their deepest values. They change when endurance—pacing, renewal, and meaningful connection—becomes part of how success is defined.

For too long, companies have focused on perks, benefits, and retention strategies to keep employees engaged. But those don't get to the root issue. People don't want more free snacks or yoga in the middle of a stressful day. They want purpose, belonging, and the ability to create real impact.

When individuals reconnect with meaning, organizations change from the inside out.

The Opus Way offers a new path:

- From hustle to harmony.
- From performance alone to purpose-driven excellence.
- From short-term wins to long-term fulfillment.

And this shift doesn't begin with corporate initiatives. It begins with one person at a time. One choice at a time. One Opus at a time.

When leaders operate from a place of Vitality and Alignment, they don't just drive performance; they build cultures where people want to stay. When organizations embrace this shift, they don't just retain top talent; they create environments where people thrive.

THE FUTURE OF LEARNING—AND HUMANITY

If the future of work is self-authored, why don't we teach people how to write their own story? Right now, our education systems prepare students for school—not life. We measure achievement in the form of exams and college acceptances. We don't teach people how to:

- Align their work with what actually matters to them.
- Cultivate and restore their Vitality so they are healthy.

- Adapt to change without losing themselves.
- Sustain success in a way that fuels, rather than depletes, them.

In fact, we don't teach people self-mastery. Instead, we expect people who have largely been prepared by rote learning to navigate well-being, meaning, career evolution, a rapidly changing and unpredictable world, and success, without ever giving them the tools to do so. And this problem starts long before people enter the workforce.

As my friends, Jenny Anderson and Rebecca Winthrop, explore in *The Disengaged Teen*, many young people are high achievers on the surface, but disconnected underneath.

Some are in happy-achiever mode, developing strong skills in goal-setting, organization, and execution. They know how to work hard and achieve results. But because they're so focused on meeting external expectations, they often miss out on a critical piece: discovering what actually drives them. They've mastered success as defined by others but may not be equipped to define success themselves.

Others tip into unhappy-achiever mode, where the drive for excellence turns into a relentless pursuit of perfection. Instead of resilience, they develop fragility. They tie their worth to their achievements, struggle with failure, and push themselves toward burnout—often at even higher rates than students who actively resist school. Here, their Vitality is traded for success.[30]

Both modes have the potential to create challenges later on. Happy achievers may enter the workforce well-equipped to succeed, but unprepared to ask if they're on the right path. They may follow impressive career tracks for years before realizing they're disconnected from their own deeper purpose.

Unhappy achievers enter the workforce driven, but may soon become exhausted. They are prone to burnout, self-doubt, and anxiety when external validation fades or when they must chart their own course.

In either case, they've been trained to win, but not to ask why. And they've rarely been taught how to cultivate their energy: how to listen inwardly, pace wisely, and align their effort with what brings meaning.

No wonder so many early-career professionals feel unmoored so quickly. They were prepared to succeed, not to flourish.

We need to teach people, from the beginning, how to:

- Claim and replenish their energy on every level—physical, emotional, mental, and spiritual.
- Define success on their own terms.
- Cultivate meaningful relationships with others and with themselves.
- Align their energies and attention with what matters most to them.
- Adapt to change in healthy ways, steadying rather than losing themselves.
- Build a life that truly matters.

Imagine a world where schools and workplaces taught self-mastery. Where meaning, energy management, and alignment were woven into how we prepare young. Where workplaces prioritized lifelong learning, not just to build skills or improve performance, but to help people grow in ways that keep them engaged and aligned over time so that they can sustain healthy, meaningful careers.

Imagine if people didn't have to navigate years of frustration, but had a framework to navigate it all, from the start.

Because knowing how to reclaim your energy, define success on your terms, and build a life that's truly meaningful? That's not just good for careers. It's essential for the future of humanity.

BUILDING A NEW MODEL OF SUCCESS

When I began this journey, I asked the questions so many of us carry: Can I build a full, ambitious life without being depleted all the time? How do I stay true to myself and steady as the world changes? What is success, really—and can I define and create it on my own terms? How do I build a meaningful life?

I didn't just want answers; I wanted a new way forward, not just for myself, but for you, and for all of us. This journey has taught me that success isn't about chasing someone else's definition; it's about creating your own. And at the heart of that journey sit these truths:

- **Success is more than external validation; it's alignment.** The most fulfilled people aren't those who've achieved the most, but those who know themselves and live in integrity with who they are.

- **You are your greatest work.** Your greatest achievement isn't out there. It's you. Your story—every success, failure, reinvention—matters. The more you own it, the more powerful you become.

- **Ambition and well-being are not opposites; they're allies.** The highest achievers, the ones who sustain success over decades, are the ones who take care of themselves physically, mentally, emotionally, and spiritually. They know when to run, rest, and relax. They have mastered themselves. They honor the rhythms of endurance so they can serve from a full cup. They know that rest isn't weakness; it's wisdom. And they've mastered the art of present focus, allowing space for stillness, integration, and recalibration.

- **Change is constant; self-mastery is your compass.** You don't control the waves. But you can chart your own course.

These are more than just truths I've read—they're truths I've lived. And now, they're yours too.

YOUR OPUS, YOUR WAY

You don't need permission. Not from your employer, your spouse, your parents, or anyone else. You don't have to keep following a version of success that no longer fits. You don't have to settle for who or where you are today.

If the old playbook no longer fits, write a new one.

You are the composer of your life. You always have been.

And while this book is ending, your Opus is just beginning.

So, go. Become the person who builds something that matters.

Live Your Opus. Choose your rhythm. Stay connected. Protect your energy. Because the only success that truly matters is the kind you can sustain.

TOOLS TO LIVE YOUR OPUS

Tool One

EXPLORE CHANGE AS A CONTINUUM

Change is a constant—but it's rarely predictable.

Sometimes we chase it down. Sometimes we resist it with everything we've got. And sometimes it finds us before we're ready. No matter how it arrives, change always asks something of us: attention, energy, courage, clarity. And, increasingly, the pace of modern life requires us to respond without the tools we need to do so well. That's where the Opus Change Continuum can help.

As the first component of the Opus Way, the Continuum helps you to do something vital: locate yourself, emotionally, energetically, and behaviorally, and consider how you might move through this instance of change with intention, care, and the right kind of energetic support. Each of the five archetypes within not only reflects a behavioral pattern, but reflects a particular energetic posture, which refers to how your energy is being accessed, blocked, or misdirected.

The Continuum is built on real experience, both lived and observed. I created it after noticing recurring patterns in my own life, the lives of my clients, and in my research. I saw that people tend to relate to change in distinct ways, not as fixed personality traits, but as *modes of engagement* that shift depending on the context, our energy, and the meaning we assign to the moment.

No matter how you relate to change, whether you crave it, avoid it, or are just trying to survive it, you've been shaped by it. Which is why understanding how it works is so important.

In this section, I'll walk you through the five modes in detail. But first, let's understand why change feels the way it does and what's happening under the surface when we find ourselves resisting, hesitating, or, even, burning out.

THE INNER MECHANICS OF CHANGE

Let's start with the basics: Change isn't just something we decide to do. It's something we feel in our bodies, our emotions, and our sense of identity—it's a full body experience.

Neuroscience tells us that when we encounter change, our brain kicks into gear, reacting instinctively. First, the amygdala lights up. This is the part of the brain responsible for detecting threats, and processing emotions like fear and uncertainty. That activation triggers a physiological stress response: Your body releases cortisol, a stress hormone, your heart rate increases, and you might feel on edge or overwhelmed.

At the same time, your prefrontal cortex, the part of your brain responsible for reasoning, planning, and long-term thinking, is trying to restore calm and create order. This internal tug-of-war is why change often feels emotionally charged, energetically depleting, and cognitively draining, even when it is "good change."

But here's the encouraging news: The same brain that resists change is also capable of incredible adaptation. Thanks to something called neuroplasticity, we know the brain can change, grow, and rewire itself through new experiences and intentional practice. That means resistance to change isn't a dead end—it's a doorway. This is the tension we all live inside: Change feels destabilizing, and it's also the very thing that enables our growth and transformation.

Even though we often think we can reason our way into new behaviors, decades of research by experts like William Bridges, Carlo DiClemente, Elisabeth Kübler-Ross, James Prochaska, and others show us that change requires more than logic. It requires an adaptive shift in mindset, belief, and behavior. Most of us don't just need new steps to take; we need a new orientation.

Leadership expert Ronald Heifetz distinguishes between technical and adaptive challenges: those that can be solved with known tools, and those which require us to evolve. [31] So when the change we seek isn't just about skill but about how we see ourselves and the world, we need more than a plan, we need to grow.

So why is it that change is hard even when we want or try to grow? Harvard psychologists Robert Kegan and Lisa Lahey find that we often carry competing commitments, deep-seated fears or beliefs that act like brakes even when we logically know what to do and are trying to move forward. They call this an "immunity to change." We say we want something, but, deep down, something is pulling against us, something we don't even know we're carrying.[32]

For example, a Hesitator might truly want to launch something new, but unconsciously fear what will happen if they fail, succeed, or get rejected along the way, keeping them stuck. A Catalyst might crave a more sustainable life but secretly believe that slowing down means losing relevance or power.

These internal conflicts don't make us broken. They make us human. And you won't find the path forward with more overthinking—you'll find it in action.

Herminia Ibarra's research in *Working Identity* points to this truth: Change isn't something we *think* our way into. It's something we *act* our way into. We try on new roles. We test new narratives. We experiment, shift, and iterate until our outer life starts to align with who we're becoming on the inside. That is to say: We practice becoming the person we want to be before we feel fully ready.[33]

That's what the Opus Change Continuum is here to help you do: recognize your current relationship with change with compassion and clarity, name your patterns, and take one (or more) grounded step forward.

THE FIVE ARCHETYPES

How we engage with change is deeply personal. Each of us has our own relationship to it, shaped by our past experiences, our wiring, and our beliefs about what's possible. Some of us move cautiously, testing the waters. Others dive in headfirst, hungry for transformation. Some crave stability and build from a strong foundation. Others thrive on experimentation and new ideas. Sometimes, we're all of these things, just in different areas of our lives.

Let's take a closer look at the five archetypes of the Opus Change Continuum. These are not personality types or fixed identities. They are patterns of how we relate to change at any given moment, depending on the context, our energy, and where we are in the arc of our story. Each archetype reflects not only a mindset but a set of energetic conditions—how your physical, emotional, mental, and spiritual energy are being supported or strained.

FIGURE SIX. THE OPUS CHANGE CONTINUUM

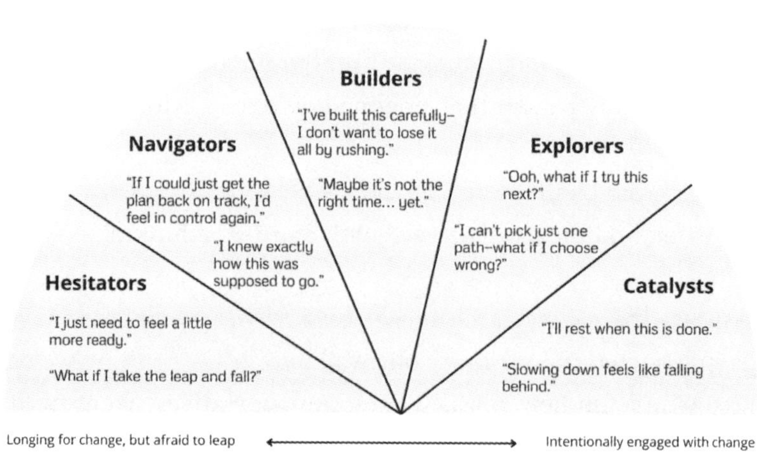

You may recognize yourself in more than one; that's expected. The goal isn't to box yourself in, but to see yourself more clearly so you can meet yourself with the right kind of support. Doing so will allow you to steer yourself more skillfully using the Opus 8 principles you'll explore in depth in the next chapter.

- **Hesitators** are discerning and thoughtful but may become paralyzed by over-analysis or fear of getting it wrong. They long for clarity and safety before acting.

- **Navigators** are expert planners. They feel most grounded with structure but struggle when plans go awry. They may resist improvising even when it's needed.

- **Builders** move slowly and deliberately. They thrive on stability but may hesitate to take bold steps, even when opportunity knocks.

- **Explorers** are idea-driven and curious. They generate energy through ideation and possibility but often struggle with focus and follow-through.

- **Catalysts** are fast-moving visionaries. They're built for bold action, but often neglect rest and pacing, which can lead to burnout.

None of the archetypes is better or worse than the other. All have wisdom. All hold a mirror to your current relationship with change.

For most of my career, I moved through the world as a Catalyst—fast-moving, future-focused, driven by purpose and possibility. My friends even used to refer to me as a "change junkie." I loved newness. Whether it was moving to a new city, starting a new project, or rearranging all the furniture in my house, I didn't just embrace change—I drove it. Organizations even hired me for that trait.

But after the sudden death of my mother and my experience with burnout, everything changed. I found myself hesitating for the first time in my life. It wasn't laziness; something inside me had gone quiet. I no longer knew what I wanted and I couldn't access the drive that once felt effortless. For a while I was a Hesitator, but I didn't want to admit it. Eventually, after being each of the archetypes, my Catalyst-self returned, but wiser, more rooted, and with energy that is far more sustainable.

I'm sure you can look back on your life and find moments where you leaned more toward one archetype than another. What about today? Which archetype feels most like you now? You may relate to one mode at work and another in your personal life. You might shift from one to another over time or even in a single day. That's normal. These archetypes are signposts rather than containers. And like all good signposts, they're here to help you move forward.

FIGURE SEVEN. THE FIVE ARCHETYPES OF THE OPUS CHANGE CONTINUUM MAPPED TO THE OPUS 8 ENERGY TIERS: WHICH ONE FEELS MOST LIKE YOU TODAY?

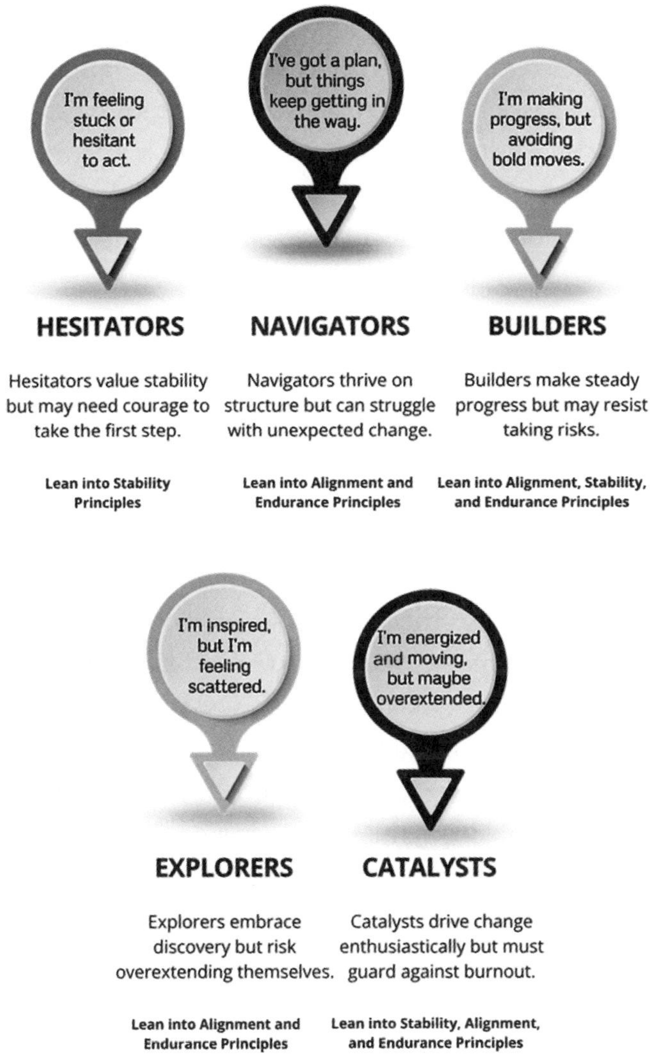

Use the diagram above to locate yourself today and note the Opus 8 energy tier which you can practice for support. In the following pages we're going to take a closer look at each of the archetypes, meet people who have navigated change from each place, and learn what they did to support themselves along the way.

Hesitators: Thoughtful and Cautious, Ready to Act

Alex had dreamed of starting a small coaching business for years. He had the training, the passion, and even a few people ready to become his clients. But every time he got close to launching, a new wave of doubt crept in: "What if I'm not ready? What if I don't get any clients? What if people don't take me seriously? What if I'm exposed and my business doesn't work?"

So, he kept preparing. He enrolled in another certification course. Built a website. Researched marketing strategies. Reworked his bio. Behind the scenes, though, Alex was exhausted by his own hesitation. "I kept telling myself I was being responsible," he said, "But I was really just scared." Six months in, he had everything—except clients. His hesitation hadn't made him more ready; it had kept him stuck.

Things shifted when Alex reached out to a friend who had already made a similar career pivot. His friend met Alex with compassion, because he had also gone through moments of doubts when he first set up his consulting business. But then he asked, "What's actually stopping you?" The honesty of that question landed hard.

With support, Alex began to lean into Grounding practices: daily walks, breathwork, and journaling. Those helped to quiet his anxiety and bring him back to the present. Through Connection, he became intentional about his circle, surrounding himself with people who believed in him, people who reminded him that he didn't have to know everything about running a business to be effective.

Eventually, Alex welcomed his first client, then another. The clarity he'd been waiting for had been waiting on him. "I thought I needed confidence before I started, but it was starting, taking action which led to landing my first client; that's what gave me confidence."

Alex learned a valuable lesson: Clarity and confidence come from action, not endless preparation.

Are you a Hesitator?

- You think things through and make thoughtful decisions.
- Your careful approach means you tend to overanalyze and delay action.
- You feel torn—wanting change, but fearing the cost of getting it wrong.
- Deep down, you know that staying still is a choice too, but you're not sure how to move forward.

Hesitators aren't indecisive; they're discerning. Beneath all that caution, there's often a fear of failing, of succeeding, or of being seen in the in-between. You want certainty before you leap. But that certainty rarely comes first. It often shows up *after* you begin.

Overthinking can lead to what's frequently called "analysis paralysis," when the weight of too many choices becomes overwhelming. With analysis paralysis, doing nothing feels safer than doing something that might not be what you consider to be "right." The longer you wait, the louder the self-doubt becomes. But there's no perfect decision, just the best one you can make with what you know today.

That's where action becomes your medicine. A single, imperfect step can break the cycle. Often, Hesitators are low in emotional or spiritual energy. They may feel unsteady or disconnected from a sense of purpose, making risk feel threatening. Using the Opus 8 energy principles can enhance emotional and spiritual energy. Grounding practices, like breathwork, journaling, or simply walking, can help you reconnect to yourself and feel steady. Connection through mentorship, community, or honest conversations can lift your spirits and remind you that you're not doing this alone.

If you feel overwhelmed by what-ifs, start with this: Take a few deep breaths to clear your head and open yourself to calm. Feel your feet on the floor, notice the weight of your body, and remind yourself that you are safe in this moment. Then, instead of trying to solve for everything, commit to just ten minutes of forward movement.

Every step you take, no matter how small, builds momentum. So, just begin.

Navigators: Expert Planners Who Shine When They Embrace Flexibility

Maya was a master planner. When she decided to shift industries, she crafted a six-month transition plan down to the week including certifications, networking events, and even a script for interviews.

But life didn't cooperate. Her company restructured and she was laid off three months into her plan and suddenly found herself needing a new job *now*.

Instead of adjusting, she froze. "I kept staring at my calendar as if I could will things back into order," Maya admitted. "I had done everything right, but reality had other plans."

For weeks she stalled and kept trying to salvage her original plan, resisting what was happening. "I felt like I'd lost control," she confided. "I was so focused on what should've happened that I couldn't deal with what was actually happening."

Things started to shift when Maya paused long enough to ask, "What's needed *now*, not what was supposed to happen, but what *is* happening?"

With Present Focus practices, Maya learned to respond to the moment instead of trying to control it; that helped her to stop obsessing over her disrupted plan. Then, by putting Pacing practices in place, she started taking smaller, less perfect steps instead of freezing under the weight of her original vision.

It wasn't the path she planned for, but it became the path that fit. "I used to think success meant sticking to the plan and achieving it," Maya reflected. "Now I know it means adapting with grace."

Are you a Navigator?

- You feel grounded when there's a clear plan. Without one, you feel unmoored. Unpredictable events make you anxious, especially when they disrupt progress.
- You prefer to analyze before acting and often resist improvising.
- You worry that flexibility means you've failed to plan well enough.

Your ability to create structure is a strength. But life rarely follows the road map. When things change, what if your confidence didn't come from having the *perfect* plan, but from knowing you can pivot when needed?

Navigators are excellent at solving technical challenges, the ones with clear steps and solutions. But most meaningful change is adaptive. It asks more of you: a shift in mindset, behavior, or identity. Pivoting isn't abandoning the plan. It's adjusting to reality.

Oftentimes, Navigators' mental energy is over-invested in planning and under-supported by emotional flexibility. The Opus 8 Alignment and Endurance energy principles can help. Present Focus practices will keep you anchored in the now, so you respond to what *is* instead of obsessing over what *was*. Pacing practices ensure you don't burn out trying to control what you can't. Both help you build resilience for the long haul.

Try this: Take your current goal and list at least three flexible routes to get there. Then ask: If this doesn't work, then what? You're not giving up on direction; you're becoming adaptable. That small shift changes everything.

The best Navigators are the ones who can reorient and keep moving when the plan they created no longer fits. Trust that you can adjust. That's what makes you unstoppable.

Builders: Steady and Strategic

Lauren had spent two years building her dream: an eco-conscious home goods product line rooted in sustainability. Every decision was thoughtful, deliberate, and researched. She tested products in small batches, built a website, and slowly, but steadily, grew her brand on social media, where she regularly sold out. Her careful, grounded approach was working: her brand was gaining traction, and her steady approach had built something real.

Then came the big opportunity she'd been hoping for: A national boutique wanted to feature her products. But taking the deal meant scaling production quickly. So Lauren paused.

"What if I can't keep up?" she worried. "What if I stretch too far and fail?"

So, she turned it down. "I told myself it wasn't the right time," Lauren said. "But deep down, I knew it was fear."

A few months later, she watched another brand, one that had said yes to the offer, gain the visibility she'd been dreaming of. It wasn't until she reconnected with a former mentor that she realized what she was doing. "You're not protecting what you've built," the mentor said. "You're hiding behind it."

That conversation helped Lauren return to her Vision, why she had started her business in the first place, and her aspirations for it and for herself. She zoomed in and realized that while her steady pace had gotten her here, the growth she wanted would require a bit more risk.

With support and Connection, a few months later she slowly stepped into the unknown. She approached another national brand that was even more aligned with her product values. When they agreed to collaborate, Lauren ran a pilot with limited stock, hired help, and learned as she went.

"I used to think playing it safe was smart," Lauren reflected. "But it turns out that, sometimes, playing it safe is the riskiest move of all."

Are you a Builder?

- You thrive on stability and progress over time.
- You like to feel fully prepared before making a move.
- You build strong foundations but hesitate when the next step feels uncertain.
- You are more comfortable with steady steps versus big leaps.

As a Builder, you're an architect of sustainable change. You're thoughtful, grounded, and strategic. But sometimes, your caution can keep you waiting for the perfect moment—a moment that may never come.

No one ever feels fully ready for big moves. But, as Ibarra's work reminds us, identity shifts don't happen through thinking alone; they happen through *action*.

Builders often conserve energy by staying within known territory but miss out on the energy that comes from stretching toward something meaningful. Using the Vision principle from the Opus 8 can help you reconnect with what you're working toward and why it matters. Engaging in Service and Connection can help remind you that taking a bold step isn't just about you; it's about the impact you can make.

So, don't worry; you don't need to leap forward wildly. But what if you stretched just a little? What if you trusted that the foundation you've built is strong enough to hold you? Try stretching, even if it's just a little. What happens next might surprise you.

Explorers: Curious, Open, and Learning to Focus

Sam was the kind of leader whose energy lit up a room and inspired everyone easily—at first. Each week brought a new idea, a new priority, a new sense of urgency. At first the team admired their creativity. But eventually, the constant pivoting took a toll. Sam's team members felt overwhelmed. Progress stalled. Trust frayed. Sam, who once prided themselves on being a visionary began to feel the quiet weight of disconnection, not just from their team, but from themselves.

"I thought I was energizing and inspiring them," Sam admitted, "but I realized I was unintentionally scattering their focus, and my own. We were running in circles instead of making progress."

The turning point came during a conversation with a colleague who offered, with kindness, a mirror: "We don't need more ideas right now. We need to believe in one and work together as a team to see it through."

That moment prompted Sam to start working with a coach who helped them clarify their deeper vision and distinguish excitement from alignment. Sam started asking, "Does this idea align with our long-term goals, or is it just exciting to me in the moment?"

Then Sam agreed with the team when they wanted to implement a new rule: no more than one major initiative at a time. With Present Focus practices, Sam stayed engaged in what the team was building, right here, right now, rather than jumping ahead to the next shiny idea. They also committed to a "not-now" list for new ideas and gave their team space to breathe and build.

The results were striking. Not just in output, but in how the team and Sam began to feel: clear, energized, and deeply proud of what they were building. Team morale soared as momentum returned. "I realized that leading well wasn't about generating endless ideas—it was about collaborating with the team to see the right ones through."

Are you an Explorer?

- You thrive on possibilities and love starting new things.
- You're energized by ideas, but often feel pulled in too many directions.
- You start strong, but lose momentum before crossing the finish line.
- You don't want to choose wrong, so you keep exploring instead of committing.

Your curiosity is a gift. You see options others miss. But, without focus, even great ideas fizzle out. Psychologists refer to the ability to generate many ideas and see endless possibilities as divergent thinking. It can be a gift, but left unchecked, it can lead to option paralysis when too many exciting paths make it hard to commit to just one.

Explorers often have high idea-generation energy but low containment—they burn bright but fast, unless grounded in mental focus and emotional calm. They don't need fewer ideas. They need structured focus and ways to stay grounded.

If this is you, start by choosing just one project or goal to commit to for the next thirty days. Not forever; just for now. Use your Vision to guide that choice. Which idea aligns most with your bigger picture? Which one helps you become the person you want to be?

Write that one idea down. Then give yourself permission to focus on it—fully. When new ideas arise (and they will), capture them on a "future" list. You can come back to them later. But, for now, focus your energy on what you've chosen.

Clarity doesn't come from exploring everything. It comes from going deep with something that matters. What might open up if you focused, not forever, but just for this season? Pick something. Try it. See where it leads.

Catalysts: Bold, Fast, and Learning to Sustain

André is a force of nature. As a senior executive, he drove global projects with nonstop energy, saying yes to everything, setting the tone for urgency and results. His pace and bold vision inspired but also intimidated.

Over time, the cracks started to show. His team, once inspired by his energy, struggled to keep up. Deadlines slipped. Meetings blurred together. And André? He didn't notice until his own body forced him to.

"I ignored the signs," he admitted. "The headaches, the sleep issues, the irritability. I thought, I can push through, I always have."

Until one morning, he couldn't. The crash wasn't dramatic; it was silent. He sat down for a meeting and realized that he had nothing left to give. "I had always believed my energy was my superpower. But I had burned right through it."

Recovery began with restoring his Vitality. He started prioritizing exercise and recovery—two key tools for boosting his physical energy—not as a reward for work done, but as a requirement. He scheduled rest the way he once scheduled deliverables. Present Focus practices helped him notice his limit before he crossed them. And, through Connection, he began relying on his team in a new way, sharing the load instead of shouldering it all.

And something surprising happened: His leadership got better. André still leads boldly, but now with rhythm. "I thought slowing down would make me irrelevant," he said. "But it made me more effective. And more human."

Are you a Catalyst?

- You love momentum and spark it everywhere you go.
- You move fast, make bold moves, and inspire others to follow.
- You forget to rest, recharge, or even slow down long enough to reassess.
- You dive in quickly and don't always consider the resources required to sustain what you begin.

Catalysts are built for action. You lead from the front, create impact fast, and energize people with your drive. But that fire needs fuel. Without recovery, clarity, and connection, your pace eventually becomes unsustainable—for you and for the people around you.

That's because Catalysts often run on adrenaline rather than true energy, bypassing recovery and confusing motion with progress. If that sounds familiar, take a breath. You don't need to stop. You just need to lean into the Pacing principle.

The best performers, athletes, leaders, and creators don't sprint all the time. They train in cycles. They rest with intention. Neuroscience backs this up: Cognitive recovery is essential to long-term performance. And if your body's been sending warning signals? Don't wait for it to shout. Rest now, so you can keep going.

Start by scheduling recovery the way you would a key meeting. Block time. Turn off notifications. Let yourself refuel. Then practice the Opus 8 energy principles to sustain your work and your well-being:

- Vitality practices bring your physical, emotional, and spiritual energy back online.
- Pacing practices keep you moving without burning out.
- Practicing Present Focus helps you notice what's actually needed.
- Connection reminds you that you're not in this alone.
- Engaging in Service anchors your drive in purpose.

Power requires speed and endurance. The best leaders and changemakers know when to pause, refuel, and realign. Rather than slowing down, work to build a rhythm that sustains your fire so it burns clean and bright for the long haul.

A FLUID CONTINUUM

Each archetype brings unique strengths—and challenges. They help you see where you are, what might be holding you back, and how the right support can move you forward.

None of us lives in just one mode. You might be a Catalyst at work, but a Hesitator in your personal life. Or maybe you started as a Navigator when launching something new, but now find yourself exploring unfamiliar territory as an Explorer.

That's the beauty of the Opus Change Continuum: It's not a fixed identity—it's a mirror. These archetypes reflect how you're relating to change in a particular season or moment. And because life changes, you do too.

You don't have to get it all right. And, as you've seen, you don't have to move mountains to make progress. Small shifts, like leaning into adaptability, taking one imperfect step, or giving yourself permission to pause, can lead to lasting transformation.

You're here to change your life in some way. Know that wherever you are on the Opus Change Continuum, this framework is here to meet you. As you move forward, the Opus 8 Energy System and the four-stage transformation process will give you the structure, insight, and cadence to move through change with clarity and intention. And, because each archetype reflects a particular energetic pattern, your Opus 8 practices should adapt as your needs shift.

Before you move forward, take a moment and ask yourself:

- Which archetype feels most like me right now, and why?
- How has this mode helped me—and where might it be holding me back today?
- What is one energy principle or action step I have learned here that I can lean into and move forward with this week?

Here's a quick reference to guide you as we move to Tool 2, the Opus 8 Energy System:

Table Two. Matching Your Change Archetype with the Right Energy Support

Archetype	Helpful Opus 8 Energy Principle
Hesitators	Stability principles, Grounding and Connection, help you move from overthinking to gentle action. Start small, stay steady.
Navigators	Alignment and Endurance principles, Present Focus and Pacing, allow you to build flexibility when plans change. Let structure support you, not control you.
Builders	Alignment and Endurance principles, Vision, Service, and Connection, can pull you toward what's possible, not just what feels safe.
Explorers	Alignment and Endurance principles, Vision, Pacing, and Present Focus, offer focus without stifling your spark. Choose one thing. Stay with it.
Catalysts	Full-spectrum energy support from principles across the Opus 8 energy tiers—Vitality, Pacing, Present Focus, Connection, and Service—help you sustain your energy and lead from wholeness.

Knowing your archetype is just the beginning. But real momentum comes from action. That's what the Opus 8 energy principles are here for: to help you support yourself and your energy in a way that feels real, doable, and deeply human.

Let's explore them together in the next section.

Tool Two

HOW ENERGY FUELS WHAT MATTERS MOST:

The Opus 8 Energy System

I didn't set out to build a framework for living a meaningful, healthy life—not consciously, at least. I was simply trying to answer my own questions.

Maybe you've asked them of yourself too: Why do I feel so disconnected, even after working so hard to build this life? Can I keep building success without sacrificing my well-being? What does it *actually* mean to thrive, and where do I even begin?

These weren't abstract reflections for me. I was burned out and searching for a way forward that didn't just patch the surface but helped me rebuild myself from the inside out.

What surprised me was how many others were asking the same things: leaders, creatives, entrepreneurs, caregivers, and professionals across industries. Their stories echoed my own.

- "Everything looked good on paper, but it didn't feel good."
- "I was always running on fumes, but I didn't know how to stop."

- "I hit a wall and realized I didn't even know why I was on this path."
- "I couldn't stop thinking about the future. I never felt grounded in the present."

What became clear was this: Most people weren't just trying to *change*. They were trying to do something far deeper: to build a life that felt healthy, meaningful, and *sustainable*.

Like me, most people I spoke with were taught that the key to progress was to create momentum. Keep moving. Find the next step, take the next step. Pass to the next level. Push forward.

The truth is that momentum is often mistaken for progress. But real progress isn't just about forward motion—it's about having the energy capacity to sustain that motion over time, across your physical, emotional, mental, and spiritual domains.

That's why when you're going through real change, burnout, reinvention, or a period of feeling stuck, momentum stalls. Before you can move ahead, you need to replenish your energy and *steady yourself*.

When I started rebuilding my life after burnout, I was desperate to feel like myself again. I was convinced that if I just found the right next step, everything would fall into place. That's why the moment my energy returned, I did what I knew best—I took action. I started a new degree. Launched a business. And said yes to almost everything.

On the outside, it looked like progress, even momentum. Inside, however, something still didn't feel right. It wasn't until I nearly crashed again that I realized that my momentum was unsustainable; I was repeating old patterns.

And I wasn't alone. In listening to others navigating transitions, I saw the same struggles repeat themselves. Some people were too depleted to move forward. They needed to *restore* before they could act. Others had energy but lacked direction. They were *moving*, but not toward something meaningful. And some started strong but couldn't sustain their momentum. They had vision, but no structure to support it.

Over time, I saw the same three essential needs show up again and again:

1. **A strong foundation**: energy, connection, stability.

2. **True alignment:** clarity around what matters and how to move toward it.

3. **Endurance**: the ability to maintain momentum without burning out.

These weren't just personal patterns; they're found across disciplines. Neuroscience shows that our capacity to change is deeply tied to our physiological state: When we're chronically stressed, burned out, or otherwise depleted, we lose access to creativity, decision making, and future vision. Positive psychology reminds us that change is identity-driven and doesn't start with intention alone, but with aligned action. And high-performance research, like that of Tony Schwartz and Jim Loehr, reveals that recovery isn't the opposite of progress; it's what makes progress possible. In fact, without recovery, momentum isn't sustainable.

THE OPUS 8:
AN ENERGY SYSTEM FOR SUSTAINABLE, ALIGNED LIVING

Back then I didn't fully understand that healthy, meaningful, sustainable success isn't powered by willpower or effort alone. It's fueled by energy across four essential domains: physical, emotional, mental, and spiritual. These four types of energy form the baseline for how we show up in our lives, our leadership, and our relationships.

According to Schwartz and Loehr's pioneering research, burnout doesn't come from stress itself, but from insufficient recovery across the four essential domains. It's not the demands of our lives alone that undo us; it's the absence of recovery cycles, across the four essential domains.[34]

This framework revolutionized how we think about effectiveness, not as a function of time or effort, but of energy. Schwartz and Loehr's work showed that energy is not only renewable, but essential to sustainable high performance. And, when one energy type is depleted, others are affected. When they're well-nourished, your capacity to lead, create, and connect, to yourself and to others, expands exponentially.

The Opus 8 builds on this foundation and expands the lens. Where Schwartz and Loehr focus on managing and recovering energy to power and sustain performance, the Opus 8 goes further. It helps you align your energy with who you are and what matters most.

Because once you cultivate physical, emotional, mental, and spiritual energy, the question becomes: Where will you direct it? And to what end?

Energy is the raw material. Alignment is the design. And the outcome—when energy, action, and meaning converge—is a life that's not only healthy and productive but deeply fulfilling.

The Opus 8 is an integrated system of eight principles across three dynamic tiers that help you generate, renew, and focus your energy. Practiced consistently, they don't just power performance, they support a life of clarity, coherence, and intention. They sustain not only what you do, but who you are. And, critically, they activate meaning.

THE THREE TIERS OF THE OPUS 8

The eight principles are grouped into three powerful tiers. These are energetic thresholds: Stability is for when you're depleted or dysregulated. Alignment is for when your energy is steady and ready for direction. Endurance is for sustaining momentum and meaning over time.

Each tier reflects a different energetic need, one that may become primary at different phases of your journey. But they're not steps you complete; they are dynamic dimensions you live in, often simultaneously. Let's look at them more deeply here and in Figure Eight:

- **Stability** (Vitality, Connection, Grounding) principles form your energetic foundation. When practiced, they nurture and replenish your physical, emotional and spiritual capacity. When life feels unsteady, they ground and restore you.

- **Alignment** (Vision, Coherence, Present Focus) principles help you aim your energy. Drawing on your mental, emotional, and spiritual energy, they sharpen your focus and reconnect you with purpose, ensuring that you're not just moving, but moving in the right direction, for the right reasons.

- **Endurance principles** (Pacing, Service, with renewed Connection and Present Focus) ensure that your energy is sustained across all four essential domains, so you can keep healthy, meaningful momentum without losing yourself along the way.

Each tier prepares the way for the next, but, because the relationship between them is dynamic, none of them become obsolete as you progress. As you're practicing Endurance, you'll still invest in Stability and Alignment. The Opus 8 is a system to live by.

Figure Eight. The Opus 8 Energy System

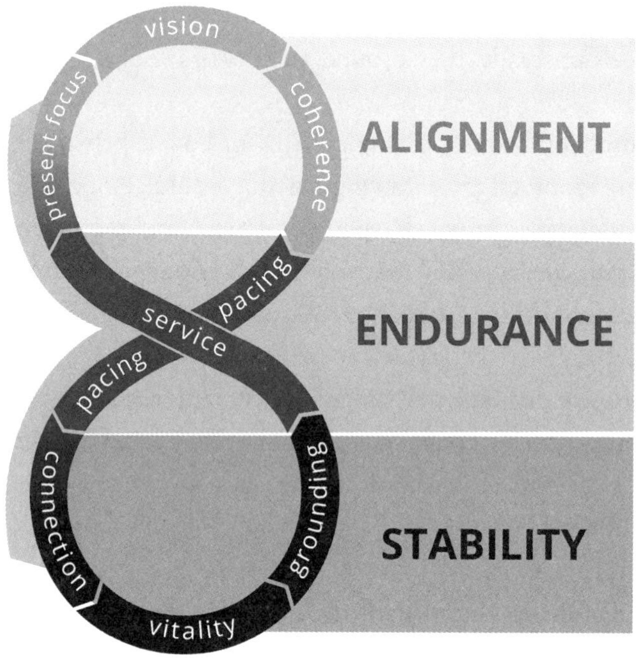

And you don't need to master all eight energy principles at once. Most people should start where they feel most depleted. If your energy is low, start with the Stability tier. When your energy returns, and you feel steady, the Alignment tier helps guide your focus. And from there, the Endurance tier becomes your strategy for long-term momentum and joy.

PRINCIPLES TO PRACTICE

These principles aren't abstract ideas or personality traits to admire. Each one becomes real only when it's lived. These are practices to embody through habits, boundaries, rhythms, and choices that shape how you move through the world.

Most energy systems focus on how to refuel so that you can perform. The Opus 8 shares that commitment but goes further. This system is not only about what you do; it's about how your energy aligns with your identity, values, purpose, and vision.

When practiced with fidelity and care, the Opus 8 becomes much more than a framework; it becomes a way of being, living, and working that helps you flourish with more calm, clarity, presence, integrity, and ease. You'll move from friction to flow. From urgency to intention. From striving to living in resonance with yourself, your work, and the life you're here to live.

So, let's begin at the foundation: building Stability through Vitality, Connection, and Grounding. Before you run toward what's next, you need solid ground beneath your feet.

STABILITY PRINCIPLES: KNOWING WHO YOU ARE

Everyone talks about well-being, but what does that really mean? Why does it matter? And how do we sustain it, especially in a world that constantly demands more of us?

There's a reason why seven out of ten people experience chronic stress or burnout: We're disconnected from what truly fuels us, from people around us, and often from ourselves. The result? We push forward, but at a cost.

That's why the first energy principles in the Opus 8 are about regaining and maintaining stability. When practiced, these principles are the ones that steady you when the world is spinning. They help you restore your physical, emotional, and spiritual energy. They bring you back to yourself before you race ahead to what's next. Without these in place, any success we build risks crumbling away.

Think of these principles as the legs of a tripod; remove one, and your stability suffers.

- **Vitality is your fuel.** It powers your physical and emotional energy so you can show up in your life fully. Without Vitality, the other principles falter. A state of being strong and active, Vitality is the generator behind your ability to connect, to focus, and to endure.

- **Connection is your anchor.** It supports your emotional energy by keeping you linked to yourself and to others. Connection renews your emotional energy. It reminds you that you're not alone and that you are, in fact, whole.

- **Grounding is your stability.** It supports your emotional and spiritual energy, helping you stay steady in the face of uncertainty. Grounding isn't just emotional steadiness—it's energetic regulation. It calms your nervous system so your energy can flow to what matters most to you.

We live in a culture that glorifies productivity but rarely teaches us how to sustain ourselves. From the time we hit kindergarten, we're learning how to suppress our needs, how to fit in with others and the way things are. We're taught to push through, handle setbacks, and keep moving.

As children we learn how to make success look easy, even if we are suffering along the way or are miserable when we arrive. Most of us aren't taught how to truly care for and center ourselves.

Real success—the kind that lasts and feels good when you arrive—demands real care and a strong foundation. These are your building blocks. And the first, and most important of those principles, is your Vitality.

Vitality: Fueling Your Energy

You can have the best ideas, the most inspiring vision, all the right skills, but none of it matters without energy.

Vitality is the foundation for everything you want to build. When you're drained, even small tasks can feel like mountains. When you're energized physically, mentally, and emotionally, you move through life with clarity and strength.

Again, science supports this: Chronic stress literally impairs your brain's ability to focus, regulate emotions, and imagine a better future. But when you restore your energy, you restore your ability to create and respond meaningfully to life.

More importantly, Vitality isn't just about functioning; it's about how you feel. Think about the last time you felt fully alive. When you were fully energized, your mind was sharp, your body felt good, and you moved through the day with ease. Now compare that to a time you were completely drained and struggling to get through basic tasks.

The difference between those two states? That's the power of Vitality. It fuels our resilience, creativity, and ability to engage fully in life. Yet, in a culture that often rewards busyness over well-being, we tend to treat our physical, emotional, and mental energy as an unlimited resource—until we crash.

Energy isn't something you *have*; it's something you *cultivate*. Not through perfection or optimization, but through steady care.

But how do you do that? Start with these three essentials:

- **Sleep.** Seven or more hours a night supports memory, focus, and emotional balance. Even one night of poor sleep affects decision-making and impulse control.

- **Movement.** Just ten minutes a day can boost your energy and improve your mood.

- **Play.** Unstructured joy, the kind that comes from doodling, games, or playing with a pet, for example, fuels creativity and resilience.

Beyond these basics, there are two other factors that impact your Vitality:

- **Mindfulness.** Just a few minutes of stillness can downshift your nervous system and sharpen your focus. From neuroscience to ancient traditions, the message is clear: Learning to regulate your attention and emotions is key to your long-term well-being.[35]

- **Nutrition.** Your body runs on what you feed it. The energy crashes we blame on work or stress often start with what's on our plate. Whole foods, hydration, and less sugar and caffeine keep your energy steady.

When we don't tend to our energy, we enter what experts call "power stress," a type of stress that happens when we're always giving to work, family, clients, or community without restoring ourselves.[36]

The antidote to power stress is practicing what researchers call the "renewal cycle," a rhythm of mindful breaks, compassion, connection, hope, and joy that resets your system.[37] Vitality is an important piece of this cycle. It is a biological necessity, and the first step to enduring success.

To build Vitality, you won't need to massively overhaul your life; instead, you can make small, intentional shifts that fuel your energy over time.

One of the biggest shifts you can make is noticing when your energy is off before you feel depleted. Try it. Use a simple stoplight check-in to monitor your energy throughout the day.

- Green (7 to 10) means you're energized and focused, thriving.
- Yellow (4 to 6) means you're getting by, pushing through. It's time to recharge.
- Red (1 to 3) means you're running on empty, and it's time to stop and reset.

Of course, your Vitality alone isn't a predictor of health, happiness, longevity, or a meaningful life; relationships are essential.

Connection: Anchoring in Meaningful Relationships

If Vitality is your fuel, Connection is your lifeline. Research tells us that the strength of our relationships—not wealth, not status—is the number one predictor of long-term well-being.[38] And yet, we're more disconnected than ever.

Even when surrounded by others, people feel emotionally isolated. The numbers are striking. Over half of Americans and 35 percent of Europeans report feeling lonely.[39] Nearly half of Americans say their relationships aren't meaningful.[40] And, single or not, 57 percent eat every meal alone.[41]

Disconnection doesn't just impact your emotional state; it erodes your energy. Without supportive relationships, stress rises, immunity weakens, cognitive abilities decline, and even your lifespan shortens.

But research also shows that being part of a community, even a small, trusted group of friends or colleagues, boosts your mental health, reduces loneliness, and helps you feel grounded. The famous "Harvard Study of Adult Development," which has tracked participants for more than eighty-five years, found that the biggest predictor of happiness and longevity isn't wealth or success—it's the quality of our relationships.[42]

But Connection is about more than just knowing people. It's about being present, with yourself, your values, your hopes, and with others.

I once coached a senior executive who felt exhausted, stretched thin, and unsure of what was missing. One day, she had a spontaneous conversation with a colleague. It wasn't a scheduled meeting or a high-stakes discussion, just two people talking in the office lounge over a cup of tea.

"That's what I want more of," she shared. "Not just meetings or updates, but *real* connections that energize me rather than drain me."

That's just it: Connection doesn't have to be big or dramatic. It just has to be *real.* A moment of presence. A conversation without an agenda. A check-in with a friend or with yourself.

How to practice Connection:

- Who gives you energy? Prioritize time with them.

- Who might you connect with this week? Call or message them.
- And most importantly, check in with yourself: How are you doing today? What do you need most?

After all, equally important, and often overlooked, is the relationship we have with ourselves. A positive relationship with ourselves is foundational to sustained health and well-being. Research across neuroscience, psychology, and ancient wisdom confirms that self-connection is essential for well-being, clarity, and resilience.

When we reconnect inwardly—through mindfulness, meditation, journaling, or simply pausing to notice our thoughts—anxiety is reduced, we can better regulate our emotions, and we gain clarity. We quiet the noise. We return to center.[43]

But when we neglect this relationship, we lose clarity, react impulsively, and struggle to align our actions with what truly matters.

Ancient wisdom has long recognized this. Stoicism, Buddhism, and Ayurveda emphasize self-inquiry as essential for emotional resilience, while indigenous traditions highlight the importance of cultivating inner harmony.

Across cultures, the message is the same: Thriving is about more than external achievements; we thrive when we are in alignment with ourselves.

If you feel disconnected or struggle to hear your inner voice, try one of these approaches:

- **Create space for stillness.** Spend (at least) five minutes with yourself each morning before reaching for your phone. Try a solo walk without distractions—no podcast, partner, music, or dog.

- **Engage in self-reflection.** Throughout the day, check in and ask yourself what you need in the moment. Listen to your first instinct. Or try the Morning Pages form of journaling, as Julia Cameron suggests in *The Artist's Way*.[44]

- **Get creative and play.** Do something creative without an outcome in mind: sketch, cook, play music, dance, or write just for yourself.

- **Tune in to your body.** Try movement that helps you reconnect: stretching, swimming, yoga, running, anything that helps you feel rather than think.

Connection is both a grounding anchor and a source of renewal. It's how we remember that we matter—not because of what we achieve, but because of who we are.

Grounding: Creating Stability in a World of Change

The world isn't slowing down. So, we must learn to steady ourselves *within* the motion. That's the work of Grounding.

Grounding is the ability to stay centered, especially when things around you feel chaotic or uncertain. It means being able to pause, breathe, and reset so you can respond to life from a place of clarity rather than reactivity. Practicing this principle supports your nervous system, your emotions, and your sense of spiritual steadiness. It anchors you before and when things feel off-balance.

Emotional regulation is one of its most powerful tools. Think of your emotions like a car. If you're always accelerating and reacting impulsively to everything in your path, chances are you'll crash. If you're always braking and suppressing what you feel, you'll likely stall.

Grounding helps you to drive smoothly, to know when to slow down, when to accelerate, and how to steer through challenges without losing control. When you are emotionally regulated, you can feel things deeply while still responding thoughtfully.

You can build this through:

- **Mindfulness and breathwork:** Calm the nervous system in real time.
- **Movement:** Stretching, walking, swimming, or yoga, for example, help shift reactive energy.
- **Self-reflection:** Reconnects you to what matters.

These practices will help shift your nervous system out of stress mode and into clarity.

At its core, the Grounding principle allows you to create stability from within. Don't worry about controlling everything around you because, let's be honest, that's impossible. Instead, build routines and systems that help you stay resilient, steady, and open, no matter what's happening externally.

If you're new to the idea of Grounding, or when you're feeling scattered, unsteady, or overwhelmed, try the five-senses reset. This is a well-known practice called by many names. It works by using your senses to move your brain out of reactive mode and into a calm, observational mode.

To get started, pause, breathe, and name:

- Five things you can see.
- Four things you can touch.
- Three things you can hear.
- Two things you can smell.
- One thing you can taste.

Or reframe your focus to what's going right, another well-known practice that interrupts negative thought spirals by directing your attention to what's working. The result: a better mood and more emotional resilience.

It's easy: Grab a piece of paper and write down three things that are going right today, even small things, like a comforting cup of tea, making the morning train on time; two things you're grateful for, like a friend's text, a book you're reading, the shining sun; and one thing you're letting go of, like the need to control how today unfolds.

By integrating simple practices like these, over time you build an internal foundation that keeps you stable, resilient, and ready for whatever comes next.

Embracing the Stability Principles

So, where do you start? If you're physically exhausted or lack energy, start with your Vitality. If you're feeling isolated or emotionally drained, begin with Connection. If you're overwhelmed or reactive, start with Grounding.

Your archetype from the Opus Change Continuum might offer a clue to what you need:

- Hesitators often need Grounding and Connection to move forward with courage.
- Catalysts need to restore Vitality to avoid burnout.
- Builders benefit from reconnecting to their "why" through meaningful Connection.

We live in a world that rewards constant doing at the expense of being well. But remember, being well is not the reward for living your Opus—it's the requirement. These energy principles are your foundation, and they create the base layer of sustainable success. They stabilize your energy, your focus, and your capacity to create a life that matters. So, before you run toward what's next, come home to yourself.

Once your foundation is strong, you can turn your focus toward the next tier of the Opus 8, Alignment, the energy principles which ensure that your actions reflect your values, your purpose, and your vision.

ALIGNMENT PRINCIPLES: THE CLARITY TO ENSURE YOU'RE MOVING IN THE RIGHT DIRECTION

Here in Opusland, you are the CEO of your life. Every choice you make shapes your journey. But here's the challenge: Many of us are so focused on achieving that we don't pause to ask if we're actually building something we want. That's where Alignment comes in. Alignment is the practice of directing your energy toward what matters most, clearly, consciously, and consistently.

The Alignment principles help you turn inward to check your direction. With practice, they support your mental and spiritual energy by helping you to think clearly, act with integrity, and stay rooted in your deeper purpose. And they invite you to ask yourself three questions:

- **Vision.** Where am I going, and why?
- **Coherence.** Are my actions aligned with what I believe in?
- **Present Focus.** Am I fully engaged with what's happening now?

When these three principles are in sync, you feel clear, calm, and purposeful. When they're not you may feel off without knowing exactly why.

You might feel pulled in too many directions. Or find yourself achieving goals that don't feel fulfilling, even if they once did. These are symptoms of misalignment, a gap between your external life and your inner truth. That gap creates friction and drains your energy. Over time, it can lead to frustration, dissatisfaction, confusion, or burnout.

Alignment isn't fixed; it evolves with you. And because you're also always changing, what matters to you is always changing too. What mattered five years ago may not be what matters now. That's why these energy principles aren't one-time tools. They are practices for checking in, course-correcting and choosing your path with intention. They give you the clarity to move forward, not just productively, but meaningfully. They also provide you with hope, which helps you imagine and believe in the possibilities for your future.

To use the Alignment principles well, you must first be grounded in practices supporting your Stability: Vitality, Connection, and Grounding. Those ensure that you have strength, a full energy charge, and clarity about who you are and how to steady yourself. Once that energy and steadiness is in place, Alignment guides your next steps.

Let your current experience be your guide. Lost or unclear? Start with Vision. A clear direction will guide your next steps and inspire you to action. Working hard but feeling off? Explore Coherence. You'll feel different when your actions align with your vision, values, and your deeper purpose. Scattered or anxious? Ground in Present Focus practices. Learning to be fully engaged in the now will help you make steady, meaningful progress.

Your Opus Change Continuum archetype can also help:

- Navigators thrive with Present Focus; it helps them adapt when plans shift.
- Builders need Vision and Coherence to see beyond the next step.
- Explorers benefit from Vision to reduce overwhelm.
- Catalysts often need Present Focus to stay rooted in the moment.

Just like the Stability principles, the Alignment principles of Vision, Coherence, and Present Focus work as a system. Together, they help you move with clarity and consistency, directing your energy toward whatever matters most to you. If one is missing, progress feels harder than it should. Let's take a closer look at each.

Vision: Defining Your North Star

Vision is your North Star. It asks: What am I moving toward, and why does it matter?

Without a clear vision, it's easy to chase what looks good on paper but feels empty inside. Vision helps filter distractions, clarify your direction, and keep you from climbing the wrong ladder.

And it doesn't have to be grand. Vision might mean building a more spacious life, deepening your relationships, or creating something you've long dreamed about. Whatever brings meaning and direction to your life—that's Vision.

The science supports this: having a sense of purpose has been shown to boost longevity, resilience, and overall well-being. And spiritually, having a Vision connects us to something larger than ourselves, a sense of future, contribution, and meaning. [45]

If you're still discovering your Vision, that's okay. We've got a lot of time together in the four-stage transformation process in part two to explore what it may be. Start with curiosity.

- **Look back.** When did you feel most alive? What were you doing? Who were you with?

- **Look forward.** Imagine a day in your life one to three years from now. What's happening? What are you doing? Who is with you?

- **Look inward.** What excites you? What are you naturally drawn to or energized by? What sparks something in you?

If you already know your Vision, connect with it daily. Whether you write it down, visualize it, or speak it aloud, staying close to your vision boosts your energy and helps you live it.

Vision offers clarity, but it's Coherence that ensures that what we aspire to aligns with how we live, creating a sense of inner harmony that fuels sustainable progress.

Coherence: Aligning Actions and Purpose

It's one thing to have a Vision. It's another to live it like it matters.

Coherence is the harmony between your actions, your Vision, and your deeper purpose, your "why." If Vision is your North Star, Coherence is the compass that keeps you on course, day by day.

When Coherence is strong, your choices reflect who you are and where you're headed. Psychologists call this cognitive consonance: when our actions match our identity, energy is released—not drained. When Coherence is missing, stress rises and motivation wanes. That's because you're spending energy on things that don't align with your values. Over time, that misalignment creates friction or even burnout.

The key to Coherence is consistency, not perfection. It's about making small, daily decisions that reinforce not just who you are, but who you are becoming and why it matters to you. By practicing Coherence, you can build trust in yourself and more sustainable motivation.

Here's how to start:

- **Use Vision as a filter.** Before saying yes to something, ask yourself: Does this align with and move me forward to where I'm headed?

- **Practice identity-based habits.** Don't just write—be a writer. Don't just run—be a runner.[46] Let your daily actions reflect who you are becoming and connect you to that identity.

- **Reinforce your "why."** Keep it visible. On days when motivation fades, purpose will carry you.

- **Create rhythms, not just goals.** Build a structure that supports who you are, not just what you want to achieve.

Why does this matter? Because identity shapes our actions, and our actions shape our identity.

We often assume that change is all about external actions, such as setting goals, making plans, and following through. But lasting change doesn't come from doing more. It comes from becoming more aligned with your values, your goals, and your identity.

Psychology tells us that habits tied to identity are the most durable. When we see ourselves in a certain way, such as a writer, an entrepreneur, or an athlete, we naturally take actions that reinforce that identity.

Our brains crave alignment between our self-concept (who we think we are or what our identity is) and our behavior. When our actions reinforce who we want to be, change becomes sustainable.

For example, if your goal is to start a business, don't just set milestones; start thinking like an entrepreneur. If your vision is to write a book, shift from a statement like "I want to write" to "I am a writer." This powerful reframe builds self-trust and reinforces behaviors that align with your long-term goals.[47]

As James Clear wrote in *Atomic Habits*: "Ultimately, your habits matter because they help you become the type of person you wish to be. They are the channel through which you develop your deepest beliefs about yourself. Quite literally, you become your habits."[48]

Identity shapes our actions, and our actions shape our identity. When your days reflect your vision and your values, you're making progress, and you're becoming the person who can sustain it.

While Coherence is about becoming the kind of person whose actions reflect what matters most, Present Focus ensures you're clear about what that is in any given moment.

Present Focus: Anchoring in the Now

Let's be honest. We spend a lot of our time in the future. What's next? What's coming? What should I be doing? We often neglect the only moment that actually exists: now. The only moment we ever actually live in is *this one*.

Present Focus is the ability to engage fully with what's happening now. Practicing it helps us move through life, not reactively, but with clarity, calm, and intention. It's one of the most powerful tools you have for regulating your energy and bringing your full self to the moment. Present Focus practices reduce anxiety by interrupting the future-focused stress loop. It restores both mental and emotional energy.

Without it, you rush, react, and lose track of what matters. With it, you make thoughtful decisions, savor what's unfolding, and tune in to your internal compass.

Why does this matter?

When we are fully present, we are happier, less stressed, and more mentally sharp.

- A Harvard study found that people spend nearly 47 percent of their waking hours thinking about something other than what they're doing.

- That mind-wandering directly correlates with lower happiness levels.[49]

- Neuroscience shows that mindfulness, the practice of bringing attention to the present, physically changes the brain. It strengthens the prefrontal cortex, the area responsible for focus, emotional regulation, and decision-making.[50]

And if you've ever felt yourself rushing through a task and making careless mistakes, there's a reason for that. Research on stress shows that when we're too future-focused, we operate in a heightened state of anxiety, making us more reactive and impulsive and less able to make thoughtful decisions.[51]

Presence not only boosts mental clarity, it fuels resilience, emotional steadiness, and creative flow. Presence isn't passive; it's a high-performance strategy.

The Link Between Presence and Peak Performance

For high performers, like athletes, musicians, creatives, and leaders, presence isn't a luxury. It's a core skill.

Research on peak performance makes the case for Present Focus. Athletes describe moments of *flow*, that state of focused immersion where action feels instinctive and effort fades. Artists experience greater creativity. Both groups develop increased resilience to stress.[52] Think of a tennis player anticipating a serve—not by overthinking, but by being fully in tune with the game's rhythm. The same is true for musicians. A pianist can't afford to dwell on a missed note or worry about the next one. Presence is what enables mastery. In fact, studies show that musicians who cultivate mindfulness report less anxiety and more creative freedom.[53]

And in leadership? Presence is a hallmark of those who excel under pressure. Emotionally intelligent leaders who stay grounded in the moment make better decisions, build more trust, and connect more deeply with others. Research consistently shows that present-moment awareness improves performance, empathy, and decision-making in high-stakes environments.[54]

Across disciplines, presence isn't passive. It's a *high-performance tool* that fuels focus, trust, and creativity.

Becoming Present

While the idea of "being present" sounds simple, actually *doing* it requires effort—especially in a world that's built to distract us. The good news? Presence is a muscle, and you can strengthen it with small shifts.

Here's how:

- **Interrupt autopilot mode**. Between meetings or tasks, pause. Take one deep breath. Reset.
- **Limit multitasking**. Focus on one thing at a time; it boosts energy, accuracy, and clarity.

- **Savor small moments.** Sip your coffee. Listen deeply. Look up. A few mindful minutes a day rewires your brain for clarity and calm.
- **Check in.** What's here right now? How do I want to feel?

If you find yourself constantly thinking ahead, struggling to stay engaged, or your day feels like a blur of screens and tasks, try this micro-reset:

- **Inhale and notice.** Where are you? What do you see, feel, hear, or smell?
- **Exhale and release.** Let go of tension, distractions, and the mental clutter.
- **Set an intention.** How do you want to show up in the next moment?

This practice takes less than a minute, but it can redirect your whole day.

When you practice Present Focus, you don't just get more done. You become more present, connected, and whole.

Putting Alignment into Practice

These energy principles work best together. When you're clear on your Vision, you can filter what matters. When your Coherence is strong, your habits reflect who you're becoming. And when you live with Present Focus, you move with awareness and power.

Alignment means you're checking in regularly. Listening. And, when you're aligned, your energy doesn't leak—it builds. This is the clarity that allows you to keep going with joy as well as intention.

From here you're ready to sustain your performance. Let's move to the final tier, the Endurance principles, which protect and renew your energy, enable you to stay connected, and ensure you can sustain momentum over the long haul.

ENDURANCE PRINCIPLES: THE ENERGY TO GO THE DISTANCE

Being well, connected, grounded, and aligned are the cornerstones of meaningful success. But to sustain that success over time, to stay in the work, in the game, in your life with presence and energy, you need something more: endurance. Endurance is what transforms bursts of effort into lasting impact. It keeps your energy whole over time. That's what these principles are all about.

At some point, every ambitious person learns this lesson: Working harder, grinding longer, and pushing through exhaustion works . . . for a while. Then everything breaks. Sometimes slowly, sometimes all at once. And what breaks isn't just your body or focus. It's your joy. Your clarity. Your connection to *why* any of it matters.

When I began studying high performers who had stayed successful at sustaining their impact over time, I noticed something: They didn't just build success. They built systems to preserve their energy, protect their purpose, and prioritize relationships that mattered. They weren't just driven; they were strategic with how they drove themselves forward.

Of all three energy tiers in the Opus 8, the Endurance principles surprised me most. As a long-time Catalyst, the idea of slowing down felt counterintuitive. Why would recovery, rest, or reflection be as essential as momentum?

But now? I'd say: Of course they are. Without them, momentum turns into burnout. Bold action becomes scattered urgency. And eventually, we stall creatively, relationally, or physically.

The most powerful transformation I've seen in clients isn't just from starting something new. It's learning how to *stay* in it, aligned, energized, and whole.

The best in the world don't just go hard; they go long. And that requires these four energy principles: Pacing, Service, Present Focus, and Connection, each one supporting your physical, emotional, mental, and spiritual energy.

Let's begin with the one many of us resist most: Pacing.

Pacing: How to Sustain Peak Performance

If you've ever hit an afternoon slump after deep focus, that's not a flaw—it's biology. Our brains follow ultradian rhythms, natural cycles of about ninety minutes of high focus followed by a need for rest.

But most of us override these rhythms with coffee, screens, and sheer force of will. We push through fatigue and wonder why we can't think straight, why we're irritable, or why creativity has vanished.

Many high achievers take pride in pushing through fatigue. Catalysts, especially, feel most alive when running fast. I used to believe I could operate at that speed indefinitely. But research—and lived experience—says otherwise. The longer we ignore recovery, the less effective we become.

When we ignore rest, everything suffers: cognitive performance, memory, decision-making, and even empathy. Creativity, one of our greatest assets, drops significantly. Mistakes rise. Relationships strain.

Eventually, our bodies call time-out, whether through burnout, illness, or a creeping sense of disconnection we can't quite name. And if you're in leadership, the effects ripple. Burned-out leaders create burned-out teams. Over time, the collective impact of running on empty is not just detrimental to individuals and the team, but catastrophic for the business.

The paradox is this: The very people who claim they "don't have time" to slow down eventually lose time. They work longer, feel uninspired, and make more avoidable mistakes.

At the far end, they may even get sick or burn out.

True high performance doesn't require you to just push harder; it requires you to pause strategically so you can keep going.

That's why elite athletes build their training around cycles of renewal and recovery. They know: Sprinting through the whole marathon doesn't work. Neither does sprinting through a quarter, a creative season, or an entire career.

Researchers have also confirmed this in the business world: The best leaders operate in rhythms of pulse and pause.[55] They treat energy as a resource to renew, not deplete. And by renewing it, they create resonance, which bolsters clarity, trust, and creativity that then ripple through their teams.[56]

Pacing is energy intelligence in action—knowing when to drive, when to pause, and how to fuel your capacity rhythmically.

Creativity: The Need for Space

One of the most fascinating discoveries in my conversations with high performers? Many of their biggest breakthroughs came not during deep work, but during intentional breaks.

When you step away from a task, your brain enters "incubation mode," where the subconscious continues solving problems. The default mode network (the same one active during daydreaming) kicks in, making unexpected connections and insights more likely.[57]

You know this feeling. You're stuck on a problem . . . and then the answer hits you in the shower. On a walk. While cooking dinner. That's the Pacing principle at work.

When we step away, our brains integrate information in ways they can't when we're intensely focused. In the research on flow states, psychologist Mihaly Csikszentmihalyi found innovative ideas emerge right *after* people take deliberate breaks.[58] For teams, this means designing rhythms that include renewal, not just output.

Whether it's a ten-minute walk, a screen-free lunch, or a day off, strategic rest enhances performance. This break provides recovery, yes, but it also houses insight waiting to happen. Rest isn't a reward; it's a strategy.

You don't have to work less to incorporate Pacing into your life. But you do have to work smarter. Knowing when to push forward and when to step back is a strategic advantage.

If you are new to the Pacing, or perhaps you are skeptical, try this:

- Work in focused ninety-minute blocks (this aligns with your natural physiological rhythms). Then take a fifteen- to

twenty-minute break—no email, no scrolling. Move your body, step outside, hydrate, eat if needed, and breathe.
- Try it for one day. Then a week. Track how your energy, focus, and mood respond.

Pacing isn't about slowing down your ambition. It's about working *wiser* to sustain it.

Present Focus: Your Adaptability Partner

We've already talked about how Present Focus supports clarity and creativity. But as part of your Endurance toolkit, this principle offers something even more essential: it helps to ensure that your energy remains sustainable over time.

When you're present, you notice the subtle signs of strain before they spiral into stress. You catch the tension in your shoulders, the creeping fatigue, the detour from your values. And you adjust.

It's the inner equivalent of a pilot making small mid-flight changes. You don't wait for the crash. You notice, respond early, and stay on course.

From an Endurance perspective, Present Focus is your adaptability partner. It allows you to respond dynamically, moment by moment. Like an elite athlete making a snap decision in a game, staying present lets you make real-time course corrections, preventing exhaustion and misalignment before they happen. With practice, this awareness can become your edge, protecting your time, your energy, and your direction.

Service and Connection: Anchoring in Meaning

We are wired for Connection, one of the core Stability principles. But in the context of Endurance, it's not just about support, it's about fuel.

The relationships that nourish you can also steady you. They remind you of what matters, offer perspective, and share the load.

But the something deeper happens when Connection turns into Service—when your energy, wisdom, or presence is shared for something beyond yourself: Meaning.

Many high achievers resist the Service principle because they see it as one more demand on their time and energy, or they are moving so fast they forget how much they have to offer someone else.

Service doesn't just benefit others; it re-centers you in your own values. It's how your energy becomes meaning.

Research confirms what many of us feel: People who regularly give back, whether through mentorship, caregiving, volunteering, or purpose-driven work, report lower stress, greater well-being, and even longer lives.[59]

That said, even the most service-driven among us can burn out when we give too much without renewal. That's why Pacing matters here, too. If you overextend, you can't serve. But when you give from a grounded, intentional place, Service fuels you right back.

Connecting to Contribution

You don't need to take on more to activate the Service principle. Instead, notice how you're already contributing and what that gives you in return. You can do this through a simple exercise.

- List how you currently serve others, professionally or personally.
- Reflect on the energy, wisdom or time you give.
- Ask yourself: How does this act of Service feel? Fulfilling? Draining? What might make it more sustainable?

Then, bring this awareness into your next act of Service. Let it guide how you give, how you renew, and how you align your effort with meaning.

BRINGING IT ALL TOGETHER

To thrive in your Opus Life, you'll need more than vision, willpower, and effort. You'll need practices in Pacing to protect your energy, Present Focus to help you adjust, Connection to anchor you, and Service to remind you why this all matters.

These aren't just recovery tools. They are practices that help you live aligned, lead whole, and endure with clarity and care. Endurance is what lets you show up again and again with your energy, clarity, and joy intact.

LIVING YOUR OPUS, LIVING INTENTIONALLY

The Opus 8 Energy System provides a gentle, powerful way for you to come home to yourself again and again.

They help you move through your day, your relationships, and your decisions with greater presence, care, and coherence.

You'll return to them often, not because you're lost, but because this is what it means to lead yourself with heart, integrity and courage. This is how you'll cultivate and sustain the energy to define success on your terms, and build a life that truly matters.

Tool Three

THE OPUS 8 COMPASS:

A Guide for Real-Time Alignment

The Opus 8 Supports meaningful, aligned, and enduring success. You don't need to master all eight at once. But how do you know which one you need right now?

Your archetypes can help, and so can the Opus 8 Compass. The Compass is about realignment, not performance. Think of it as your personal rhythm-based check-in, helping you to ground yourself and notice where your energy is flowing well and where it needs care.

You can return to the Opus 8 Compass regularly throughout your journey: weekly, monthly, or anytime you need them. Whether your energy dips, your clarity fades, or you're simply not feeling like yourself. Used weekly or monthly, the Compass becomes a practice of energy intelligence—helping you notice, adjust, and return to what matters most.

Before diving in, take a quiet moment to arrive. This might include a few deep breaths, a sip of something warm, or a brief pause. You're tuning in, not rushing.

Then, walk yourself through each of the eight principles. Each table offers a short description of the principles within each tier. Our familiar simple stoplight rating system helps assess your current energy and alignment levels:

- **Green (G):** I'm thriving. I feel energized, aligned, and consistent.
- **Yellow (Y):** I'm functional but not flowing. There's room to grow in this area.
- **Red (R):** I'm struggling, depleted, or disconnected. This area needs my attention.

As you reflect, jot down what you notice. No need to overthink. Just pay attention to what shows up. You're gathering insight, not grading yourself.

THE OPUS 8 COMPASS

Table Three. Stability Principles: The Energy and Stability You Need to Replenish and Restore

PRINCIPLE	ENERGY PRINCIPLE IN PRACTICE	G	Y	R
Vitality	I wake up feeling replenished. I'm sleeping, moving, eating, and restoring my physical and emotional energy in ways that support me. I feel physically steady and emotionally resilient in daily life.			
Connection	I feel supported, seen, and emotionally connected to myself and others. I spend time with people who uplift me.			
Grounding	I have go-to practices that help me reset. I feel emotionally steady, spiritually centered, and responsive rather than reactive.			
Exploratory Prompts **Vitality:** Where is my energy strongest right now? Where is it leaking? **Connection:** Where do I feel nourished? Where might I need more support? **Grounding:** What helps me return to center when things feel off?				

Table Four. Alignment Principles: Directing Energy with Clarity and Purpose

PRINCIPLE	ENERGY PRINCIPLE IN PRACTICE	G	Y	R
Vision	I'm clear on my top priorities. I am energized by where I'm headed and clear on why it matters. My daily and weekly choices align with what excites and challenges me.			
Coherence	My actions reflect what matters most to me. I live in alignment with my core values. I feel like myself in the way I work and live.			
Present Focus	I'm engaged with the moment. I make space for presence, creativity, or reflection each day.			
Exploratory Prompts **Vision:** What excites me about where I'm going? Has anything shifted? **Coherence:** Where do I feel in flow? Where are my values and actions misaligned? **Present Focus:** When am I fully here? Where am I distracted, rushed, or checked out?				

Table Five. Endurance Principles: Sustaining Energy and Meaningful Momentum

PRINCIPLE	ENERGY PRINCIPLE IN PRACTICE	G	Y	R
Pacing	I move at a rhythm that honors both ambition and energy recovery. I feel steady, not strained.			
Service	I contribute to others in a way that feels fulfilling and sustainable. I know my "why."			
+Connection	I nurture meaningful relationships over time. I stay connected while honoring my energy.			
+Present Focus	I'm present in my work and relationships. I act with intention and awareness. I notice when I need to pause, reset, or reengage with the moment.			
Exploratory Prompts **Pacing:** Am I forcing progress, or am I honoring my natural rhythm? **Service:** Where am I making a difference? How can I serve in a way that feels fulfilling? **Connection:** Where am I feeling most connected to myself and others? Where might I need to reconnect or re-source my energy?				

Choosing One Principle to Focus On

When you're done, look at your notes. Which energy principle is calling for your attention?

If any of your Stability principles show up as yellow or red, start there. You can't build forward without fuel and steadiness. If your Stability foundation is solid, move to the Alignment or Endurance principle that feels most essential right now.

Trust what your body, heart, or intuition is telling you. When you notice something calling for attention, that's not failure—it's feedback. That's the wisdom of this system: you're never behind; you're always being invited back into alignment.

So, ask yourself: What's one small action I can take this week to nourish this principle and my energy? Write it down. Say it aloud. Place it somewhere you'll see it. Let that simple act be your way forward.

Tool Four

MY OPUS LIFE

This is where your vision becomes practice. *My Opus Life* is your personal blueprint—a living, breathing framework designed to help you sustain your energy, deepen your alignment, and stay engaged with what truly matters. Here, you'll name the habits, relationships, rhythms, and reflections that support the life you're creating so that even on hard days, you have something steady to return to. This is how you move from intention to embodiment. This is how you live your Opus.

MY OPUS VISION STATEMENT IS: ENERGY, WELL-BEING, AND HEALTH

How will I care for my well-being and health each day and each week, not just as maintenance, but as nourishment? How will I cultivate and replenish my energy on all levels—physical, emotional, mental, and spiritual—so that I can show up with presence, resilience, and joy? What rhythms support me when I'm thriving? What anchors steady me when I'm not?

My health and well-being goals, as linked to achieving my Year One plan and living my Opus include:

- My morning routine.
- My evening routine.
- My daily movement or exercise routines.
- My nutritional habits.
- How I will work each day so that I ensure that I replenish my energy throughout the working day.
- How I will cultivate an abundance mindset daily.
- How I will cultivate a gratitude mindset daily.
- My Opus Reboot routine.
- These are the signs that my energy is being depleted and what I will do to gently reset.
- When life gets messy, this is how I'll care for myself without judgment.
- Other routines that will generally sustain my well-being and health.

ALIGNMENT

How will I ensure that my actions align with my values, my identity, my goals for my Opus, and, most importantly the deeper rhythms of who I am becoming? How will I recognize when I've drifted, and what will I return to in order to recalibrate?

My approach to alignment, as linked to achieving my Year One plan and living my Opus include:

- These are the goals for my Opus over the next year.
- These are actions I will take daily to connect to my Opus.
- These are the specific habits I will use to carve out time regularly to take stock, connect with and work on my Opus.

- These are the financial habits I will adopt to maintain peace of mind with money as I pursue my Opus.
- These people will form my inner circle, champion my success, and challenge me in healthy ways as I move to attain my goals.
- These people will receive less of my attention, and I'll remove them from my life if needed to prioritize my energy.
- This is my criteria for making decisions about how I spend my time, so that I engage in activities that align with my true self and my Opus goals.
- These are the signs I'm living out of alignment—and how I will respond with compassion and curiosity.
- These are the old identities or patterns I'm releasing to make space for who I'm becoming.
- These are the "North Star" values I'll revisit when decision fatigue or doubt creeps in.
- Other habits of mind or ways of working which will support alignment.

STAYING THE COURSE

Staying the course doesn't mean always moving fast or getting everything right; it means returning, again and again, to what grounds you, reconnecting with yourself and your Opus through presence, compassion, and the quiet courage to begin again.

These are the promises I am making to myself as I begin to live my Opus, and this is how I will stay the course.

My promises to myself are:

- I will share what I've learned from this book and The Opus Way with these people.
- This is what a great day looks like: habits, well-being, work, and all else I love in life.

- This is what a great week looks like: habits, well-being, work, and all else I love in life.
- Here is my plan to keep myself moving toward my Opus in the next fourteen days—critical activities.
- This is how I will revisit this plan (My Opus Life) regularly (monthly, quarterly, or yearly) to check in, refine, and realign.
- When I lose momentum, this is the simple practice I will return to reconnect.
- This is the mantra or affirmation I'll hold when I need to steady myself.
- On hard days, this is how I will be kind to myself while staying committed.

Tool Five

OPUS VISUALIZATION

Visualization is a powerful tool. By mentally stepping into your future each day, you begin to shift your energy and attention toward what matters most. You create a path toward it not just through your actions, but through your presence.

This practice will help you embody your Opus so that you don't just chase success, but live it, feel it, and become it. You can access the audio recording of the visualization at LiveYourOpus.com.

Before you begin, settle into a space where you feel relaxed, perhaps in bed, during the quiet moments before sleep or upon waking.

- Breathe deeply.
- Inhale, exhale.
- Inhale, exhale.
- Inhale strength, exhale fatigue.
- Inhale love, exhale any worries.
- Inhale calm, exhale any stress.
- Inhale possibility, exhale any resistance.

Now, I want you to envision yourself in the future that you created, standing in the midst of your Opus, grounded and open, radiating the energy of a life that's fully aligned. Feel the energy of this masterpiece that is your life.

Picture yourself living your most ideal day; a day where you are feeling healthy and comfortable in your body and at ease in your mind and in your heart. Can you see yourself?

On this day, all of your actions come with ease and flow, fueled by clarity and sustained by presence. You and your vision are in harmony.

- What is it that you wanted to accomplish?
- What is that big dream that you have?
- Who is it that you wanted to become?
- What rhythms does that version of you engage in to honor your energy and stay connected?

Picture yourself moving as that person, your future self. Think like that person. Engage with the people you love as they would.

Notice how your future self moves through the day. How do they carry themselves? How do they speak? What do they no longer stress over? Embody that now. Breathe it in, let it settle into your bones. Let it become your natural state.

There are no worries in this vision. You have the confidence and the power to stay steady, to overcome any challenges, and to seize any opportunities.

You walk with confidence, feeling the steady rhythm of your steps. Each one carries you forward, effortlessly, naturally.

How was it you wanted to feel in your Opus? That is how you feel. Feel that emotion—now. Let the emotion guide your energy. Trust it to remind you of who you are becoming. If it's joy, let it bring a smile to your face. If it's pride, let yourself beam. If it's satisfaction, let your heart be full.

Breathe in that emotion, inhale it. Exhale anything not serving you.

As you move into your day, carry this vision of yourself living with joy and with ease and flow, your energy, strong and sustained, and your dreams fully in motion. Let it set your pace so it's not hurried, but intentional.

Remember that your Opus is not something you achieve in a day or in a week or in a month or in a year; it's a new way of living with intention. Reclaiming your energy. Respecting and following the definition of success you have for yourself. Putting yourself first, raising the bar to where you want it, aligning your actions each day with your vision, and trusting that every step you take today and each day after brings you closer to who you truly are and what matters most to you.

Your Opus is not a destination. It's a way of being. Every step today, tomorrow, and beyond is shaping you for the life you were meant to live.

So, if you've closed your eyes, open them gently now. Step forward with intention. Your Opus is waiting.

NOTES

1 Ben Wigert and Corey Tatel, "The Great Detachment: Why Employees Feel Stuck," Gallup, December 3, 2024, https://www.gallup.com/workplace/653711/great-detachment-why-employees-feel-stuck.aspx; "Global Meaningfulness Index, 2024," Voluntās, https://globalmeaningfulness.report/wp-content/uploads/2024/11/Global-Meaningfulness-Index-24.pdf.

2 Johann Hari, *Lost Connections: Why You're Depressed and How to Find Hope*, (Bloomsbury, 2019).

3 William Bridges and Susan Bridges, *Managing Transitions (25th anniversary edition): Making the Most of Change* (Balance, 2017).

4 Bridges and Bridges, *Managing Transitions (25th anniversary edition): Making the Most of Change*, xiii.

5 Jim Loehr and Tony Schwartz, "The Making of a Corporate Athlete," *Harvard Business Review*, January, 2001, https://hbr.org/2001/01/the-making-of-a-corporate-athlete.

6 Dorie Clark, "The Real Reason We're All So Busy (and What to Do About It)," TED Talk, Boston, MA, November 2021, 7 min., 47 sec., https://www.ted.com/talks/dorie_clark_the_real_reason_you_feel_so_busy_and_what_to_do_about_it.

7 James R. Doty *Into the Magic Shop*, 103.

8 *Neha Sangwan, Powered by Me: From Burned Out to Fully Charged at Work and in Life* (McGraw-Hill, 2023), chap. 2, Kindle.

9 Wendy Wood, *Good Habits, Bad Habits: The Science of Making Positive Changes That Stick* (Farrar, Straus and Giroux, 2019), chap. 1, Kindle.

10 Arianna Huffington, "Evicting the Obnoxious Roommate in Your Head," *Huffington Post*, May 10, 2014, https://www.huffpost.com/entry/evicting-the-obnoxious-ro_b_5303112.
11 Morten Albæk, *One Life: How We Forgot to Live Meaningful Lives* (LID Publishing, 2021).
12 Michael Gervais, *The First Rule of Mastery, Stop Worrying About What People Think of You*, (Harvard Business Review Press, 2023), chap. 2, Kindle.
13 Susan Jeffers, *Feel the Fear . . . and Do It Anyway: Dynamic Techniques for Turning Fear, Indecision, and Anger into Power, Action, and Love* (Harvest, 2023), chap. 1, Kindle.
14 Gervais, *The First Rule of Mastery*, chaps. 3, 4, 5, and 6, Kindle.
15 Gay Hendricks, *The Big Leap: A Guide to Transcending Personal Limits, Overcoming Fears, and Unleashing Your Authentic Greatness for a Better Life* (HarperOne, 2009), chap. 1, Kindle.
16 Doty, *Into the Magic Shop*, 75.
17 Doty, *Into the Magic Shop*, 75.
18 Napoleon Hill, *Think and Grow Rich* (Tarcher, 2007), chapter: The Sustained Effort Necessary to Induce Faith (Kindle).
19 Dorie Clark. *The Long Game: How to Be a Long-Term Thinker in a Short-Term World.* (Harvard Business Review Press, 2021).
20 Mary Catherine Bateson, *Composing a Life* (Penguin Group, 1990).
21 Jeffers, *Feel the Fear*, chap. 2.
22 Jeffers, *Feel the Fear*, chap. 7.
23 Jim Loehr and Tony Schwartz, "The Making of a Corporate Athlete."
24 Joe Dispenza, *Evolve Your Brain: The Science of Changing Your Mind.* (Health Communications, Inc., 2007).
25 Hendricks, *The Big Leap*, chap 1.
26 Hendricks, *The Big Leap*, chap 1.
27 Hendricks, *The Big Leap*, chap 1.
28 Doty, *Into the Magic Shop*, chaps. 3 and 7.
29 Bronnie Ware, *Top Five Regrets of the Dying*, https://bronnieware.com/blog/regrets-of-the-dying.
30 Jenny Anderson and Rebecca Winthrop, *The Disengaged Teen: Helping Kids Learn Better, Feel Better, and Live Better* (Crown, 2025), chap. 3, Kindle.
31 Ronald A. Heifetz, Marty Linsky, and Alexander Grashow, *The Practice of Adaptive Leadership: Tools and Tactics for Changing Your Organization and the World* (Harvard Business Press, 2009).
32 Bob Kegan and Lisa Lahey, *Immunity to Change* (Harvard Business Review Press, 2009).
33 Herminia Ibarra, *Working Identity, Updated Edition, With a New Preface: Unconventional Strategies for Reinventing Your Career* (Harvard Business Review Press, 2023).
34 Loehr and Schwartz, "The Making of a Corporate Athlete."
35 Daniel Goleman, *Focus: The Hidden Driver of Excellence.* (HarperCollins, 2013), chaps. 8 and 9, Kindle.

36 Richard E. Boyatzis and Annie McKee, *Resonant Leadership* (Harvard Business Review Press, 2005), 7.
37 Boyatzis and McKee, *Resonant Leadership*, 62.
38 Robert J. Waldinger and Marc Schulz, *The Good Life: Lessons from the World's Longest Scientific Study of Happiness* (Simon & Schuster, 2023).
39 "Loneliness Statistics: By Country, Demographics & More," The Roots of Loneliness Project, updated March 27, 2024, https://www.rootsofloneliness.com/loneliness-statistics; "Loneliness prevalence in the EU," European Commission, 2022, https://joint-research-centre.ec.europa.eu/scientific-activities-z/survey-methods-and-5analysis-centre-smac/loneliness/loneliness-prevalence-eu_en#:~:text=The%20first%20ever%20EU-wide,Loneliness%20prevalence%20differs%20across%20countries.
40 "Loneliness Statistics."
41 "Loneliness Statistics."
42 Interview with Dr. Robert Waldinger, episode 161, "What Makes a Good Life? Lessons from the Longest Study on Happiness," *The Mel Robbins Podcast*, April 4, 2024, https://www.melrobbins.com/podcasts/episode-161.
43 Judson Brewer, *The Craving Mind: From Cigarettes to Smartphones to Love—Why We Get Hooked and How We Can Break Bad Habits* (Yale University Press, 2018).
44 Julia Cameron, *The Artist's Way: A Spiritual Path to Higher Creativity*, (Souvenir Press, 2020), chap. "The Basic Tools."
45 Dr. Aditi Nerurkar, *The 5 Resets: Rewire Your Mind and Body for Less Stress and More Resilience* (HarperOne, 2024), chap. 3, Kindle.
46 James Clear, *Atomic Habits: An Easy & Proven Way to Build Good Habits & Break Bad Ones* (Avery, 2018), chap. 2, Kindle.
47 Clear, *Atomic Habits*, chap. 2.
48 Clear, *Atomic Habits*, chap. 2.
49 Matthew A. Killingsworth and Daniel T. Gilbert, "A Wandering Mind Is an Unhappy Mind," *Science* 330, no. 6006 (2010): 932, https://www.science.org/doi/10.1126/science.1192439.
50 James R. Doty, *Into the Magic Shop: A Neurosurgeon's Quest to Discover the Mysteries of the Brain and the Secrets of the Heart*, (Avery, 2016), 102–104.
51 Nerurkar, *The 5 Resets*, chap. 5, Kindle.
52 Mihaly Csikszentmihalyi, *Creativity: Flow and the Psychology of Discovery and Invention.* (HarperCollins, 1996).
53 Frank M. Diaz "Mindfulness, attention, and flow during music listening: An empirical investigation." *Psychology of Music* 41, no. 1 (2013): 42–58.
54 Goleman, *Focus: The Hidden Driver of Excellence*, chaps. 14 and 15.
55 Tony Schwartz and Catherine McCarthy. "Manage Your Energy, Not Your Time." *Harvard Business Review* 85, no. 10 (October 2007): 63–73, https://hbr.org/2007/10/manage-your-energy-not-your-time.
56 Boyatzis and McKee, *Resonant Leadership*, chap 2.
57 Sio, Ulrich, and Thomas Ormerod. "Does Incubation Enhance Problem Solving? A Meta-Analytic Review." *Psychological Bulletin* 135, no. 1 (2009): 94–120. https://doi.org/10.1037/a0014212.

58 Csikszentmihalyi, *Creativity: Flow and the Psychology of Discovery and Invention* (Harper Perennial 1996), chaps. 3–4.

59 George E. Vaillant, *Aging Well: Surprising Guideposts to a Happier Life from the Landmark Harvard Study of Adult Development.* (Little, Brown and Company, 2002).

ABOUT THE AUTHOR

Janine Mathó is a former Harvard and Pearson executive, award-winning leader in global learning, and trusted advisor to changemakers navigating growth and transition.

Over her twenty-five-year career, Janine raised $30 million for education innovation across sectors. She shaped global strategy for the future of work and guided organizations through transformation.

Her turning point came in 2020, after corporate burnout and the sudden loss of her mother—a season that led her to reimagine life, work, and success. A guiding question emerged: How can ambitious people build meaningful lives and lasting success without losing themselves or what matters most, or burning out?

Janine now works at the intersection of leadership, well-being, and transformation, helping ambitious professionals reclaim energy, align with what matters, and build sustainable success. Her debut book, *Live Your Opus*, helps high achievers who look successful on the outside but feel depleted or misaligned. It offers a practical, soulful framework for building a life that feels better inside than it looks outside.

A first-generation Cuban American, Janine has lived in three countries and led work on four continents. She brings a cross-cultural lens and rare integration of strategy, science, and spirit to her work. Janine lives in Provence with her husband and two Labradors, and travels often to London and Boston, where they raised their three grown children.